HOT TYPE

HOT TYPE

Icons, Artists and God-figurines

Bongani Madondo

PICADOR AFRICA

DEDICATED TO

Nomvula

You should have been here but would I have turned up this way –
a dreamer?

&

Sandile Dikeni

When I grow up I would like to write like you.

First published by Picador Africa 2007
an imprint of Pan Macmillan South Africa
Private Bag X19, Northlands, 2116
www.picadorafrica.co.za

ISBN: 978-1-77010-063-3
© Bongani Madondo 2007

Author photograph courtesy of Sabelo Mlangeni
Cover design: Donald Hill of Studio 5
Printed and bound in South Africa by Pinetown Printers

Contents

Introduction

Not since Jesus has a baby [the Brangelina baby] been so eagerly anticipated. Actually, forget Jesus. Only three wise men turned up to greet him in the manger.
– Jason Zengerle, *New York* magazine
Story titled 'Not Since Jesus'

If pop culture were a country, it would, on the promised Judgement Day, either be wiped off in one huge flame of fire, or as a forgiveness gesture, embraced – rivers, volcanoes, people and their blings, and dreams – by God The Almighty.

That is, He is bigger than pop, and not that I doubt.

That is, He can pull it. Whip it and slam it where it hurts most.

But because, at core, it is business; with the best of its expressions underpinning and sustaining the best and worst that capitalism has to offer, it would not – trust me – be diabolical to suggest that God is big business in pop.

Either as a quote, bearer of good news or a force to pitch your wares – say a pop song, a film – against. Contemporary culture is in a love and hate, or love and hasty affair with God, so much that, quite frustrated they aren't quite able to reach the heights He has set, or the heights He supposedly inhabits, the very egotistic, talented and simply mad, of our favourite pop personalities have dared to make cheap pot shots at the Almighty Himself.

Have they forgotten Babel? Is that why most in pop culture still speak in tongues — or just allow a computer doctored-photograph to speak for them?

Others evoke God in such a way that audiences, or interviewers are led to believe that they, and only they, are big chums with the big force up there.

Who can forget the father of funk and The Godfather of Soul, James Brown at his peak, telling *Rolling Stone* magazine:

'But you know, once you be lucky enough to do some of the things I've done in life, there is a lot of stress. Christ went off — he didn't want to be around other people when he was praying. I ain't no Christ ['am only his pal'?] but at least I got to go off and think.'

He continued: 'If Christ had to do it, what about me? I am no prophet. [I just posses the same wisdom as one.] I'm just a good person trying to do the right thing. But I got to have time off. I thank God that I know what I know.'

All that was said during The Godfather's beyond-hedonistic days, when he beat countless women, cheated countless people, snorted bagfuls of coke down his nostrils, blacked out in countless strange places and cheated with countless women, while going in and out of jail for this or that misdemeanor.

God, clearly, was cheering him all the way.

And there was that rather naive, sometimes radical, and talented lyricist, John Lennon, patron saint of harmless pop: in 1966 he caused the Beatles, then at their peak, huge album sales and a plummeting career when he boasted to the press that 'The Beatles are more popular than Jesus Christ'.

Said at the beginning of his band's tour of the US in 1966, American zealots burnt their records, radio erased them from the playlists.

A quarter century after his death from a crazed gunman shooting him point blank — sent by Jesus' gang, no doubt — his loyalists still regard the block of flats where he lived, Dakota, in Manhattan, as some kind of shrine.

Non-commercialised Graceland, but a spiritual trip[ping] nonetheless.

Introduction

An hour after he was gunned down, thousands of fans sprang from all corners of the globe to pour grief, in the form of postcards, bouquets of flowers, music and all sorts of paraphernalia outside his flat.

It wasn't the last day the world would express its collective hurt, appreciation and thus secularist canonisation of a popular culture icon in that manner — only 25 years later, a menacing and playful rapper, street poet, ex-thug and something of a legend in New York City, Christopher Wallace, a.k.a. Biggie Smalls' funeral was attended by close to a million people, blocking the streets of Brooklyn, New York.

The comedian Chris Rock has this cutting send off: What the heck, Biggie and Pac were killed, Martin (Luther King) and Malcolm (X) were assassinated — get that?

Still he could not account for why another iconic rapper — not even the best — actor, and something of a Holy Son-Devil-The Redeemer and revolutionary icon and thug messiah to the entire world, from Sierra Leone's rebel soldiers, from street thugs in Oakland, West Coast, to rapist gangs in Soweto, from Hollywood million dollar-milking films to religiously symbolical murals in the Cape Flats, Tupac Amaru Shakur, attained a Christ-like, if not Elvis-like mythical allure.

Today top university courses teach his *poetry* in an age when Malcolm X and Martin Luther King's speeches had, but assumed fossil status in political and cultural Africana.

Though Fela Kuti never quite claimed to know God, he believed he had special powers, and of course he consorted with marabouts and African medicine charlatans, who claimed the powers of God.

So popular was Kuti's daring, reckless and *über* hip fuck you attitude to the several oppressive Nigerian governments that when he died, over a million people attended his funeral, though government count is a conservative 200 000.

Still, how many people attended General Sani Abacha's funeral? Or how many people would have remembered the name 'Sani' compared to 'Fela' were Sani not the beast of Lagos that ate up the life of Ken Saro-Wiwa?

Icon worship is not restricted to radicals only. Die-hard collectors would know of this powerful photograph, depicting a nondescript old woman passing a corrugated iron wall in the London borough of Islington scribbled with graffiti declaring, 'Eric Clapton Is God.'

Also that was the time he played something of a mean blues, white boy-angst guitar, but nothing as soul tormenting as Jimi Hendrix, who subsequently arrived on the British Isles shores and got God, I mean, Clapton, to play second fiddle in his own heaven.

There are lots of examples where pop enters the murky areas of religion and is not content spending time singing hosannas at the back row, but challenges Jesus and, or God for the throne, or in the case of Kanye West's February 2006 *Rolling Stone* magazine cover — wear a crown of thorns, cultivate the same beard as Christ — how do we know how he actually looked, I mean, for real? — all in the name of keeping it real.

Though it was pop culture's most blatant run at religious symbolism, a moment where pop came to gamble and play dice in church, for Kanye it was a culmination of his rather bizarre exploration with Christianity.

Two years earlier, he had a massive pop song, 'Jesus Walks', that had nothing to do with Christ but with the fact that Kanye, a fresh voice in a morally suspicious, gangster and materialist hip-hop world, would soon walk straight to the bank over 10 million times, a fancy strut taken via Grammy avenues and countless magazine covers.

Like the wickedest pop image-makers, self-publicists, artists, con-artists and manipulators of the age — Don King, Muhammad, Mobutu Sese Seko, Quentin Tarantino, Samuel L Jackson, Marlene Dietrich, Marilyn Monroe, Louis Farakhan's Nation Of Islam, P. Diddy, Papa Wemba, George Clinton, Prince, Miles Davis, Andre 3 000, Fela Kuti, Colonel Muammar Gaddafi, Mao Tse Tung, Frida Kahlo, Madonna, Miriam Makeba and now Osama bin Laden, and others — West has a cunning internal compass wired to the root of his brain.

It is this natural compass that enables the best to read and ride the fluctuating socio-cultural, as well as political and religious currents in the niche world they trade in.

Alert to the fact that his mainstream appeal pulled him closer to throngs of suburban white teenagers and apolitical college campus middle-class blacks, Kanye, who had a blingy neck chain with Jesus icon — a Jesus Christ with aquatic blue, diamond eyes — tried, unsuccessfully, to get the jeweller to turn Christ's eyes darker and the whole icon a shade darker than it was.

In his attempt to repent and appeal to black folks, Kanye opted to repaint his Jesus black, so as to maintain his otherwise non-existent tough street exterior and turf market, even if it's in the psychology of hip-hop lore and not in actual cash-till realities.

A son of a university professor and political activist, he is smart enough to know that though hip-hop might go Hollywood, all forms of hip-hop and their wealth / struggle / drugs and guns mythology must return, or pay tribute to the streets, flippant as it may be, to remain relevant.

The streets are hip-hop's life blood, which is why it is such an oddity, today, to listen to or watch a cursing Jay-Z: his skin is too smooth for that, and were it not for his deft poetry, his party has all but imploded when he put on a suit and had the actual bottom line to care for, and not only a line of coke, as has been the case a decade ago on the streets.

Religion, the streets, *where art is the juncture*?

As an art, religious symbolism can be a spiritually, intellectually and creatively engaging subject. It can be the crossroads unto where subversion meets the sublime. It can also be where the atheists could express their deepest spiritual, transcendental interpretation of a super being they do not quite recognise, even.

Also, it can offer the most powerful platform for art to attain two seemingly repellant virtues — craftsmanship and purpose — as early Catholic as well as Roman / Greek and Egyptian public and religious art, has shown in the pre- and post-Renaissance eras.

This is something many so-called style makers and revolutionaries in today's pop culture, such as Kanye West, have failed to maximise or explore.

Closer to home things are not even promising a whiff of change or a display of creative risk. The best effort was Akin Omotoso's film, *God Is An African* but even then, the dare lies in the title and not so much in the dramatisation of his story narrative.

In music, things are in an ice capsule, worse in so-called revolutionary sounds and imagery of young black arts. Back in 2000 there was a video of Mandoza's and his Soweto street toughies Chizkop, who were clearly motivated by a search for controversy, thus free album promotion, in which they re-enacted the Crucifixion.

Their cruci*fiction* video of the song, '*Umuntu Omnyama*', in which they were depicted as Christ and the two criminals, was rather coarse and vulgar, far from being boundary-pushing.

Watching it you could not be enticed to ponder the issue of religion in the townships, the notion of sacrifice, greed, or urban black folks' contradictory obsession with white Christianity on one hand, and its need to create its ghetto paradise, filled with ghetto imagery, ghetto icons and a supposed black cultural way of life, on the other.

The video had none of those. In fact, they would have done much better by studying another thug — but soulful — image revolutionaries', Bones Thugs and Harmony's, video, a tribute to their mentor, Eazy-E, titled, 'Crossroads'!

Clad in white, making a beeline towards the peak of a mountain carrying the coffin, the video has all the symbolism one finds in one of the biggest denominations, Church of Nazareth, popularly known as Shembe Church, in Inanda, KwaZulu-Natal.

Mandoza and his gang, like Madonna, later in her comeback, in which she staged a non-convincing crucifixion freak dance piece in her performance just outside of the Vatican city in Rome, was dead on arrival.

The kwaito boys, like Madge, are not Lou Reed, David Bowie, or even George Clinton of Parliament. Even Mzekezeke's infantile gambit paid off more than the kwaito-rock star from Soweto.

Introduction

Pop Among The Believers

If popular culture as well as political personalities bizarrely evoke God and Christ for their own crass ends, how come then, society and the media accord those 'stars' reverence befitting early prophets, sages, shamans, the true social conduits to a higher forces, huh?

Why is it that, in the last half century, charismatic, sometimes talented, figures in sports — Pele, too, believed he was chosen by God [*Four Four Two* magazine, August 2005] — Muhammad Ali; politics: Félix Houphouët-Boigny, Ayatolla Khomeini; film: Cary Grant, and now George Clooney and Leo DiCaprio, Mariah Carey, Lauryn Hill — who has a song 'Forgive Them Father For They Don't Know What They Are Doing' — Britney, X-Tina, and now the world famous philanthropists, Angeline Jolie and Brad Pitt, tabloidly known and Brangelina's every move, religious belief, scripture, announcements, sexcapades, secret weddings in imaginary faraway African lodges, edicts, lyrics, and almost everything they touch, so obsessively scrutinised as though for some illusive wisdom or answers?

Why is it that millions of teenagers do not believe a thing their parents tell them, but make up unquestioning billions of consumerist masses lapping up every product a specific star sells on the telly?

Why is that the majority of populations in democracies voice out their disdain about the cult of personality, especially as it pertains to a popular leader — say Bill Clinton — and yet go ahead to venerate another leader, Nelson Mandela, who had divorced and remarried in his 80s?

Why is that we despise self-promotion by leaders who are all sheen and no substance, yet are inherently opposed to those hard-working types we tag as 'lacking in charisma'?

So Many Questions

Why is that millions believe that television and the media in general cannot be trusted, yet the same consumers purchase publications such as *Heat, Hello, People, Daily Mirror* and *Us Weekly*, most of which, and some broadsheet stories, mainly rely on hearsay and twice-removed anonymous sources?

Why have popular soapies, such as *The Bold and The Beautiful, Days of Our Lives*, and so forth, been running over a decade now, without any sense of closing shop or developing the story further?

Why is that audiences get affected personally when, in the televised drama, their favourite characters go through hardship, death or fail to snog a woman / man in an affair with his brother? Why do people care?

Why do the masses believe in articulate, talented, believable pop icons such as Bob Marley, Marvin Gaye, Gilberto Gil, Salif Keita, Hugh Masekela, Miriam Makeba, Caetano Veloso, and others, and specifically why have their very words become, so to speak, gospel?

Is it because of their lived experiences, in areas they might be singing or commenting about? Why is that Hugh Masekela is being listened to when he speaks against drug abuse, and, possibly be vilified if it is found that he still indulges in those narcotics himself?

No, Hughie is not on the rocks again, I am just keen on why we have given up on the notion of human beings' fallibility. Is that why we are so floored, disappointed when we are caught out?

Why is it that some daring pop figures with their own religious sects, or faiths they believe in, draw unprecedented attention, more than, say, traditional religious faiths, case in point Tom Cruise?

Is it because people have given up on God, on religion totally or are just star-whacked? Is it because we do not care about Scientology, but only in TomKat's role in it? Why? What about the rest of the faithfuls in there?

More significantly, why is that our fascination with stars and all the products they communicate / sell to us — Playstation games, biopics, from

Eminem's *8 Mile* to documentaries on Brenda Fassie, food, health and beauty endorsements some do not even use — borders on the worship, of almost religious type?

Why have we turned our beloved screen, music, sport personalities from favourite actors to idols, then icons, up to little god-figurines of our age, which we can purchase, display up on our mantelpieces, beside bedposts, in our lounges, and hide them away in a suitcase or magazine pile down the attic or garage?

Why do we collect them? Why do we discard or hide them when they are no longer articulating or representing our desire? Was the whole racket about them or our dreams, illusions, all along?

Do we leave them to hang dry, scandal after scandal, because we pay to watch them express the freakiest of imaginations and behavior we are too civilised, shy or just ugly and non-interesting to subject ourselves to?

Dear Editor, That's My True Confession
— a hodgepodge of Brook Benton's lyrics

I, for one, do not have a clear, let alone a blurry answer to all of these. You see, I am one of the culprits. One of those who tells you never believe in a flesh-and-blood being, and yet, spends sleepless nights interviewing or even worrying about people I deem extraordinary, characters I — and a tiny few elite in the media — have decreed are 'stars' or 'newsworthy'.

I am one of the guilty ones who bemoan the death of spirituality, the death of faith, the death of moral compass and centre, and yet would be the first in the queue to interview or search for a most dangerous criminal, just because outlaws are sexy and sexy outlaws make for sexy copy — regardless of how many people the sexy outlaw might have killed in his or her selfish outlaw spree.

If you, the people, ask, I would turn around and *sayeth* with conviction: 'the death by the numbers, the revelation, the ultimate trip to the jail . . . that's my motivation,' clearly knowing, once he goes, so too dies the story, unless — and that's where the showbiz in us hopes for a sequel — he escapes.

Lord knows that I am one of those who believe that, quite frankly, famous artists' self-righteous lyrics and, or public announcements, smell of a naked ambition and promotion, a kilometre, or a radio channel away, and yet bemoans artists' lack of political convictions.

'They just believe in themselves!' we coo away in self back-patting.

I am one of those bemoaning public icons' obsession with freed and expensive automobiles, but am the first in the queue to see what sort of futuristic jalopy the new Bond is driving in *Casino Royale*.

I am one of those who believe Naomi Campbell is obnoxious, and yet given a chance — which in fact happened twice in my career, once in Sandton City, once in Rome, Italy — I am one of those who push and shove, or even run after Naomi as she tries to dodge the media, or change from one micro-mini, to another micro-mini.

In short, I am, sadly, embedded unto the demands, silliness and rigorous pursuits of popular culture.

The Page / Bulletin Is A Stage: Showbiz, **Baby!**

Journalists — the sorry, proud and often disingenuous worldwide family I belong to, often with strange uncles, bribe-taking half-brothers thrice removed, star ass-kissing sisters, all those writers, radio and television, blogospheres, etc. — are an interesting human DNA.

Like politics, the arts, and sometimes the academies, journalism is, at best, performance arts. Its practitioners, by their very nature, perform for a gallery for a quid or two — whatever the price, we can give it to you.

Of all aspects of this performance — name by-lines are as good as old theatrical poster star billings, or public announcements on community halls or graffiti splashed on bridges — culture, politics and sports, journalists are the best of the media's in-house performance artists.

The three aspects, called beats, make up what is called show business journalism, though if you could listen to their protests, you'll be convinced that both political and sports journalists are engaged in some lofty, or too low a level to qualify as showbiz's journalists — while, in fact, all the trappings and evidence points to the contrary.

They write about public figures upon whom the masses have placed their lives and dreams — and in that lies the original ingredients of a Greek tragedy and, or African, oral, dramatic tales — the basis of which is love, hope, belief and betrayal.

Both — politics and sports — have, in the last 20 years, woken up to the inherent, self-promotional, chutzpah previously thought to be the soul forte of show enterprises such as film, theatre and live-music stagings.

The contents might differ: a Minister responsible for providing water to the poor; from, say, a dramatic soccer coach, think of Jose Mourhino; to a promotional tour of a classic music star, Dame Kiri Te Kanawa, but the ingredients, scripts and outcome are the same.

It's about selling the message, and as glossy as possible. The core drive and aim of, for example, classical music on one hand and politics on the other, are not dissimilar, in the arithmetic of the hearts — both are concerned with tradition, survival and prosperity, or growth.

They are about further commitment among the believers, and the recruitment of a new flock, though both are too proud and pompous to agree to that — beyond the high noon of electioneering, or lobbying stakeholders.

Classic music elites will tell you they are targeting the high-end market, but like a politician representing a constituency, its promoters derive their satisfaction not in an empty hall, but a hall bum-full of seats!

Where does all that leave showbiz journalists — those who own up to the crassness, as well as those self-anointed princelings of the craft? Hear, hear, hear us denying it: We are the biggest free riders.

Free-riding *performers*.

We are the great tag-alongs as our subjects, and, interchangeably, our co-performers, surge forth into their different types of ruling the world.

Both political journalists and showbiz sorts share one core element: how we love to be loved, and respected — with the carrot being a face recognised enough, and name trenchant enough to warrant that much sought-after invitation from subjects we report about.

As noted above, often journalists become co-performers — part of the show-piece. Usually a *hot* journalist and *hot* subject make for a doubleheader, a double bill that's too great to turn down, from a performance arts perspective.

Dear friends, I do not suppose I am a hot journalist, neither do I strive for cold layers, but, I too believe in the hot types, hot stories, hot gossip, hot ideas.

I believe in this embeddedness — unfortunately as fraught with landmines, career corpses, egos on the runaway and moral judgement lapses as it is — of the whole nature of the beast.

And — *yebo* — I agree: it is pungent, but we are all in it, otherwise we would not be in this industry and you would not be reading this.

Join me as I harass, pray with, dine with, debate with, attend, interview, and generally hop on a multi-fold, and different paths, back alleys, and highways, as well as aboard several Boeings, as I tour with my fellow performers in show business: icons, the God Figurines Of Our Age.

Check the smirk — aahh! Just like you, I am keen to milk out what makes them tick, and what makes them cheap. Performers that is, and it's not like me and you are immune . . .

Bongani Madondo, 2007

The Hip

Don King in Soweto
I lurve *S-a-we-doo*, son!

At his best and worst — always interchangeable in the life of the super Don— he is like a fresh paint freshly splattered on the walls.

Bright, nose-thumping, in-your-face paint. Its scent attacks the nostrils while its pupil-dilating colour leaves your visual senses permanently razzled and dazzled.

From the moment he and his entourage — personal assistant, lawyer and son John Carl Renwick or 'Carl King' — went aboard in Cleveland, Ohio in United States, his fellow passengers knew all about how Teflon Don was on his way 'down south' for two things: to stage a fist fest at Carnival City, and to meet 'my hero, Mr Mandela', which he pronounced like 'Mao' and 'dealer'.

A minute after his arrival, Johannesburg International Airport experienced a mini-frenzy as the one-man tornado shot straight through the crowd to address a congregation of local press about how 'happeee' he is to be in the 'muthaland. Land of hope, land of liberation'.

And just when they were lapping it all up — bearing in mind this was not King at his legendary rap-operatic best because at 72 his theatrics have lessened in proportion to the size of his silver Afro — King shifted his motor mouth into promo-speak for his international non-event, All the King's Men, live at Carnival City.

This would feature two men you'd never heard of before King touched down: Virgil Hill challenging WBA cruiserweight champ Jean-Marc Mormeck. And from south-side, Philip 'Da Bomb' Ndou versus Isaac Hlatswayo.

'Tell 'em all, tell the Xhosas and Zulus to come out of the bushes to come watch a show they will never ever forget', cried King.

When told that South Africans are a lot more than Xhosas and Zulus, he improvised: 'This show's about showing confidence in this country, its great people, its . . .'

Nobody in 35-plus years in the bashing business has told Donald King to shut his trap. Not his friend, 1950s rock star Lloyd Price; not King's match in the ego stakes and one-time host, Mobutu Sese Seko; not fellow bad boy, the Rev Al Sharpton; not soul-funk king James Brown; not J Edgar Hoover, who investigated him for years and never managed to get anything to stick; and certainly not his two most prized fighters, Muhammad Ali and Mike Tyson.

At his peak, Ali told the world's mightiest army and politicians to go and find the shortest way to hell, rather than force him into the Vietnam War. Tyson crushed the skulls and dreams of men twice his size. But neither man had the nerve to tell King to 'shut up'.

But there was one exception: Sam Garret. Garret was a tubercular alcoholic, a fellow gambler and a good friend of King's. Garret owed King $600 from a bet he lost by foul means. On a beautiful spring day in April 1966, King parked his Cadillac convertible and sauntered into the Manhattan Tap Room at 100th and Cedar Avenue in the Cleveland ghetto.

'Using size and girth — he weighed over 240lbs to Garret's 130lbs — to intimidate Garret', writes Jack Newfield, who investigated the case and penned an unauthorised biography, *The Life and Crimes of Don King*, King shouted at Garret, calling him 'scumbag' and his favourite, 'muthafucker!'

The small man told him in no fewer words to: 'Shut the fuck up'. Garret should have known better than to disrespect the ruler. King urged him outside, where he rammed a fist and, it is suspected, the butt of a gun into Garret, before kicking the small, writhing man to the ground and jumping on him.

When two cops, detective Bob Tonne and his partner John Horvath, approached the scene of the 'fight', they saw a man's head bouncing off the pavement like a rubber ball.

And they saw a large man standing over the figure, holding a gun and applying another kick to head. 'Hands up! Stop it!' they commanded, approaching with pistols drawn. 'Drop the gun!'

King looked around, gritted his teeth, muttering 'muthafucker!' and then gave the bloodied Garret one last, vicious kick that Detective Tonne later remarked, 'I will never ever forget'.

After a few days drifting in and out of consciousness, Garret died at 11.15am, April 25. Instead of the initial 'aggravated assault', King now faced a murder charge.

But after his lawyers made several visits and engaged in closed-door talks with Judge Hugh Corrigan, King's expected life sentence was whittled down to three years, time he spent reading William Shakespeare, Friedrich Nietzsche and Jean-Paul Sartre. Not WEB DuBois. Not Marcus Garvey.

The detectives who arrested him were furious. And that was the last time anybody told King to 'shut up'.

Fast forward, four decades later. Orlando's Hector Peterson Square is a riot of photo-journalists' camera clicks as the King presides. I'm late but catch up with the man at the Apartheid Museum, still panting, him doing his impressive ballerina-meets-Harlem shuffle-strut: pure theatre.

He's bedecked in silky blueish pants and a star-studded denim jacket embroidered with cartoon cut-outs of himself grinning in a tux, holding the title, and flashing his famous grin. US flags are stitched all over, front and back, and King looks like a hybrid of a demeaning modern Steppin' Fetchit, or post Y2K ageing minstrel — *flash da smile, boyo!* — and the cloning of 1970s rapper, Melle Mel gone awry.

This Thursday though, he is high on his own version of black consciousness. The more he preaches it, the more it sounds like al-Qaeda singing a hip-hop version of 'God Save the Queen' — i.e. a complete show of nonsense.

His train of hangers-on (the helper, the pompous son, the short blonde with the J-Lo figure) moves outside where nearby school pupils, teachers, media, police and loafers jostle for a space to see, talk to and touch the King. All hail the King.

'Aaaiman-dla-hhhhh,' he roared, ramming his blinged fist skywards. 'Yee know, it's so spiritually uplifting to be here. On this soil. Here. *E-k-a-ya!'*

It is clear King the hustler is in remission and King the Malcolm X of boxing has taken over.

'The youth of this country must realise that lots of people shed blood for 'em. Like Hector, here. Your bruvvas died, so you can be free. Yeah? Free! To all black people South Africa signifies one thing: never again. Never! These are my roots. Unless black people stand together, we are nuffing.' Somebody asks him about Tyson.

'Oh, Mike? Abbaah!' his voice rises and abruptly stops, as if preparing it to scale a new register. This is a skill sopranos like Dame Kiri Te Kanawa utilise to stun audiences in little vacuous doses. 'Mike! Good question. I'm talking to Mike. You know, me, Mike, same blood.'

By now I had done my fair share of pushing and was up front looking him straight in the eye. 'Mr King, two questions. How true is your "Mike Tyson one blood" talk? From what I gather, he's lodged a $100-million case against you, that's not so neighbourly is it?

'Mike aside, sir,' by now I'm sweating like a pig, 'I dig your thing about black power, black vision, roots and stuff. D'ya reckon you and your one-time buddy, Rev Al Sharpton are the shining examples of black America's leadership? In the vacuum left by Louis Farrakhan's silence, a void where rappers are paraded as black America's political pioneers, would you . . .'

There's no time to ask if he'd consider running for, say mayor, governor or even president.

'As I say', thundered King, 'unless we bond together we are nuffing. This is a great country, I love Souwedoo. Really do.' He ignores my questions with a straight face, grinning and looking at me, as if to say, 'Who the hell you think yee are? Scram off!'

Thirty minutes later and 300 metres away, the world's most famous grin is about to be wiped off King's face.

By the time his entourage arrives at Nomzamo Winnie Madikizela-Mandela's mansion, the lensmen and the rest of the media are already stationed at the gates.

A few words are exchanged between 'Mama's' omnipresent security and a man in a suit and a Pajero. Clearly, King had not made the necessary appointment to drop by Nomzamo's. But that is not the reason access is denied. 'She's not around', King's entourage is told.

Ten minutes later, photographer Dudu Zitha and I drive back to the queen's gated palace.

'Is it true mama is not in?' Her security guards smile conspiratorially.

At 2pm on the bullhorn, the King struggles back. Carrying both an SA and a US flag and surrounded by his people, he steps into (where else?) Wandie's for lunch, his grin firmly in place. But he's lost a round and is feeling it, eating little and speaking even less.

Is his mind in Las Vegas? Is he thinking of Tyson's $100-million lawsuit? Has his mind slipped back to the deafening African chants, *'Alee Bom-a- ye, Alee, Bom-a-ye* [you will die]' from the 1975 Rumble in the Jungle in Kinshasa?

The one-hour lunch passes with little more than a sentence of King's rap-opera. The few words uttered are anecdotes about Mandela's garden in Qunu.

Just then, a group of Joburg-based US expats approach the table to say hello to the King.

'Hi', says one of the young beefcakes, rather cautiously. 'I'm Larry Scott, from Atlannah. Jus' passing to check how's the folks doing down 'ere.'

King nods his head and bends as if to whisper something you are not supposed to share with anybody — except that his baritone cannot be reduced to a whisper. 'You from Atlannah? Lissen 'ere, man: this place, Souwedoo, is like the cradle, man. When you are in Souwedoo, you're where the soul is at brutha. Oh yeah. Yep.' Few words.

The intruder, Scott, and his equally star-struck buddies vamoosed.

King sits silently, chewing on a toothpick, like the baddies used to in 1950s gangster films. Though the image recalls a smart and alert inner-city rogue pose, without the cameras flashing, King looks like an old man surrounded by his grandchildren. For a moment, the most flamboyant character in sports cuts a sad and lonely figure.

When it is time to leave, he quickly dons his 'love-black power' mask. The restaurant bill is R2 451.

Outside, in the shiny Merc and 4x4s the King's clan bopped and weaved to the sound of DMX's gruffy voice, 'Blood O' My Blood Niggah', to which a band of South African photographers, contracted by King's host Golden Gloves, responded by bopping their heads back, enjoying a syrupy made-in-the Bronx guitar loop, 'Blood O' My Blood . . . Niggah . . .'

King's next move is plain goofy. He is scheduled to attend Parliament's opening, the idea being to meet President Thabo Mbeki.

King himself wrote in a super-gloss brochure, 'I'm honoured to be presenting an important award to a man I hold in the highest regard, former President Nelson Mandela, and to have an opportunity to meet your new President, Thabo Mbeki.'

On Friday morning, Parliament is fish-packed: politicians, business sorts, cultural players, all in a riot of various Africana colours. But is Don King in the house?

By midday, dignitaries pour out to pose 'n pout for pictures. But King is nowhere to be found. Back in Joburg, his people say: 'He opted to meet Tokyo Sexwale instead.'

Saturday night and Carnival City is at its kitschiest. Slot machines are chiming and thousands of dreamers, gamblers and aspirant kugels are sashaying around, rubbing shoulders with the new black business czars like Tokyo and his beauteous wife, Judy.

About 12.35am, after a few inconsequential fighters knocked each other's brains around and just before the Ndou–Hlatswayo fight, the man of the night, the King himself, is ushered to the ringside and instantly joined by Sexwale, leaving Dali Tambo to fend for himself. Better to be seated next to the King than the Prince.

By 2am I can't wait at the King's palace cheering '*moer hom,* bomb him' anymore. Somebody shows me the exit sign. My legs are jelly strong and eyes puffy red.

The following morning, somebody calls to say, 'Of the two palookas you missed, one, Mormeck, retired the other one, Hill.'

Bored and sleepy I mumble back, 'What the heck, smart boy was over the hill long before he arrived, isn't it?' before banging the receiver down. King left the following night without even a goodbye. No media, no nuffing. The truth is, in the stratospheric opera world of Don King, me and you are nuffing. Without a bond we are nuffing.

John Perlman Uncensored

This writer has a love / hate relationship with radio. And what heightens the feeling is the fact that I have a personal history with it. My own stint in radio ended rather . . . er, better let sleeping dogs lie. But since then I swore never to tune into radio, let alone go anywhere near a studio.

But really, would you say no to going into a studio when your subject is the reigning emperor of talk radio? The man whose daily work is akin to that of current affairs shit-stirrer, political garbage-disposal specialist and delivery man all in one?

The idea was to catch SAfm's John Perlman before he left for work, at home, hot from the bath, in the voodoo hours. Just after he had splashed the last dash of shaving cream on his face.

The Diary

3.20am: (Yawning, and cursing journalism) I kick the duvet off. Zig-zag to the bathroom. Slump into the bath. Still cursing.

3.40am: Where's my cab? Gawd! Nothing materialises. Emergency call to a friend. A documentary filmmaker, his adrenaline rush is wired to the madness of journalism. In five minutes, he pulls up outside.

3.55am: We are lost in Melville.

4.17am: Getting itchy, we . . . oh, yeah, this must be Perlman's place, mate. It's the only house in the street with lights on and curtains wide open.

4.20am: 'Yo, you are late, mah man. Don' you worry though. I don't leave before 4.30am. Coffee, tea?' Coffee. Keep it real. Black.

I steal a glance at his bookshelves. Scott Turow, James Ellroy, Michael Cunningham, Margaret Atwood and JM Coetzee.

Reporter: 'Ahh, so you are into fiction, heh?'

Perlman: 'Man, good fiction makes for exciting escapism. Brilliant fiction just transfers you to somewhere deeper. Anyway, I deal with reality issues 24/7. This helps to go somewhere deeper without being there.'

4.40am: We bundle into his blue Renault. He tells us he's been presenting AM Live for six full years. 'In fact, today is my sixth anniversary on this show.' The man's remarkably upbeat. Where does he get all this energy so early in the morning?

'Man, I wonder how many people look forward to their day at work, every day, at the time that I wake up or even later, without a grudge or grumble. For me, ahh, each and every day piles up the previous day's ecstasy. I wake up for that.'

Reporter: 'Six years, waking up at 3am? What's your goal? Ten years?'

Perlman: 'I don't look at life like in numbers. I live my life and work for as long as it challenges and excites me. I dunno for how long I will be doing this. Right now, I'm blessed.'

4.50am: We enter SABC Radio's basement parking lot. It's empty and spooky.

5am: Thirty minutes to go before AM Live goes on air as we arrive in the

SAfm studios. In the producers' studio adjacent to the on-air studio, I learn that Rhulani Mgwambani, the show's senior producer, and Mark Preller, the technical producer, have been here since 3am. They are supposed to be there at 3.30am. Don't they have a life? The show, it turns out, has 13 producers working on it. Thirteen! At most stations two producers is a luxury.

5am: Hush. Preparation time. Perlman runs to his computer. 'Shucks, I'm late,' he mutters under his breath.

5.10am: He's at his computer, checking the wires and writing his own headlines: 'The BBC in turmoil over the Hutton Inquiry'; 'Rape survivors could get antiretrovirals'; 'Shoes Moshoeu believes SA can match Nigeria'; Really? I mean, besides the money players are paid, do they really believe what they say?

Perlman reads all the wire-service copy. Consults with his team. Everything's planned with military precision. Isn't this supposed to be theatre of the mind? Where's the drama? The noise, the shouts, the strained exchanges?

5.30am: On the bullhorn, 'Good morning, you are waking to John Perlman on AM Live.' Perlman kick-starts the day. In the studio, he reads headlines and quirky little items that offset the serious veneer of newspapers' front pages. Many of the headlined stories — if you listen to Perlman talk — are newspaper follow-ups of news first broadcast on AM Live's *After 8 Debate*.

5.45am: It's election time and AM Live is already on the ball 'towards the 2004 general elections in April', Perlman says. April? Does he have a hotline to the president?

In any case, AM Live's been doing a profile of all nine provinces, in the last weeks. Today, it's 'Focus on Limpopo'. Somebody files a five-minute profile of Premier Ngoako Ramatlhodi.

The show picks up pace. Perlman's voice is still calm though a perfect conveyer of his sharp mind. He thinks quickly, offers a different take on obvious issues and communicates with his producers by sign language.

I am itching. Where's the controversy? The heat? Okay this isn't Jerry Springer on radio but . . . yep, something was bound to pop up. It's Uncle Bob's crying the beloved country.

'Seven and a half million people in Zimbabwe need food assistance to stay alive.' The show connects to a World Food Programme expert. Can't remember the name. But not to worry. He's another whitey expert on Zim. Granted, he sounds like he knows his story.

Just before 6am: A big, bald, black man shuffles into the studio. Name's Bongi. The sports presenter / producer. Two minutes on Bafana, one on tennis. Exit Bongi; in comes Ivan le Roux. Le Roux is an expert on bus disasters. Topic? Phuthaditjhaba bus disaster. Le Roux is breathtaking, if not too deep for radio. But this is AM Live. His memory rolls back with impressive recollections . . . the 1985 Westdene bus disaster, the Natal bus disaster, and this disaster, that disaster. He tackles bus companies head-on. And hits the government transport regulations where it hurts most. Nothing self-righteous about his expert views. Quick, crisp and insightful. Gee, where do they get these white men — I mean if the brain drain that we have been told about is true, there shouldn't be any available white man in this country.

Le Roux gets two minutes flat. And he probably woke up at 5am. For two minutes? That's radio for you.

6.35am: The show is at full blast now and exciting.

7.30am: A big, tall and smiling black woman saunters into the producer's booth. It's Onke. Onke Zembe. 'Onke — the producer of AM's liveliest section, *the after 8 debate* — is one of the pillars of this show and the station,' Perlman volunteers this info. 'Without her, we are a mess.'

Ashwin Desai refused to feature in today's debate, titled 'Why do we care about the American election?'

'He feels that he's not an expert enough on this topic,' Zembe offers.

But there are substitutes, like Jubilee 2000's quotable radical MP Giyose, the Centre for Policy Studies' dial-a-quote expert Chris Landsbergh and the SABC's man in Washington Simon Marks. All but Marks are ready to Michael Moore President Bush down.

Still, beating on Bush is best left to the show's regular callers. Every show has its own expert callers, who aren't different from the most over-zealous soccer and rugby fans. In their mind, they can choose and train the country's national team. These expert callers have an opinion on matters varying from skin lighteners to George Soros, from Tito's economic philosophy to the landless in Limpopo province.

8.07am: Calls open. At last, time for drama.

First caller: 'Ai, no. You guys, we are making a meal out of nothing here. Why should we care? What about Palestine's occupation?'

Second Caller: 'America is not clued up about the rest of the world.'

Third caller: 'I would like to know if we can send election observers to the US; I mean there's no democracy there. You can't trust that those people won't steal the election.'

On and on, the anti-American theme song plays.

This is where Perlman the skilled broadcaster really emerges. 'But you are talking as if Clinton was better. He wasn't. Clinton talked the talk but could not walk the walk. There was no more aid in his tenure than in Bush Junior's. Republicans are not flashy but they provide the cash aid.'

MP Giyose: 'No, John, the oil chiefs are in power in Bush's America. They put their candidates in power to run the government.'

Perlman: (Still calm, but spikier.) 'At least they are open about it. We don't even know who gives our parties money here. It is all under the table.'

The show goes on like that, Perlman obviously enjoying himself, sharing banter and illustrating examples. He drives the lorry, but his callers are the hollers in the back of the lorry. They haggle, agree, cut each other off and offer nuggets of wisdom. When time calls for it, he brings the issue back into perspective. Next caller?

8.35am: Perlman doesn't skip a beat. Breaks no sweat. Even on the most contentious issues, he remains cool, hard working and throws no verbal gymnastics around. Were he a boxer, John Perlman would be the Marvin Hagler of talk radio. Calm, but he gets the job done. Not flashy or full of drama, he packs a great punch.

9am: 'Hi. I'm John Perlman. Enjoyed being with you. Good morning. And have a good day.'

It's all over. That simple. That difficult. That impossible. The photographer has long gone. And it really feels like a replay of that 3am duvet-kicking motion. My head feels like it has survived a 30-round bare-knuckle war with Mike Tyson. I make my way out of the SAfm studios. Legs strong as jelly. Zig, zag, zag outside. What a day.

Hi, I'm the New Bob Mabena

Pleased to meet'cha

It was just a few days ago when this broadcasting 'multitasker', one of the key spokes in the wheel of a media giant, husband and father, braved the cameras' flashlights, the make-up artist's tool kit and that stuff they put on metrosexuals appearing on magazine covers.

Only difference is that Bob Mabena is not your typical metrosexual, or a metrosexual at all. But a 'metro man' — in the old sense of the word — he is. Metro = urban, driven, cosmopolitan, assured, always seeking, always on the move, always in the mix, and really not only studio mixes, Mabena is much more than that.

This is how things swing today on Planet Bob: he is scheduled to do this interview, he has to play host to his best childhood friend recently blessed with a bouncing baby boy. Also, the man and his family — yes, he is still married to his equal, Zandile Nzalo-Mabena, yes, they give off an energy of a mature couple, together in this, and no, they are not about to break up *again*, and yes, this none of your business, with deepest apologies, dear reader. Well neither mine, but more about that later.

The family is about to vacate its dwelling in Ferndale, Randburg to one of those China-walled developments: Broadacres, near Dainfern. And that's not even half of it. The chap has to do all those things and be ready by the following 10am for his weekly communion with God.

Yep, Bob Mabena is a church man. Alright, alright, not like that *über* metro man, Ray McCauley, but a church man in that he is a believer and does what he needs to do to construct a balance in his spiritual and family life — period.

Is the church bit an antidote to the black version of a rock 'n' roll persona, action man, car-racing adrenaline junkie, hot shot DJ, a Tupac Shakur fan and party man? Does wifey drag him to the Lord's house?

'Look, being centred means a lot to me,' he would later say. 'I am not a child anymore.' But that's after storming through his schedule, which I wasn't too sure of, considering all those things happening on Planet Bob. And then comes the phone: 'Tell you what,' Mabena's voice is crisp amid traffic rush, 'mah brother, seeing that things are so tight, why don't you just come to this little party-gathering I'm hosting for this chap, and we'll see if we can get words in edgeways in there. Sorry man, that's just how it is.'

'Perfect!' I thought.

Later in the evening, I'm greeted with cackling laughter as I knock at the door. The man himself welcomes me. No, let me retrace my steps and do the obligatory celebrity-envy thing: in the driveway I spy a display of beemers of all shapes and sizes, an X5, Z4, all sorts, as if this were a piece cut adrift from Bavaria, Germany.

I'm expecting a party full of posers in golf shirts and women in strapless tops shimmering around. How wrong I am! The music is old style R & B — the 80s happened 20 years ago, right? — of Atlantic Star and Mighty Clouds of Joy variety and not 'You remind me of my Jeep' modern soul-crunk passing as rhythm and blues.

And the laughter I heard earlier did not come from anybody you have seen on the society pages of *BL!NK* or *Style* magazines. It is Mabena and his old Atteridgeville pals, wrapped in stitches, telling a variety of stories. It is male middle-agey fraternity chat: traffic fines, the life on the fast lane they ditched just a few years ago, and of the current black middle-class rap — white folks struggling to cope with their new rich, brash, black and African ritual-practising neighbours.

Okay, a few of Bob's hot shot buddies — I mean hot shot according to South African media standards — Lesley Sedibe of CCP / EMI Records and later Blueprint's Groovin Nchabeleng would pop in, say 'Halo ma Gents', tear into a T-bone steak, throw in a joke and blast off.

So I didn't get an interview. Mabena was being the host and I was busier rolling on the floor with laughter — Pretoria humour is sickeningly peerless.

'Can we do it in the morning before church, then?' the heathen in me proposed. 'Come around, bhut', came the retort. Hardly twelve hours later, I arrive at the Mabena residence with a drunken face — from yester night's laughter — to meet him for breakfast in his study. Still drunk from lack of sleep too, he is more on top form than I am.

Context: it's been almost a year since Mabena left the Gauteng adult contemporary station, Kaya FM's most coveted slot, *The Morning Show*, while still a hit with the fans, critics and advertisers alike. Put it this way: in the way he handled social, political, economical renaissance issues, fresh-as-morning dew music, and his irreverent, Don Imus-meets-Chris Rock old commentary, bits of philosophical observation and still remaining relevant to listeners dashing to work, Bob Mabena was, to be precise, lightning-rod hot!

Writing in the Jo'burg-based tabloid, *Sunday World*, radio critic Bongani Mahlangu lamented last year: 'I would have enjoyed painting a glowing picture about local radio, but that would have meant giving the wrong impression. The year began and ended sadly for black radio. First, Bob Mabena retired from radio broadcasting prematurely.

'What is puzzling' he rolled, 'is that many of those who add no value to radio continue to cling to the microphone.'

But some of us were not that impressed with Mabena's studio trapeze act.

18

Was it not only a year ago when he joined Jozi's favourite black station from the lily-white Highveld (one of Primedia's shining assets) mature, steaming and inspirational, what with that seminal Telkom-sponsored Africa Tour, with which he stamped his name on adult listeners' memory forever?

Then King Bob returned to Highveld with a huff, and rumours swirling back at Kaya of power play, unfulfilled positions and bad blood? For him to come back for the second time, charm and work his trust again to the top of the listeners, only to leave and join the corporate headquarters of Primedia, was, well ... I wonder if his listeners have forgiven him much. I haven't.

But that's old hat. We are here to talk about the new Mabena; old Bob, but new challenges.

He occupies a very influential post; that of Primedia's Business Development Executive. Essentially what that entails is that he is the business equivalent of an effective Premier League midfielder — the engine.

He is responsible for bringing off-centre creativity, spotting new opportunities before they become opportunities, as well as sitting on the executive committee that runs all assets, including all radio stations.

'It goes beyond radio. Basically I'm responsible for maintaining and expanding current accounts, including looking for new business. Media is not only about mere entertainment. Other than managing current assets, I'm the company's point man in liaising with government, the government communication body (GCIS), as well as exploring new business avenues in the public sector.'

He explains how easy and dangerous it is for media behemoth to grow or burst.

'It is all about new technology as well as an eye and ear for turning what others see as a dormant area into a creatively attractive, developing business. The industry is getting edgier, media convergence is no longer another by-word for globalising the communication world's business.

'It is business reality, with dire consequences for those businesses not better positioned to take advantage of new technologies.

'You need to be able to create a balance. It is not always about rushing headless into new technologies and new markets without understanding and mastering what your core business is and how best to manage rapid change.' Mabena raps up a pretty savvy and minty-tasting language — but what does all this techno-jargon mean?

Sure, these post Y2K fancy-pantsy buzzwords — dotcoms, media convergence, global networking, etc. — have had their setbacks.

Some five years ago, Primedia, then thought to be the slickest kid on the media block as opposed to old horses such as Naspers and Johnnic, which were then still gobbling up what turned out to be useless assets they would later be happy to see the back of, fell from the top. A victim of too much enthusiasm on the part of their chief executive, Willliam Kirsh.

Also, there was a fear of a takeover bid by European-based minority shareholders, things looked pretty awry for the media giant. Was it not convergence that almost destroyed it? Also, didn't we learn that growing conglomerates with too many assets and limited expertise as well as power battles can be its own enemy?

Didn't the American Online and Time Warner merger and break up, the fairly dim Dreamworks SKG and other Silicon Valley examples point out that not all that's converging in the dotcom boom was not really a pot of gold?

'Primedia is strong in terms of content, and content is where convergence is not growing but bearing good results. We still have a stronghold over conventional media such as outdoor advertising, cinema and radio, but we are saying we are open to new technology.

For example, there's a direct link between movie business, cellular phones and internet technologies. That's part of where the excitement is, and of course I am not going to give it away, telling you what our projections and strategies are, to remain edgy and better-placed for fresh thinking. All those though are challenges facing the team I am with. It feels good.'

It should. Corporate talk is that, Mabena either enjoys his work so much, or is pressurised to prove his worth, or both, that he is often to be found at the office at 6am. *Gawd*, doesn't he have a life? He laughs at the question.

Face to face he is still the old, opinion-flinging Bob Mabena. Right now he is thinking aloud about the challenges facing the Africanisation of business and corporate culture. Also, the fallacy of black economic empowerment in changing the entire economic reality of the country is his concern, or so he would like me and you to believe.

No, he did not use the word 'fallacy', instead he prefers 'the pain of transformation'.

'Don't get me wrong, I am a proponent of black pride. Retracing and seriously taking time off to study the inspirational aspects of African cultures. I am big supporter of what Mathole Motshega's Kara Institute, cultural intellectuals and community bodies are engaged in, making sure our children will grow black, informed and proud.

'There's no beating that, otherwise we'll end up being clones of every other more formulated, rooted culture such as the Japanese, the Chinese, continental India and so forth.

'But that – Africanisation – in its shape should be questioned: What is it we are aiming to achieve, what are the timelines, how will that impact on people – those we are trying to Africanise – is economic reality? Is that sustainable, does it bring bread to the table, how can Africanisation bring in a totally new approach to the way we are doing business, how can we grow from it? These are what I'm keen on.'

Since he posed the question of our times, I put it to him: what do you think is the correct approach? Do you really think there is that sort of process, Africanisation, and how do you implement a cultural philosophy in a modern enterprise? Didn't white liberal media and black skeptics kill it, that *dream*, some years ago?

'Problem is, there's no growth without personnel. All great economies, the Afrikaner economy after the Anglo-Boer War, the German economy after Hitler, the American economy as spearheaded by Franklin D Rooseveldt's New Deal, the current Chinese dragon, all those are people driven.

'People like me and you. South Africa, especially black South Africa has no tradition of grooming talent. We do not have people currently being prepared, mentored, exposed to the numbers and complexities of the economy. Individual drips and drabs, but there's no political process, where business interests converge with the political programme of the country.

'First of all, for this Africanisation to really happen you need money, no doubt. It's all about capitalism, whether you are interested in creating African Capitalism or whatever sort of capitalism you have in mind, money is the catalyst and we do not have it.

'But also, it's a legacy issue: there are no big super-wealthy black families in this country. The Motsepes are the closest to the Kennedy, Du Pont or the Vanderbilt mogul families in the US.

'See, it's alright to join the Joneses in the 'burbs, but even the Motsepes are far from being the Ruperts or Oppenheimers. What happened to black family wealth, the Maponyas, Ramolopes, Shikwanes (Habakuck), all those?'

Rhetorical question, one which he answers: 'Most were overtaken by new economies. Most of those white giants started as minnows. They struck political and religious deals with the previous governments, pension funds were channelled into their enterprises, because those were then regarded as *die volk's* enterprises. We need our own *volk* wealth.'

He says that it's all about patriotism ultimately. Thabo Mbeki's bourgeoisie patriotism that has given birth to the ANC-com-BEEs — greedy bunch, is that what you are pushing for?

'I'm thinking as we speak, do these things like *Proudly South Africa* really work? It — patriotism — should be entrenched deeper than that. For example, why can't we have Ster Kinekor cinemas all over the country playing the national anthem before each and every feature they show?

'Why can't every school, say, once a week sing the anthem? How many children, black children know the lyrics of the national anthem? We have a way to go. Wealth creation begins there. Convergence of ideas, spirits. We have to have a programme.' Mabena's programme, it turns out, entails

22

understanding and respecting European — as in white — corporate culture as is.

'We need to respect established business practices blended with our own way of doing things. We have to master the beast, the way the inner machine works. The greater part of all world economy succeeded based on its — Anglo-Saxon, therefore American capitalism — models. Not all of it is bad, but clearly it served its time. There's a need for new thinking. Are we ready to take advantage of that?'

Suddenly, something strange happens. Confession time. Quite startling and unprovoked, the man decides to centre the discussion back on the dance floors and on radio studios, party poppin' and yet this time, he is speaking the language of the late 1980s rapper, Chuck D, and Thabo Mbeki's black consciousness — and not necessary, P. Diddy, Bob Mabena ain't your fun daddy no more.

For the record, he is so done with radio — especially black radio — that he sees no point in discussing whether he'll go back to radio or not. 'To do what?' he asks, as though bewildered by the question. 'You see, its like Muhammad Ali, boxing and Parkinson's. I have done it, got the T-shirt and took a hell lot of punches, much as I dished.'

Worse still, a few disc jockeys excite him. Names such as Rudeboy Paul, Mesh on Thobela, Fresh trickle off, not much. 'I am not happy at all with my contribution to South African pop culture.

My days at Radio Bop, Metro FM, Studio Mix and being the country's number one deejay for a long time were fraught with filthy Americanisms, bad cultural influence on the youth, inspiring them through music, towards foreign norms, a very sad perception of what a superstar is. Yep! That was me out there.'

'It is sad,' he clears his throat. 'I feel guilty for that. Of course, there were positive things I did as a young man — I started radio at 17 — but the mess outweighs the positives. It went on for over ten years! I do not mean that I am the be-all, but I am aware that I played a major role, sort of a cottage industry of what you hear on black radio today.

'I drafted the blueprint to what today's celebrity deejays believe is the way to be hip, cool, be the best in the game and hold on to their thrones in showbiz, and it's all tragic. Crap! I hope the young ones never walk this line. The Bob Mabena line was a screwed line! So much growth, I mean, really, Bob Mabena was just a deejay, no?

'It is all about my family. I am very blessed with the wife I have, the person she challenges me to be. No, I am not afraid of talking about my divorce and re-marriage.'

Mabena, who is the father of five children — Reneilwe, Clementine, Kamogelo, Sihle and Dimakatso — opens up his heart again.

'I was a wreck, a plane coasting dangerously off the runway after breaking up with my wife. That's when the period of growth, soul searching began. I was wasted. The pits. Getting back to her, accepting the honesty she needs to live her life with me, challenged me to ask myself: What exactly do I want in this life? No prize for guessing, it's her that I'm content with.

'Thing is, I am father of teenagers you know . . . they are creating their own Bob Mabena personas, I mean I can't compete with them on who's the best Bob Mabena, you know?'

Here, the name Bob Mabena is not used as third person display on an ego, tripping off the runway again, but playful metaphor, for a blind but adventurous thrill seeker and urban hedonist of days gone by.

It's way past church time, and no he didn't make it: one more sin on my part.

It's time to go.

* * *

Days after finishing this piece, I chance upon a little nugget of information, after days spent scraping the barrel, investigating the future of SABC TV channels. Classified information within the top echelons reveals that Mabena is being head-hunted by the broadcaster.

It is said that they even went to the extent of offering the post to run, lead and turn SABC 3 into a combination of 'brains-with-entertainment value', as it aims to create a new face and territory for itself. Thus I called again:

Writer: It is true that you are going to the SABC?

Mabena: No comment.

Writer: Nice meeting you, Mr Mabena.

Listening to radio one lazy day, soon after the interview, an announcement was made: Bob Mabena has joined the SABC in some corporate capacity.

Just then, somebody asked, 'Mhhhh, Bob Mabena? Isn't that the name of a once-famous deejay?'

Free Mbizo, Freedom, Free Jazz
Elegy for Johnny Dyani

No road is an easy one, but they all go back to God – John William Coltrane, from *A Love Supreme*, 10 December 1964

The heat wave – at about a million-plus degrees, mhhh, not quite, but you get the drift – threatens to melt the whole of eMonti, as East London is known, on the day I hit town searching for the spirit of a 'dead man' grooving, Johnny Dyani.

Like the village dreamer-healers, spirit mediums who speak in tongues, I am mad enough to assume it is possible to look for, find and interpret the souls of the dead . . . or what in African folklore are referred to as 'the living dead'.

Ever since I was bewitched by the song '*Magwaza*'; a pulsatingly mad, disturbing, healing, high-voltage 13-minute recording of rituals, chants and instrumental pyrotechnics, I swore, one day I would meet its creator: the creator.

Yep, it was that religious an experience. Hallucinatory even. The sort of 'high' thousands of rock 'n' roll and jazz fanatics are prone to evoke in their countless 'I saw Elvis' or 'it rained horizontally the day Miles Davis died' tributes.

So, who is this high priest of music?

Johnny Dyani — 'Mbizo' to close associates — was born in Ezilini, Qonce, near King Williamstown. He grew up in Duncan Village, a semi-urban Eastern Cape village named after Sir Patrick Duncan, the British Governor-General. A sort of born-to-groove, born-to-inspire-the-world child prodigy, Dyani grew up to become a leading singer, pianist and a way-out-of-this-world talented double bass player.

The story of how Johnny — who was then chums with young musical talents such as Mongezi Feza from Queenstown and Dudu Pukwana and Nick Moyake from Port Elizabeth — joined a young white bohemian pianist, Chris McGregor, drummer Teboho Louis Moholo and later, Makaya Ntsoko, on a one-way ticket invitation to perform at the Antibes Jazz Festival in France, is the stuff of hip-jazz lore.

A good two years after kicking Europe in the pants with their mule-strong blend of stripped big band sound (a variation of what was referred to as African Jazz back home) and isiXhosa roots, the band split, but not before meeting the man who would play, as cliché would have it, an instrumental role in their acclimatisation with Europe, just as Duke Ellington had done for him — Dollar Brand.

Mbizo, it seemed, even as early as that had an ace of few in his bass-licking finger tips. He toured with various offshoots of the original Blue Notes, before branching out as a band leader, in his own right.

Armed with youth and a deep-rooted sense of African traditional music as well as a unique interpretation of the various elements of jazz, Europe in the late 1960s was a musical oyster for this young Eastern Cape multi-instrumentalist.

Europe, particularly Paris, London and Berlin, was a melting pot of cultures populated by established African-American jazz players, poets, writers and Third World artists, musicians and activists in exile.

Soon Dyani was not only playing with the likes of Don Cherry, Mal Waldron, David Murray and John Tchicai, but had established himself as a band leader employing many of the most highly regarded avant-garde names as his sidemen.

One, John Tchicai, says that 'Mbizo was one of the greatest musicians from South Africa and he was an inspiration, in Europe and other parts of the world, for many musicians and listeners.'

Yet back home, South Africans raised on a diet of black American soul, negro spirituals and jazz, the name Johnny Dyani is as common as seeing an Eskimo buying a freezer — a rarity.

For the record: Dyani — living in exile in Malmo, a small town in the south of Sweden — collapsed while leading a successful tour of one of his numerous outfits, The Johnny Dyani South African Jazz Project in Germany, 1986.

As is with several 'icons' — particularly in their posthumous careers as 'dead geniuses', figures such as Jimi Hendrix, Miles Davis and Kippie Moeketsi, and not Fela Kuti who lived his truths on the world headline and in his lifetime — Mbizo's life story is riddled with truths and falsities.

Alright, alright, the tales coursing through his (after) life are, proportionally speaking, not half as schizoid and mythical as those numerous Elvis Presley in the Congo, Elvis holed up Afghanistan sightings. Though he was a major star in his own life, pop stardom, was not his thing, which does not mean jazz operates entirely out of the pop firmament.

In fact, in the States it became a mask to Miles Dewey Davis's true genius, simply because he courted it somehow, what with his rock lifestyle, hitting the nights with the Jimi Hendrix posse, and finally his move to Hollywood.

Our own Hugh Masekela, lived a rock-star life; how he survived to tell the tale is the stuff of legend. Even the pioneering avant-gardist John Coltrane died a rock-star death: his liver gave up at 27, after years of pumping it with alcohol and shooting heroin.

Though still a major player in the traditionally discreet world of jazz, a world where biography is frowned upon in favour of art, Dyani's life and death, has given birth to divergent little tales, cross wiring in and out his life, to light up a portrait of an artist and a persona as complex and compelling as his art.

For example, almost two decades after his death, there are persistent claims by several who swear they were not only Johnny's friends, but were present when he collapsed and died on stage while performing.

Mkhalelwa Mazibuko, back then a student and part of Mbizo's inner circle of close-knit South Africans in exile, says, 'He had been complaining about his health. We thought the tour was taking its toll, but were taken aback when he collapsed on stage. Everybody rushed to the stage, and a few of us quickly accompanied him to the hospital.'

Singer, actor and dancer, Pinise Saul, who was not only part of Dyani's touring band but knew Johnny from Duncan Village, remembers it differently. 'We were on a break, after playing the Berlin Fabric Jazz Café, when this young man, Thabang Makubere came running in, found me with Makhaya Ntsoko and other band members.

'He told us Johnny collapsed backstage. We told him, '*Haai wena, asinaso isikhati so kudlala* – young man, don't be wasting our time, here'. Realising the gravity of the situation, though, we rushed outside, but the ambulance beat us to the scene.

'Doctors said, "It's exhaustion, he'll be okay." He never returned to the tour. Gone.'

Mystery. 'He was mysterious to outsiders because he was a man of few words', his fiancée and mother of his three children, Janne Dirch Petersen, later told me – and myth followed, but never overshadowed him to the end.

Not only his very last moments confused those who loved, worshipped and claimed ringside status in his music and life. His date of birth, for example, is still a point of contention:

Dyani believed that he was born on 30 November 1945, and celebrated the last day of November as his 'birthday'. Yet, as Lars Rasmussen, the publisher of a collection of reminiscences about Dyani called *Mbizo*, says, 'Mysteriously, his passport has 31 December 1947 as his birth date when in fact the Amathole Museum in King Williamstown offers 4 June 1947 as a more plausible possibility.'

Sipping Rooibos with his eldest brother, Fikile 'Bra Fix' Dyani — another contentious footnote in his life, since he had no 'blood brothers', only cousins — in Mdantsane, the now 75-year-old Bra Fix, told me: 'That boy never knew his mother, let alone his birthday.'

And, the stranger his story became, the longer the 'I knew Johnny personally' list grew. Over the years, his wistful bass riffing — clearly blessed by the gods from Ezilalini, the Xhosa countryside — became the soundtrack to my silent prayers, and the more his ghost or rather, spirit, seemed to beckon to me: come ye non-believer. Come to the source.

Though Johnny Dyani left his native Duncan Village precisely 40 years ago, the town is my first port of call. First, that is, if you discount many years of foolish pub-crawling in smoky jazz clubs, where both connoisseur and hedonist embraced in a mutual love for jazz. Not to mention coffee cafés where white bohemia shaped and shagged the new young Azanian dreadlocked poet, never tempering his hope that the mythical Mbizo Dyani would, finally, appear to tell his story.

His-story? Why would that matter?

* * *

Mbizo Dyani is the most eulogised artist in Europe and South Africa, particularly heralded by his fellow artists.

There are about 36 recordings — including from his friend and creative soul mate, Dudu Pukwana's *They Shoot to Kill* to Pierre Dorge's *Doctor Dyani I Presume* — dedicated to Dyani. The dawn of democracy was heralded by Sakhile's former front man, the late Sipho Gumede's chart-topping, moody, blue, bass-heavy musical beauty, *Song for Johnny Dyani*.

Still, it is in poetry that the spirit of this diminutive music shaman from the Eastern Cape reigns supreme.

It is Dyani's name that Lesego Rampolokeng brandishes as he plunges into a war with capitalism, in his meandering — some might say 'the artist as self-declared madman' — poetic tour de force, *Jazz For Johnny Dyani*:

Your bones were scattered in mutilation's wind / foreign and hostile enough to cuff the limb of your rhythm storm / where still you rise my prophet beyond the height of profit / bursting the corporate gut out of the toilet and into jazz-street.

Though exile ate at his soul, Dyani's impact as a recording artist should not be seen through the narrow microscope of alienation and hopelessness. His genius could be detected in the most natural, simple — but not easy — arrangements. In songs such as '*Ntyilo Ntyilo*', a song, at turns worn out and mutilated, and at times heralded as the *Porgy and Bess* of the yet to be put together Modern South African Jazz Songbook.

In Dyani's hands — soul, rather, for that's where his fingers seemed to be permanently dipped — the song is rendered sans the cheap-Tin Pan Alley patriotic, 'home brew' flatness it has been reduced to in innumerable concert halls.

To listen to it from *The Witchdoctor's Son's* 1978 session that included John Tchicai and Dudu Pukwana, is to experience something akin to an orchestral piece of prayer . . . evoking the memory of those folks to whom a Dyani collaborator, artist Motlhabane Mashiangwako, refers as those 'who came before us.'

This was a period that appreciated music as art, and not mere entertainment. It was during the shift from sound as mere companion to jive itself. Here, artistic grandness was stripped naked to reveal a sound as direct, disturbing and deranged art.

Ten homesick years away from their roots, Dyani and his band found a forever-shifting home, deep within their own musical chords. Such blatant self-gazing, resulted in a music that can be termed beautifully sick. Sick as in, an illness known to the wise ones, as 'the illness of the gods'. A coded gift that can only be decoded and healed by those who deign to confer it:

. . . And you ask yourself how can talent be equated to an illness? Go ahead ask the full take: Why did Hendrix die, Joplin, Coltrane expire so young and gifted?

When asked where Dyani's name fits in the pantheon of great bass players, his ex-sideman, the renowned alto saxophonist Tchicai says, 'up there with Charlie Mingus'.

* * *

East London, December 2004. The town is in the throes of pre-Christmas madness. The air is thick with the click sounds of the locals. A bad hi-fi in a nearby furniture shop blasts the latest crude rap. Across the passage leading to the Jazz Inn (my hosts), a yellow-skinned African, young bright thingy, with fried hair, wearing a Britney Spears-ish tube top, waltzes past, eager to catch a taxi to the townships.

Woza Friday!

Spaarky — as my host, the sixty-something Dutch émigré and trader in rare jazz records, Albert Spaargaren is known — is whistling an out-of-tune version of a Mongezi Feza piece, 'You Think You Know Me', which was poetically interpreted by Ezar Ngcukana.

That's when it dawns on me: Besides the theme song for the isiXhosa initiation rites, *washu Magwaza, Magwaza, yo hoo ho*, into which I don't have an insider's insight beyond being rather awestruck by its polyrhythmic layers, I know pretty much nuffing about this Xhosa man, Mbizo.

It is believed that because he left his Eastern Cape family at such an early age (14), Johnny never went to initiation school. In the city centre, I ponder aloud, do I now know Dyani?

It is 7pm. If we are not careful, we will miss the first of my interviews. Mkhalelwa Mazibuko — MK — who says he knew Dyani back in the Berlin of the 70s leads us to the beach-front coffee shop for a sundowner and a rap about Mbizo.

To MK, Johnny Dyani was many things — big brother, friend, comrade, sponsor (he paid MK's university fees) and mentor. 'I will never forget the day Johnny came from Sweden to Berlin where we — a group of South African students — lived.

'He collected us and told us to follow him to the train station. We emerged next to the most prestigious concert hall, the Philharmonic. 'He organised entrance for us. "But hey Johnny," we cautioned, "the Philharmonic *is nie mos 'n speel gontjie*. This is a serious swanky joint *jy weet?*" "Not to worry," he said. "Go inside and behave."

'Minutes later we were shocked to see our friend on stage, with the spotlight on him and famous soprano Irene Schwartz performing live at the Philharmonic!

'After the show we met Johnny's buddy, Bra Louis Moholo. He was so envious yet admired Johnny's work ethic. One day, he swore, he too would play at the Philharmonic. Three years later, Moholo was at the Philharmonic, with none other than the great American pianist, Cecil Taylor.'

Itching to link the worldly, urbane Mbizo to the young boy who grew up in Duncan Village, I arranged to meet Pulle Twak'u, Dyani's childhood friend, the following day.

'Johnny used to call from overseas quite a lot,' says Twak'u, now a dapper salesman and something of a community hero. 'He was homesick. He would call to ask me about some of the most bizarre things and people. "*Wemfondini*," I used to tell him, "all the people have moved to Mdantsane Township." He would ask, "Where's Mdantsane?"

In the streets of Mdantsane, the second biggest township in South Africa, I meet several youngsters and ask them about the area's greatest musical export. They look at me as if I've escaped from a loony bin. 'Johnny who?' Mcedisi Solomon wanted to know.

I end up at the Dyani household. At 75, Bra Fix is diabetic and half blind.

'Johnny comes from a family of ten children', Bra Fix, begins. 'Of all the ten children of Minah and Driver, all but three — myself, Noxawe and Ntsikilelo — have died. The "official" version is that Johnny was the youngest in the household of Driver and Minah Dyani.

'The truthful version is that Johnny never knew his real mother or father. In 1946 a young woman, Nonkathazo (the burdened one), was expecting and it was clear she was going to bear more than one child. She was only able to give birth to one. The next child was stuck in his mother's womb.'

The elderly Dyani spoke about the horrifying birth scene in which both Nonkathazo and the other child lost their lives — though, the account in Lars Rasmussen's book claims that Johnny believed he was a triplet. Only the firstborn survived.

In essence, Johnny Dyani believed that the lives of his mother and brother were sacrificed so that he could live. That very awareness added to the haunting aspects of his life no amount of greater artistry could rewrite.

These and other things pertaining to isiXhosa tradition inspired him to compose some of his most endearing songs — 'Does Your Father Know', 'Year of the Child', 'Grandmother's Teaching' and 'Heart with Minah's Face' — expressions of longing and alienation felt by the child in him.

Bedraggled by the emotional rain, I was glad to bid farewell to Mdantsane and the Eastern Cape. If Johnny is not here, I thought, I would search for him elsewhere. For, despite being buried here 18 years ago on 16 November 1986, his spirit has remained in Europe.

Wrapping up the research into this dynamic musician's impact, I landed up with Paul Bothata Kgabo — an insightful collector of Dyani's rare recordings.

Listening to records such as *Let the Music Take You* — David Murray on tenor sax and George Brown on drums — and singles 'The Fast Life', a fire-spitting, furious choreo-poem, you can actually hear Dyani's upright bass squeal like a million violins and the bass riffing seems to come from two basses played by one man.

'If this is not genius, then that word is useless', a man drunk on *The Witchdoctor's Son* was heard screaming in Berlin, exiles say. But he was not an angelic, subservient recipient of European applause or even American arrogance. One of the Dyani urban legends is his 1960 confrontation with the god-like iconoclast, Charlie Mingus.

Legend has it that the great Mingus asked him, 'Hey, mah man, can you read music?' Dyani answered, 'No.' Mingus bragged that he could, and so after a gig in which Dyani outplayed Mingus, the American came to congratulate him. 'That was great, man.' Dyani's response was curt. 'Thank you. You played rather flat, I must say.'

* * *

Even a zealot — like me, for whom the Shamanic piece '*Magwaza*' is the reason I was set out on the tracks of Dyani's spirit, have to acknowledge that perhaps the most spiritual exertion, anyone will ever hear, of Dyani on disc, is to be found in *The Hajj*, a recording that bears not his name, but that of countryman Dollar Brand, this time known by his Muslim name, Abdullah Ibrahim.

Here, the Free Jazz genius, known for his almost natural scaling of the peaks of African rural sounds — and yet, it was as much 'natural', as it was a result of spiritual effort and the power of memory — teamed up with a man to whom art meant a dialogue with his god . . . Allah.

Here was man for whom the pleasures of creating sound to express himself was no longer enough. Abdullah Ibrahim was, at this phase, a man to whom creating music was just another call to deeper prayer, a man to whom to create was to test the limits of earthliness, and sanity as understood by the earthlings . . .

It must be noted that, at this stage — and perhaps, that is why this record ended the way it did — Dyani had also converted to Islam and changed his name to Akhir Dyani, years after Ibrahim had changed from his District Six street name, Dollar Brand to Abdulla Ibrahim. Dyani's conversion was certainly a result of Ibrahim's influence and personal as well as musical challenges.

The Hajj — a 1978 Downtown Records release — should be seen and heard for what it is: an artistic consummation of a deep brotherly love. As far as the Johny Dyani discography is concerned, nothing is as creatively confessional as this song.

The truth, to those who rushed to the shops — hip jazz cats and music-loving squares alike — was out, dripping through the stereo speakers. As they say, the truth shall come out: Brother Abdullah, was, and perhaps is the only living artist, capable of pushing Dyani to his most exhaustive, inspirational and glorious heights.

Considering Dyani had played and swung with the best of them, Steve Lacy, Don Cherry, Charles Mingus, Mal Waldron — who had done duty with Lady Day (Billie) herself — it was not a home-boy advantage, but raw vision by Abdullah Ibrahim that inspired Dyani's flights into demonic genius — the artist not as spiritual being, but as a spirit conductor.

The title track itself in Arabic, Abdullah's religious language, translates as 'a journey'. What a bruising, uplifting, impossibly mind-defying, 21-minute piece of musical journey it became?! As far as cosmo *logical* sounds goes, here was an artwork more elegiac, elegant and epic in scale, than Salif Keita's '*Mandjou*', more sonorous than Nusrat Fateh Ali Khan's '*Mustt Mustt*'.

Intentional or not (works like this cannot be pre-determined, pre-meditated), the whole Hajj experience was up there with giants such the 21-minute 'Pursuance'and 'Psalm — Live Version', both from John Coltrane's full set of his 1964 masterpiece, *A Love Supreme*. 'Tis.

If such human endevours fail to bring down the angels from the heavens, then perhaps the latter were just but biblical fairies all along . . .

Koto Bolofo

The poet laureate of fashion photography goes to Bizana

Bizana, Eastern Cape. Those with an acute sense of the country's migratory roots refer to this area as e*maMpondweni*. With its exuberantly coloured dwellings and general dealers with their 1970s kitschy murals — *Beef, Bull Brand Gives You Strength* — in screaming red, amid the dour rural surroundings, the place could have been ripped from a Warhol pop art-gone rural. We are shadowing the doyen of European fashion photographers, Koto Bolofo, here for a ritual in honour of his late father, Makhaola Bolofo, known here as 'Dublin'.

The root of Dublin's and, and therefore of his son's, bond with the village was planted almost fifty years ago, when he briefly settled here as a teacher from Lesotho. This was before fleeing to England after the state had accused him of being a Marxist. Facing possible arrest, Dublin rounded up his family and beat it out of the country, passing back through Lesotho, and then onto Zambia, Kenya, Tanzania and France, before settling in one of damp and grey London's working-class boroughs, Ealing and later, Southall.

HOT TYPE

Today marks the fiftieth year since the family flew out, 12 since ol' Dublin and his wife, Makoto Vuyiswa Bolofo returned to the village, buoyed by Nelson Mandela's final long walk to freedom. It is also exactly a year since Dublin passed on in his late 80s, hence the ritual in his honour.

His son has a deep emotional bond with both the village and his departed father, one that was cemented almost a decade ago when Koto, experimenting with film, shot a biographical 'coming-home' documentary on his father's return to the village. *The Seed Is Black, The Land Is White* won critical acclaim, becoming a film classic on the international artsy circuit, such the Berlin and Toronto Film Festivals.

In England, Koto's parents, particularly his father, wished for the young Koto to have a career in the sciences or, at best, medicine. 'We wanted him to be a doctor, but ah, the boy had no brains for medicine,' his mother recalls. 'Then one day we were horrified when he told us he was going to study graphic design. We had no sense at all as to what the world of design really meant. Luckily I was working for British Rail and it had a division called Industrial Design Department, and that is where I first heard of that word.

'One day I arrived home in high spirits, happy to have heard of the word design,' she says. 'And when I told his dad, "Dear, in fact there is a word called design." Then papa turned around and said, "Oh, now you are siding with him now in this madness of his. And what's that, 'design'? My son's going to be a doctor."

Clearly, ol' Dublin's wish took a dive when his son ended up studying graphic design, from where he was attracted to a world of images, image-making and style. Fate had pulled one of its tricks: Today Koto Bolofo has become a rare talent within the international fashion world's explosive and ultra-competitive field.

His is a stylistic work with a touch of elegance. His work, especially material published in *L'Uomo Vogue* and his hardcover book on the sculptor Sibusiso Mbhele, shows him to be a poet with the soul of painter, an artist with an acute sense of the speed of light.

Koto Bolofo

At any given moment, his classy, sometimes playful, often spiritually evocative work can be found spread across the pages of *Italian Vogue*, *L'Uomo Vogue*, *Russian Vogue*, *German Vogue* and *GQ*, as though they are his canvass to imprint his dreams upon. His campaigns for Yohji Yamamoto, Hermes and Burberry, as well as his coffee-table books on vintage car racing, obscure sculptors, and the latest, a pictorial biographical project on what makes tennis icon Venus Williams tick, offer an insight into the world of the photographer as an alchemist.

Let's dispense with art-gallery speak and nail it for what it is: The man is, simply, shit hot!

Together with fashion photography's gods such as Bruce Weber, Nick Knight and David LaChapelle, Koto Bolofo is a *galactico*, one of the true heirs to Mario Testino and Patrick Demarchelier, and possibly relay baton holder to incendiary talents such as the Lagos / New York City hipster, Andrew Dosunmu and Mali's Boubacar Toure. In photographic terms, Bolofo's work has that rare ability to enter into and dissolve the metaphysical world, thus recreating it as nostalgic realism in the same vein as William Claxton images of 1950s bebop / jazz dandies . . . smoky blue, deep, and 'with it'. The man uses light in the manner a master painter, making do with a minimal supply of colour.

And yet — other than for a handful of social documentary collectors and artsy sorts — Koto Bolofo is perhaps one of South Africa's best-kept secrets.

I asked around. David Golblatt said he was not familiar with his work. Jozi's new pop cultural photographer, Lolo Veleko said, 'the man has this 1970s feel, but I started getting his vibe just a month ago.'

The black kids at the Market Photo Lab, said nope, he doesn't register, while a few of those familiar with him first laid their peepers on him at the annual Design Indaba gig in Cape Town earlier this year.

I got interested in him entirely by default. Ten years ago, I set out to locate a video director and photographer who had directed the American soul-disco songstress Janet Jackson's sepia video of one of the eeriest pop song cuts

39

of its time, 'Got 'Til It's Gone'. A charming photo-montage of 1950s *Drum* pics juxta*posed* with contemporary Johannesburg and New York's street postures, the video introduced the then unknown Sudanese model Alek Wek to the world, while paying homage to a period of bygone, defiant dandy-ness; high-waisted Zoot suits and outlandishly-collared shirts.

Rumour had it that it was Koto Bolofo who directed it. It turned out it wasn't, but, ah, the ill-fated chase opened a window onto a name and an artist I had never heard before.

Not that I knew of Bizana, or Mhlanga village for that matter, but it did not tally up with my perceptions of a man strutting through the fashion biz, a world confined to magazines such as *Vogue, GQ, I.D.* and such glossies known for blond-shells, bleeding mascara, from corner cafés' shelves. Excuse me: I mean this is the man who calls Venus Williams, 'my sister'. Watching him in the village today, the man — his face swallowed by his goofy academic, but 'in style' spectacles — seems one with the entire setting. Only that, for him, it's not a setting, it's home. It's here that I got to appreciate the man's fluidity. Though he has availed himself for this interview, his is an elusive spirit. Like his photographic output, Koto Bolofo is always on the move . . . movement seems to define him. He is here with me and yet, he is not.

First day's tricky. We can't talk. He is meeting a salad mix of village folks: some come for advice, some are aiming to get him to part with a dime or few quid. Here's a man, who, in his 'normal cause of events' floats around crafting poetic images in the world's capitals, and here he is, in a village with nothing going for it other than the aroma of cow dung hanging in the air. To make sense of it, you have to imagine the hissy fits of Naomi Campbell and the cat-strut of Kate Moss, and then cue in the sound of ululating village women, milling around stewing *drie-voet* black pots.

Talking amidst the singing, dancing young men — with rubbery pelvic joints perform acrobatic snake moves — with screaming dames cheering on the sidelines, a commotion of an African village at its most *carnivalesque* — felt like being unwittingly let in to the alchemist's secret room. Something about this village, or this day, seemed to stir his soul. Just as we are about to warm up to a subject, the man would spring to his feet, dash to the back kraal where a group of 20-plus men were wrestling an ox to the ground. The ox would have none of that, thus the mother of all riots ensued.

Koto Bolofo is right in the mix, his black suit and matching silk tie flapping about wildly, in a local crowd thick with click-click sounds. The next moment as he's angling for a grand view leading towards the beast's collision with the old man's dagger, a camera in hand, one could not but think of Dambudzo Marechera's *The Black Insider*. One with the crowd and, yet in reality, an observer or observed at best.

Speaking in a blend of soft and operatic vowels, gesturing as he goes about, you'd imagine you are in conversation with an actor. The man's flair for the dramatic — unexpected cackling laughter, sudden detachment when he's in deep reflection — is quite evident, and yet his work possesses a different kind of drama.

What does Bizana, or any part of South Africa really mean for him, after growing up in England?

'Uhm, uhm, it's something do with the blood you know. Home for me, is not exclusively geographical. It's something in you, man. It is what you choose. What you feel, what you yearn for, what you put into it, your life . . . it's really like a love affair. You have to work for it, take detours from it and get absorbed by it. For me, it's a matter of family spirits, that African vitality.' Though his work, as author and fashion critic Adam Levin puts it, 'is very European, very traditional, very classic, very romantic', Bolofo will never allow anyone to box him in. 'Never.'

'Oh, yeah, I am a romantic and still very African. The two aren't opposites. You see, Africans are very noble, very elegant people, and my work expresses that. You can't fake being an African. It's either you are or you are not.'

'Let's clarify this European thing,' he says, as I venture into his space as he greets this or that cousin, his anglicised, but quite eloquent, seSotho distinct. '. . . The European thing, uhm, uhm, I mean that's really a matter of cultural displacement but it doesn't alter who I am, who I want to be. You might think I am joking, and even my mom does not believe this, but I see myself ending up here in this very village. These are my roots. This is where I aim to retire to, to create something homely for my family.'

He lives in Vendee village, in a refurbished castle-like farm house, three hours out of Paris, with his wife Claudia Van Rhyssen and, as Monna Mokoena, the gallerist who visited him there, jokingly puts it, 'their Benetton kids'.

'Identity is really a personal choice,' Koto Bolofo says almost in passing. 'For instance my younger brother, Setsoto — born and bred in London — wants nothing to do with this . . .' he points around Bizana, to the sky as though capturing the country in one hand wave. 'You really can't fault people's choices.'

He would rather talk about his work, and then his beloved, his father's beloved land.

'Look, this is all I ever wanted to be — photography. I give my all. I deal with the best only. The best. I don't give a damn if you are black or white, if are shoddy I am so over you — period. Never assume just because you are pink and I am pink, then I'd be down with the pink squad, uh uh. I am a ruthless bastard when it comes to work. I don't want to sound offish, but when you are overseas, in a world of exacting standards with multi-billion dollar personalities, you do ask yourself: Africa? Mmmh, South Africa? Can they pull it off? Tha's how 'tis man, tha'sit. Reputation is everything,' he says, explaining how, for the first time in his three decades on the cutting seams of fashion, he has agreed to showcase his work at the Johannesburg-based Gallery MOMO, the free-thinking brat on the contemporary art circuit. 'See, Monna Mokoena,' he says of the gallerist, 'is full fire.'

Talk zig-zags from the present to the past, rarely into the future, for, just like all fashion photographers, the man lives his future today. In a flash, we are back in 1994 and his dad, a topic close to his soul. 'First time I came back — when was it? 1992 or thereabouts — Mandela was out, man. I will never forget the spirit of the time — gripping! I had never really been in South

Africa, prior to that. Arriving here, Johannesburg Airport, named after some Jan Smuts chap, and later Durban Airport were like these super-modern structures. Outside, on these snaking highways, I was like d-a-m-n. This is it. Home! Nothing Out Of Africa about it, so I thought we are doing fine here. The Bolofos have nice pads. Worth all the trouble spent in the cold? I whistled with joy.'

'Arriving in Bizana,' he says, 'nothing corresponded with my dreams. This place was very dry, windswept. A sad sight. I was devastated. Is this what it means to be home?' I asked myself. 'Of course, daddy was over the moon. He was deeply moved that, finally, he was back home. 'We are free, we are free,' he kept saying, meanwhile I'd be like, 'God this is terrible. This is real bad.'

'You see, this might sound like bragging, but my father was a real people's man, and he imprinted that on me, a virtue I've taken to heart, thus, to art. Anyone can feel for themselves, that there's no real distance between me and my subjects in my work.'

Of course that is bragging *Monsieur* Bolofo! And why not?

In the arts and sciences of this world, some people have their praise singers, while some are left to speak for themselves. The late cult photo-stylist Richard Avedon once acclaimed celebrity photographer David LaChappelle, as the 'surrealist of our time, our own Magritte'. Koto Bolofo tells you directly that he works with quality and class and nothing else. It's an attitude that has earned him a reputation as 'Mr. Shoot-First', ask questions later, particularly within the design and make-believe fashion scene. Fashion writer Adam Levin says, 'I have attended his workshop at the Design Indaba. All the man does is speak about himself.'

When I raised it, the man pointedly said, 'What have those people done? Look man, Richard Avedon — yep, him — has been to my house, signed my book, had tea with me. I want to ask them, hey, show me your book that Avedon has signed! Huh?' Modesty — especially of a false kind — is a virtue he has no time for. 'When I was at the Design Indaba, the only black folks I saw there were serving tea in their oversized garments, heads bowed in perpetual submission. I asked myself, do I have to be humble when I go on that stage to talk, do I? Oh no, I have never been humble! What was I supposed to say: 'Thank you ladies and gentleman, I am very blessed to be here'? They won't get that from me.'

And still, he sees himself as somebody driven to engage and share his experience with this country. 'Criticising each other will bog us all down, I tell you. We criticise each other while Europe is watching us . . . looting our creative wealth. What's the use?'

Dig him or diss him, the man pretty much walks his talk: Back in the mid-1990s he plucked a young Bergville, KwaZulu, sculptor and village outcast out of the shadows of the Drakensberg mountains and into the international art arena. The name Sibusiso Mbhele, with his sci-fi, movie set-like sculpted planes: two seaters, 'copters, jets; has since soared to become a drop-around-the-dinner-table name amongst the tuxedoed class.

What happened to the young man? 'He got punch-drunk by fame,' he responds, skipping not a beat. 'The young man was ahead of his time. We – Bolofo and his wife, with whom he made a documentary book and film on Mbhele – were also ahead of him,' he says now, with a disinterested look. 'I spent a greater part of my latter working life looking out for that bloke and it was like filling a bucket with holes. I think he was not really prepared for it.'

The man starts to move, cracks up with laughter, then suddenly stops, his gaze fixing on the dancers, as they leap and look as though frozen in a poetic picture. Clearly, the interview is getting in the way of all the local dazzle. An agreement is struck: 'Man, let's do this in Johannesburg. This is impossible. I am really enjoying this – the dance. A-m-a-z-eeeng,' man, he dragged it. 'A-m-a-zeeng.'

* * *

Jozi' s cold is dissipating. Tuesday afternoon trips to the airports are a test case of tolerance – honking hooters, swerving Mercs, a taxi trapezing on the white line, entering the game of death. I am right at the back of a flying private hire cab ferrying Bolofo to the airport, from where he'll spend the next 14 hours up in the air. What's left of the interview is conducted in a lightning speed of gigabytes.

South African glossies? 'Dead. They import lots of overseas crap.'

South African fashion industry? 'Ought to wake up to talent in the townships.'

Why don't you show them how to? 'Would love to, but you guys can't afford me. It's about the rates.'

Style Wars: US, Europe, the East or Africa? 'Africa. But it don't mean a thing. The catchphrase is, industry, ba-y-bee.'

And then he goes all anecdotal. 'Have I told you the story of my mentor, Antonella, the editorial director of *Condé Nast* in Italy, A-n-to-n-e-llahhh? I call her anytime with any shoot or idea and she just flaps her hands up in the air,' he switches to an Italian accent, "Doe eet, doe it, aneetime." When she sees me in Rome, her face lights up and she screams my name: "Koto, Koto, *Kotino*. Aahh, my *chocolatino*."

In a flash, he's gone. And I am left speechless when, back in the web of traffic, the driver cracks up laughing, asking, 'Who's that man?'

Salif Keita

The muezzin from Bamako

Known around the world as 'The Golden Voice of Mali', Salif Keita's unique sound blends the traditional styles of his West African homeland with influences from Cuba, Spain, Portugal and the Middle East.

The key factor to understanding and enjoying his music and beliefs is through his voice. His Islamic-inflected voice evokes — noted the well-known world music critic, Simon Broughton — 'the spectacular mud-brick mosque of Djenne, in his native Mali.'

Though not particularly religious — but spiritual — Keita's voice has all the piercing peacefulness and cries for redemption just like the voice of a muezzin. Keita is perhaps part of a few spirit mediums channelling the power of Islam's second most key figure, Bilal, an African slave who became Prophet Muhammad's (PBUH) prayer caller and His most trusted disciple.

Though Western African vocalists by their nature have searing, emotion-tinged vocals, it is only a few truly talented artist who are able to use it to soar beyond mere entertainment, prayer or vocal gymnastics.

In this regard, the Mansa of Mali is at home with other creative vocalists, such as Youssou N'dour, Mapenda Seck and Ndiouga Dieng of Orchestra Baobab, amongst others. These are intermediaries to whom art, religion, love, war and peace are intricately woven aspects of humanity's complex nature.

Ever since his breakout album — 1987's *Soro* — which established him as a primer of what became World Music, Keita born in 1949 in Djouba, a village west of Bamako — has enjoyed a prosperous career not only in his native Mali but in the entire West African region. Early on in his career, he was awarded the National Order of Guinea by President Ahmed Sékou Touré.

He became well known in Europe and America after moving to Paris and collaborating with other African pop stars there.

But his was not an easy path. Despite the fact that he came into the world in 1949 of noble birth — he is a direct descendant of Sundiata Keita, the Mandinka warrior king who founded the Malian empire in the thirteenth century — his albinism was considered a sign of bad luck in Mali, and resulted in his being spurned and alienated by his community and even by his family.

He spent his childhood and teenage years isolated, and turned to music as a means by which to make use of his talents and connect with others. His reputation spread far and wide, picking up momentum as he left Mali and moved to Abidjan, and then he finally went to Paris in 1984, where he has remained.

His 'Golden Voice of Mali' epithet actually has a double meaning, as many people with albinism of African ancestry have skin and hair that is light golden colour rather then the more typical deep brown or black.

This is a face-to-face interview with the artist, on the art of performance, spirituality, and the dilemma of living in Paris while one's soul is part of Africa.

* * *

BM: Monsieur Keita, one lasting impression your fans have of you in South Africa has to be that moment when you ascended the stage at the 1996 Arts Alive Festival at Vista University, Soweto .

Your searing rendition of the song '*Sina* (*Soumbaya*)' from the career-making 1987 album, *Soro*, felt like a prayer — with you as the high priest. Looking back, what was the impact of that show on your subsequent work, here?

SK: Oh yah, yah, that, ah remember yes, yes I do. I became very emotional there. I felt a powerful surge of love from the people. I will never forget that show.

BM: You are talking about connecting with the people. That's the key word — connection. How does an artist arrive at that point in which he realises an honest connection with his audience?

SK: It's all in the way they react to the music, if they make an effort to be one with the art. It's a bit difficult, telling the honesty, though.

BM: But how do you know they are not merely singing along to a familiar hit tune?

They say Miles Davis — in his Jack Johnson phase — felt the connection in the audience's silence, particularly since he tended to turn his back to the audience. It was not a case of them looking at his obvious physical expressions. In short, his was not a jive.

SK: It is difficult to tell deception, but one thing your audience will never fake is their soul. Of course, in movies there are lots of fake emotions, but not at live music festivals. Miles gave his back to them, I want to walk amongst them. Touch them. I am an African. Ours is an interactive art. Music is not mere sound: it is sharing, a way of life.

BM: Your music overwhelms. The songs linger on the listener well beyond their performance or radio play listing. I do not understand your language, thus your lyrics, but I feel like you are talking to me, and sometimes I feel like you are talking in tongues. Like the women in the traditional doctors' initiation section where I grew up. Quite surreal.

SK: Thanks, but every time I step on stage, or go into a studio to record, I do not assume that my songs will touch my audience on an emotional level all the time. Though my music comes from the bottom of my heart, I play on, hoping it connects. It's really a bonus if it does.

BM: I hear you, monsieur, but if I remember correctly, the ordinary who you really wanted to play for, the folk who adore your art, were nowhere near that now legendary Arts Alive show. Only African elites . . .

SK: True. But you see, when I compose music, I compose it for the people. I then rehearse it within myself, whereafter I perform it to the people who pay to come to gigs. But if it was within my power, I would love to perform free for ordinary people. The time will come.

BM: I realised that yourself, the late Ali Farka Touré, Youssou N'dour, Mory Kanté, Busi Mhlongo, Baaba Maal and Orchestra Baobab are heralded by the European media as 'African music royalty', while dombolo and rhumba superstars such as Koffi Olomide, Papa Wemba and are seen as the masses' acts. Who dictates what works and what doesn't? What sells and what doesn't? Is what's good for Africa necessarily good for Europe and vice versa?

SK: We are all artists, African artists trapped in Europe trying to make it in a commercial sense. But also, you should know, and now I speak for myself, I try to speak out against the colonisation and continuing oppression of our people. Of course what sells in Europe is what the Europeans want to hear – but we are more diverse than that.

I know artists you've mentioned, being able to play for all sorts of audiences. They should: they are the people's messengers. I am proud to be an African. But, also, I operate on the world stage for world audiences.

BM: Excuse me, monsieur, how do you feel about a whole lot of African music styles being lumped together with Indian, Pakistani, Eastern European vibes, Maghreb, the Australian Aborigines as well as *World Music*? Doesn't it dilute the impact of African music on the global cultural sphere?

SK: My brother, jump out of your dreams. See, although this is a nightmarish reality, we Africans do not own anything. Yes, we have rich, creative cultures and traditions. But who packages it for commercial consumption? Europe.

They have the money. So they will package our music as they please. As for me, this world music thing is just a marketing label.

BM: Your music varies from the deeply soulful, such as '*Soureba*', to epic poetry, as expressed in the Mandinka war song, '*Mandjou*'. Your art marries hard rock, funk and pop styles with traditional sounds. Is that the global aspect, or is African music just rich and diverse within itself?

SK: I play what I feel. Yes, I play for Africans, but it is not only black people who embrace my music. I am not about to allow myself to be boxed in. I do not want nobody — not you, not people in Paris, Bamako, the US market — to define me.

When I tour the States my audience is primarily made up of white Americans and African expatriates in the US — and that's how it is. American radio / media is notoriously restricted to, and promotes mainly that which appeals to Americans.

BM: What about African-Americans, perhaps the biggest black music-buying market in the world? Are they tuned into your music?

SK: Ahh, and this is not meant in a bad way, I think because of schooling and socialisation, they are ignorant of what African music is all about, what is happening on the continent. Also, they are not too clear on the connection between us and them. They still believe in CNN's jungle connection to Africa.

I am glad though, that I have met and worked with artists such as Carlos Santana.

That man is not ordinary like you and me. I suppose in a way he is, but he's more of a . . . free spirit. He's an extraordinary human being and artist. One of the greatest of all time! I met him in San Francisco, west coast US, and I will cherish that memory forever.

BM: It's touching that you describe Santana with so much awe. In fact, it's rather scary. I mean, this is the man who described you as the musician with the 'heavenly voice'. The great Salif and the icon Santana, waxing lyrical about each other. Is this mutual back-scratching or what?

SK: Banter aside; you have to feel the man, his music, and you'll have a sense of what I am talking about.

BM: Your music is filled with African pride. Does that make you an Africanist — as in, intentionally political? I notice that your cultural expression, for example your use of imagery and, and some titles — 'Africa', 'Mandela', '*Mandjou*' and '*Sundiata*', etc. — is uncompromisingly African.

SK: No, I am not an Africanist in a narrow ideological way. I am an African and proud of that. I don't care about politicians. Do you think that Bush, Blair or Mbeki care about the people suffering on the ground?

BM: I hear you. But I find it strange that you are advancing such Africanist working-class notions while you are based in Paris, Europe. Also, you perform more in Europe than in Africa. Isn't that a bit ironic? Eiffel Tower Africanism?

SK: Look, Bongani, I don't see any dilemma there. Firstly, you are wrong, I am now firmly based in Bamako, Mali. Of course my family is still in Paris, but I have relocated back home. My band is Bamako, my everyday life is Bamako.

See, Paris is for business, and sure you'd understand what I mean. Why am I so fiercely Africanist while performing in Europe? Easy! Europe is powerful, rich and still oppressing Africa. If you want to change the heart of power, you direct your message to those in power not the powerless or the converted.

BM: What would you like to achieve in your lifetime that you feel your music has not achieved?

SK: Unite in the spirit with all African artists the world over. Create music that speaks to the masses, for they have no voice. Inspire hope. That is my dream.

BM: Which is what you are doing right now, no?

SK: Merci, Monsieur Madondo. I suppose I don't want to deviate from such a fulfilling path.

BM: I am afraid we have to call it quits, before we sit and rap until the chickens grow beards. I must say, you have given me a new perspective on the role of artists . . . beyond music.

Salaam Ailaikum.

SK: *Wa' Ailaikum Salaam*!

Mbongeni Ngema
Not Sarafinished yet

Mbongeni Ngema is not known as a cat with countless lives for nothing.

It's 20 years since he created the original *Sarafina*, and 13 odd years since *Sarafina II*, as well as couple of years since his national 'storm in the tea cup' blown into a marketing *coup de grace*, theme song — *AmaNdiya*.

Gazing back over the last decade, I imagine the controversy-prone man as somebody permanently splashed with baby oil — slick, shiny and elusive. Many a rock — some of which he invited through his erratic and brave approach to life — has been hurled down his path.

Yet, as if propelled by some indeterminate force, the man has headbutted and smoothed his way from one landmine to another. As an artist — actor, director, musician, choreographer — he continues turning mundane stories and songs into . . . what's the phrase so loved by sucking-up entertainment scribes? 'Gold'.

Though Madlokovu (his clan name) has created some of South Africa's most transformative, radical and culture-altering — as well as some of its most mediocre — stage works, he has always projected a tacky political profile. Witness his attempt at evoking the memory of Steve Biko in the 1997 religious musical *Maria-Maria*.

Yet despite the rage, emotion and intended politics of his material, there's something that always propels one towards Ngema the theatre virtuoso and not Ngema the political animal.

I suspect, though, that the man's overall appeal lies in his pop / cultural split-personality. To the liberal press, Ngema is Idi Amin reincarnated; while to theatre lovers and neo-Africanists — South Africa's 'Renaissance children' — he is a hero, a cultural historian and a peerless entertainer. David Mamet, John Kani, George C Wolfe, Savion Glover — none of them has ever created such riotous, emotion-layered choreographical spectacles.

Some are very personal stories, but his best-known, *Sarafina*, is simply a dramatisation of the June 16 1976 student riots; telling the tale of how these kids took on the might of Afrikaner power and planted a seed of defiance that would become a major feature of the battle against segregation.

A gifted choreographer with a visual aptitude and an ear for bewitching music, Ngema's power has always been in what you can see, hear and feel. His stories stick in your memory like braai odours in a new lounge suite — you might be uncomfortable with the smell, but it makes you salivate.

At rehearsals at the State Theatre, school gals in hiked-up gymslips mill around talking on cellphones while angelic voices and frantic guitar loops seep through the roof. The music is as hot as a New Orleans creole dish. For once, Pretoria's happening.

Disturbed by what I thought was the man's clinging to past victories, I visit Ngema's hotel in Pretoria for coffee and a chat. Tonight is the opening and Ngema is expecting important figures. Calls from high-profile people disturb our conversation. Soon, however, we get to the bone of it: Why *Sarafina*? Isn't this hankering after lost glory?

He clears his throat. '*Sarafina* is a modern classic. Classics have a longer shelf life. Look at *Le Miserables*, *The Lion King*. Audiences just love them, regardless of when they were created. Whether in Vienna, Berlin, Paris or

London, classics are the staple diet of the theatre business. Other than that' — long pause — 'it makes sense to raid our recent past to energise the journey ahead.'

But is a decade of democracy reason enough to pull those old bell-bottom pants from granny's closet; to proclaim that the future lies in yesteryear? 'Sometimes,' Ngema says, ignoring the jibe, 'it's those old pants that tell you how fashion and style has evolved. For example, *Sarafina* was created 18 years ago. Since then, things have evolved. Children were born and raised.

'To these children, hip-hop and kwaito are the only expressions of black pain. To young whites, the past is as dim as it is to their black mates. Other than the helper at home, the only blacks they relate to at an emotional level are their black mall friends with MTV rap twangs. As the song says, to them, it's always been "this wunnerful".'

Besides educating Mandela's born-free generation, where to for South Africa's hardest-working playwright? 'It's all about exploring the roots so I can make sense of the routes we have to take if theatre is to compete with other media.'

Teatime's long lapsed and I'm beginning to feel like an intruder. But we are not yet Sarafinished — we still need to discuss the scandal surrounding the R14-million tender awarded to Ngema in the mid-1990s by the Health Department to turn *Sarafina II* into an Aids-awareness tool.

'I became a sitting duck for the media. I was naive. I didn't know anything about tenders and neither did [then Health minister] Dr Nkosazana Zuma. The idea was well-intentioned. We made mistakes and were punished. But that episode almost ruined my life. I was hospitalised and later discovered I was diabetic, depressed and drained.'

Later that night I find myself in a fish-packed Opera Theatre audience — which includes members of the original *Sarafina* cast and multitudes of freebie kings and queens — to witness if all this breast-beating is worth a dime.

Animated and passionate, the play is vintage Ngema at his deft best and the energetic young cast's fresh voices fill whatever cracks there might be. Ngema needs to ease up on his Gibson Kente-esque technique of over emphasising the burlesque facial expressions, but such creases will get ironed out as the cast settles in.

However, for it to recapture its former world domination — something Ngema still lusts after — *Sarafina* will need a combination of some of its original cast — such as Somizi Mhlongo, Dumisani Dlamini and Baby Cele — and the present fired-up and youthful line-up, possibly a dream never to be realised, as most are major headliners in their own right.

Madlokovu hasn't lost his zing; he's just more mature, more contemplative. But that's only the demenour . . . and outside appearances. Stare deep into his tiger (eyes) and you'll see an almost feline type of spirit, feigning indifference while readying itself to pounce, strut off in glory, or both.

Ooowie, Hughie!

Masekela's rock 'n' roll

Hughie — Hugh Masekela or 'Bra Hugh', a prefix pregnant with street cred that cuts the 'bras' from the ghetto riffraff — had been in New York for no more than a month when he met the world's coolest loudmouth, Miles Davis.

Their meeting came about when Masekela's benefactor, trumpet legend Dizzy Gillespie — with whom the young Masekela, long before he realised his dream to come to America, had been exchanging correspondence, decrying Dr Verwoerd's neo-Nazi country — led the 23-year-old lad into Birdland, the famous jazz club.

Masekela was in the US to study at the prestigious Manhattan School of Music. But, like his ol' squeeze, the vivacious Miriam Zenzi Makeba, he couldn't go back to his beloved mother in Alexandra township, South Africa, if he wanted to.

It took many high-placed and caring people — like his childhood mentor, Father Trevor Huddleston; Makeba's benefactor in the US, Harry Belafonte; and other figures in the British and US liberal, musical and religious arenas

— to bring him to where he now found himself.

At the time Hughie arrived — September 1960 — New York was experiencing something akin to, if not more animated than, the Harlem cultural renaissance of the 1920s. Manhattan was part of a huge underground, sweaty, creative, boiling transatlantic gumbo. With European, Asian and Latin ingredients for added taste, the place was stewing hot.

Birdland — named after bebop genius, drug fiend and hedonist supreme, Charlie Parker — was frequented by arbiters of style, hipsters and that untouchable few simply known as 'cool cats'. Drummer Max Roach, poet LeRoi Jones, composer Donald Byrd, essayist James Baldwin, band leader Charlie Mingus, eccentric pianist Thelonious Monk — all terribly cool, indisputably hip, and all regulars at Birdland.

The wah-wah riffing notes, muted and unmuted trumpet solos, smoke, sweat, rib-cracking humour, laughter and camaraderie were at an all-time high the night that Gillespie — something of an a legend in the town — led young Hughie into the joint where he, Gillespie, was gigging for two 'full-to-the-rafters' weeks.

He was eager to introduce Masekela not only to Birdland but to America's greatest musical, theatrical and literary figures — names that Hughie and his peers, worshippers of 'cool and its musical stylists', had ceaselessly dreamt about back home.

In the crowd were the Slide Hampton Band, a young Quincy Jones, the great Sarah Vaughan and — holding court with a bevy of women around him, snow-white smoke curling and swirling above his head — the heir apparent of cool himself, the 'Prince of Darkness', ladies and gentlemen, Miles Dewey Davis!

After a few introductions Gillespie left Hughie to the master trumpeter, who shook the youngster's hand with a scowl on his face, barking with his raspy voice, 'You from South Africa? You know Jeff?'

Tongue-tied and still recovering from meeting his childhood idol, Hughie stuttered, 'Who's Jeff?'

Ooowie, Hughie!

'She-e-et, you don't know Jeff?' Davis turned around to face Gillespie. 'Diz, this motherfucka don't know Jeff. He ain't from no South Africa, man.'

Turning around, his face almost in Hughie's face, he barked some more: 'You full of shit, man. You from South Africa and you don't know Jeff?'

Gillespie interjected: 'Miles, who de fuck is dis Jeff, man? Where he at an' what de fuck do he do?'

'Jeff's the baddest bass player from down there, South Africa,' replied Davis. 'I ain't never met anybody wid da kinda confidence as Jeff. He's a very baaaad ma'fucker, that Jeff.'

To Davis's delight, young Hughie did know the revered Jeff — but by his full name, Jeff 'Hoojah' Cartriers. What's more, he also worshipped the bass player's no-nonsense street reputation and musical prowess. 'Hoojah', it turned out, had counselled Hughie and the boys back home on the thisses and thats of life.

Other than the noisy Manhattan streets — skyscrapers, blaring car horns, screeching tires, dog shit on the sidewalks, noisy garbage trucks toting gigantic plastic bags — meeting Davis was a rude awakening and a sharp welcoming gesture for Masekela.

The meeting, and the harsh winter climate, imprinted the message on his mind: This is America, baby — a place where faster, bigger, smarter and wittier men and women's dreams have been made, broken or deferred; all in the wink of an eye, and sometimes with the cough-cough pace of the Chattanooga Choo Choo steam train.

The legendary meeting is lyrically retold in Masekela's autobiography, just published in the US. As one of South Africa's best-known jazz exports and one of its most enduring popular culture figures, his fame overseas is perhaps surpassed only by that of his friend, childhood sweetheart and one-time wife, Makeba.

With a title taken from Masekela's 1968 worldwide hit 'Grazing in the Grass', *Still Grazing* is, at 385 pages, a fat, tear-flowing, drug-infested window into marathons of insatiable sex, name-dropping, self-destruction, the struggle of black people against a bleak future, musical craftsmanship, big lights, big cars, bigger pay cheques and biggest egos, brotherly love and sisterly embraces — and triumphs against insalubrious odds.

It also offers insights into personalities ranging from knife-wielding Alexandra street thugs to Malcolm X, Marlon Brando and Marvin Gaye — and just about everybody who has had a ringside view and, or participated in twentieth century black popular culture, Hollywood and world radical politics.

Co-authored with the infamously temperamental D Michael Cheers, editor of the now defunct *Ebony South Africa*, *Still Grazing* reads and sounds like the voice of a very earnest man; as earnest as a man with Hugh Masekela's ego can ever be — 60 bloody, blind, dangerous and fun-filled years at the top, and bottom, of world pop culture.

Though, by design, autobiographies tend to be no more than tales of triumphs against all odds and (not so) veiled attempts at glorifying their authors, this one does what many fail to do — it denies you an opportunity to feel pity for the narrator. I often found myself screaming, rooting for life to chew and spit Masekela out. And at times I was expecting those whose women he was having fun with to materialise out of nowhere and beat him senseless.

It also leaves you wondering: How could anybody have survived the kind of life Hugh had and lived to tell the tale? Is this guy having the last laugh at life and all its moralistic fun-spoilers?

Thematically sub-divided into three sections — 'Home', 'The World' and 'Africa' — the book kicks off with Masekela's life as a four-year-old growing up in the coal-dusty streets of Witbank, 'a one-street town ... surrounded by coal mines, coal trains and coal-packed containers pulled by steam engines called '*Mankalanyana*''.

Witbank might have been conservative when young Hughie was a lil' *bangbroek*, but over emphasising its conservative nature ('a redneck, rightwing, Afrikaner town') makes the authors look lousy — even though the tone of the book makes it clear they were, to use Hugh's favourite phrase, 'cutting some slack' with his biggest support base, American readers and music buyers.

Without pretence or trying to be deep, the book describes — without outlining, without analysis — South Africa's, especially black South Africa's, racial complexities; race, racism and what constitutes blackness.

The first child of social worker Pauline and sculptor Thomas Selema Masekela, little Ramapolo Hugh Masekela arrived, kickin' and screaming, with the help of his maternal grandmother Johanna, on April 4 1939.

'I was born on a tree-lined street at Number 76 Tolman Street in Kwa Quga township and yet *The Star*, the then widely circulated white-owned daily newspaper, did not publish my arrival — or, for that matter, any news about black people,' he writes.

Hughie and his younger siblings — Barbara, born 1941, Nelson Mandela's chief of staff after his release in 1990 and now South Africa's ambassador to the US; Elaine, born 1947, who lives in Yeoville, Johannesburg; and Sybil, born 1953, who 'died of Aids' — were born half-African and half-coloured.

If it wasn't so sad a reflection of this country's racial madness, his and millions of other children's tales would be a tragi-comical story about race classification.

Coloureds are generally assumed to be of a mixture of African and European blood. By virtue of his mother Pauline — the coloured daughter of a Ndebele woman, Johanna Mabena-Mahlangu, and a Scottish mining engineer, Walter Bowers — Hugh and his sisters were a full result of that half-black, half-white ancestry, carrying their moPedi father's full African blood.

Hughie grew up seeing how his granny, Johanna Mabena-Bowers — a stocky woman and a devout Christian who referred to him as 'my little Minkie', a corruption of Mickey Mouse — hustled to make ends meet as a shebeen queen after she was dumped by her roving Scottish beau.

'She sold this mean, potent mix called Barberton, a sorghum beer that distorted her clients' faces — miners from Malawi, Angola and Mozambique — causing their lips, legs and cheeks to swell. But there was also unspiked sorghum beer, gin and brandy which were reserved for her educated friends, teachers, lawyers, preachers, thieves, and con men — the elite of the booze world.'

His story meditates on township life, from Witbank and Alexandra to KwaThema, narrating their vibrancy, pain and blood; all the while listening to old gramophone records of American jazz greats — Glenn Miller, Billie Holiday, Louis Armstrong — and the hottest of the locals, the Jazz Maniacs, Merry Black Birds and Merry Makers, with whom he would later play.

It was in his teenagehood — hanging out at Jozi's reservoir of jazz, Dorkay House, and falling in love with a woman not only eight years his senior but also the object of desire of both black and white bohemians, Miriam Makeba — that the young man became initiated into the high-rollin' life of musicians at their worst and best.

On the road together as part of *King Kong*, the biggest musical revue of the 1950s, the life, recklessness and beauty of Masekela and Makeba was a touching romance — and a dress rehearsal for the grim soul connection, the marriage, and the numerous ons and offs they would engage in 15 eventful years later, thousands of kilometres away in America.

Like that of Makeba — who was instrumental in bringing Hughie to the US, taking care of his accommodation, school fees, food, clothes, and introducing him to radical figures such as leading Africanist John Henrick Clarke and Hollywood leading man Marlon Brando (who once concocted a plan to rescue Robert Sobukwe from prison) — Masekela's destiny was predetermined. His introduction to the sepia scene of US pop culture was bound to be fraught with fatally attractive turnoffs and life-threatening curves.

His journey soon went awry and his booze and drug intake nearly achieved what apartheid had failed to — kill him.

Still Grazing is brimful of such tales of excess — and more: how he courted, slept with — no, sexed — and was seduced by countless women; black, white, Latino, African, American and European.

Their names are reeled off with regret, loving memory, pain and wonder:

Ooowie, Hughie!

Jessie La Pierre, who he had a child with; Jabu Mbatha, who he was married to for 16 years and divorced in 1997; Tshidi Ndamase, with whom he had a daughter; Pat Bannister, the Caribbean scorcher whose middle-class Trinidadian parents said she would marry a musician over their dead bodies.

And if that ain't all, there's Ingrid, the Swede stunner with whom he had a girl child he has never seen; the mad Chris Calloway, daughter of jazz great Cab Calloway; and finally his present wife, the unassuming Elinam Cofie — a dark-complexioned Ghanaian beauty whom he first saw in 1977 as a young girl, crying at a Paris airport.

And all through this roll call, Makeba was present — as sister, fellow artist, lover, wife and political teacher.

Other than the women, there are tales of millions of litres of cognac and wine, outings in Harlem, Lagos nights spent with his equally hedonist pal Fela Kuti and the Hedzoleh Soundz, freebasing with funk king Sly Stone, club-hopping with guitar icon Jimi Hendrix.

The egos of Masekela and his best friend, manager and producer Stewart Levine, swelled so big it derailed a potential Hollywood career.

It all left the yellow-skinned boy from Witbank bruised, battered and burnt out.

Oscillating between reality and a drug haze, Hugh loved San Francisco's hippie haven, Haight-Ashbury, where 'the streets were teeming with junkies walking like mummies, flying high on acid'.

At the height of flower power and hippie philosophy, he and his friend Luigi Alfano would pop LSD, go sit atop Mount Tamalpais and imagine they were American Indians or medieval sages.

At worst (or best, depending on who you ask), funky, agitative black power flew out of the window to usher in 'purple consciousness' as Hugh and the best of the black jazz hipsters popped, guzzled, smoked and injected themselves to death.

John Coltrane, Jimi Hendrix, Miles Davis, Marvin Gaye, Fela Kuti, members of Osibisa — they're all dead, while, mysteriously, Masekela still does over 200 shows a year, looking fitter than a Spanish bull.

Did his Scottish forefathers collude with his amaNdebele, baPedi and maKalanga ancestors to save him so he could testify about his show business route to hell and back?

Not only is the book honest, but — like any account told from a hero's perspective, or from that of a religious convert who has just seen 'the light' — there are parts which, in their attempts to rid Hugh of responsibility for the direction his life took, end up demonising him.

For example, he is ashamed that he missed the funerals of Dr Martin Luther King and Malcolm X and that, in essence, he never really played the cohesive role in the international fight against apartheid his star status would have allowed him to.

But he retorts in lame defence: 'This had become my lifestyle — cocaine and booze — but I wasn't alone in this. All over the world not every participant in the struggle for liberation was sober. Stress drove many radicals into their graves through booze, drugs or sex.'

What does Hughie expect of us here, to hand him a handkerchief?

A master narrator who employs his personal lilt — and the spirit that fuelled albums such as *The Americanisation of Ooga Booga* and *The Lasting Impressions of Ooga Booga*, emotion-swamped instrumentals like 'Bo Masekela' and '*Nomali*', and epic Afro-traditional poems such as '*Abangoma*' — Masekela comes out emotionally light, with no baggage or bad feelings about his six decades deep in the thick mud of all that jazz.

He is not so angelic, though, when he deals with his marriage to Makeba and the way it was 'interpreted' by her in her own autobiog, the out-of-print *Makeba: My Story*.

It's clear he has been waiting to tackle this issue for decades.

'In her book, Miriam says the reason we divorced is because I was too young; too naive and jealous of her success. Far from it. No marriage could have survived that degree of infidelity — hers and mine — ours had. I do not regret not being married to Miriam, no, even though I still love and respect her.'

A man trying too hard to be sensible while putting a red-hot sword into an affair that brought him to America and, possibly, to where he is today?

Or is this the cry of Johanna's grown Minkie, dead-set on defending his integrity?

Whichever way, it is hard not to see it as a salty but short revenge. One thing is clear, though — their bonds go further and deeper than any egotistic jibe would stab.

Clearly, *Still Grazing* — like Billie Holiday's *Lady Sings the Blues* and *Miles: The Autobiography*, co-written by Davis and Hugh's mutual pal, the poet Quincy Troupe — is a story told with a Hollywood biopic in mind.

If it is steered in that direction, nobody could accuse Minkie and his partner Cheers of hiding their ambition. With its rich imagery; its music as the 'soaring theme', as Nadine Gordimer waxes on the back cover; and the tri-continental (African, European and American) political and cultural figures intersecting the story, Masekela's tale of spiritual support across the colour bar and triumph of spirit over ego is the stuff all enduring films are made of.

Plus, his name is Hugh, y' know . . . Way ta go, Minkie!

Brandford Marsalis

Gonna kick yo' ass!

Rumours of my death have been greatly exaggerated.
– Mark Twain

Reminisces of a flak catcher

Episode I

Just over a decade ago, when we notoriously scavenged 'for sale' bins of the old Exclusive Books and record store on Hillbrow's Pretorius Street for jazz gems, one of the thrills of living in that godforsaken metropolis was witnessing the third coming, explosion of jazz, right in our faces.

Third coming? Urban lore tells us that as far as it is an expression of a lifestyle – and not only a music form – jazz has not quite actually set its foot in a major way, in this country since it (leading innovators) left after the destruction of Kofifi, Umkhumbane and District Six. The only other time it made its presence felt was through the late 1970s to mid-1980s, through the gird-like township empowerment innovations such as *Stokvels*.

A bit of digression on the second of these three cultural period instalments. *Stokvels* were weekly rituals where the dandiest and haughtiest, as well as the maddest congregated.

It is where snake loose, nifty jivers, ghetto philosophers, and petty thugs would turn out with their spotlessly shiny two-tone brogues and Hawaiian floral shirts to shoot the breeze, down the hooch and break a leg, break a sweat for their round-hipped molls — in their *phenduka* skirts and brown berets — and peacock around as though they'd patented a secret DNA chip on what it meant to be black and utterly cool.

Ah, but what a joy! It was in the late 1970s and to say we — the young ones — were mesmerised is to test the tolerance of understatement. The music? Ah. Of course to us, kwela, funk and jazz, were all the same: as they say, if it swings it swims!

For some reason, the Hillbrow of my coming of age — late 1980s, early 1990s, a blinding sprawl of blazing neon lights, gaudy dressing, reckless abandon, political assertiveness, intellectual stimulation, a crossroad where heaven and hell tangoed in their daily excesses — sort of allowed me to live my own jazz dreams.

The first batch of previously exiled jazz musos such as Hugh Masekela, young guns such as Jimmy Dludlu, Zim Nqawana and jazz court jesters such as the late ol' Jim Harris were familiar faces. Cotton Pub was the rage and being down with the exiled and jazz groupies was the *thang*.

'Tis in such climate that — like all young guns, who, just because they've bought a very bad recording by, say Big John Patton, or brogues you saw on Charlie Parker in the biopic, *Bird* — you thought you had a karmic connection with the jazz world, especially its stars, who, for the very first time, you'd bump into at a local Hillbrow corner café.

Reality was altered and the schizo feeling it effected in us was ironically sweet: it felt like some of the jazz giants had just simply walked off the LP and CD covers to stroll the city streets, just like you, just like me.

For its kitschy nature, it was quite a revelation that in Hillbrow, jazz was a religiously respected art (jazz = *jah–is*: God's music, played in both the church and the whore house, if you care for its roots).

It's round about that time that I — then a minion starting up in a weekly newspaper — first met the *insight fury* of a jazz die-hard scorned, in the form of stickman, Lulu Gontsana.

Possibly miffed by the young cat's uninformed utterances of jazz in the paper, *City Press*, the drummer invited me over to his joint in Kotze Street, for free lessons in jazz criticism and coffee, and so I beat it to his crib at the agreed time.

Before sinking on the couch, Gontsana threw me a copy of *Jazz Times* magazine, which had a controversy-courting cover story totally dismissive of critics writing on this noble, but blood-boiling art called jazz. With the bullish title, the cover line read: 'Jazz Critics Who Do They Think They Are?'

The article, and by extension, my jazz guide, Gontsana, had no time for self-anointed critics, especially those who could not differentiate between Thelonious Monk's 'Round Midnight' and Chaka Khan's 'At Midnight', or, who had no inkling of how miles apart John Trane's 'A Love Supreme' and Motown's Holland-Dozier-Holland's 'Ah lurve you b-a-b-e-e' soul recordings are.

What followed next was something I was scarcely prepared for. Gontsana, frustrated with the level of newsmedia's jazz reporting and criticism, vented out on me, throwing the child — me — with the darn water. Telling me how uninformed and not so dedicated to the art form I was, Gontsana lit a bonfire on my ambitions of becoming a critic.

All my dreams of a black beret slanted to the side, guzzling whiskey from the bottle, while talking codswallop about Kippie Moeketsi or Billie Holiday, flew out of the window, and perhaps for the right reasons.

For the very first time, I recognised how easy it is for people — especially journalists — to mouth off information on issues they know pretty much zilch about — especially the most sickening ones: 'God is dead'; 'Punk is dead'; 'Chivalry is dead'. And the one we've been hearing since the inception of bebop music in the forties: 'Jazz is dead'.

Thing is, rarely does the public scratch beyond the surface, a reluctance responsible for critics' omnipresent levitation in their ballooned-up egos. And so we don't learn – as band leader and jazz artist, Brandford Marsalis reminded me in a telephonic interview a week ago: 'Jazz critics know no shit, period', unless your name is Gary Giddins, Nat Hentoff or Gwen Ansell?

I do not remember how exactly I left Gontsana's place, or why he vented it all out on me. I mean, there were several established names, not particularly dishing out Pulitzers in jazz criticism.

What's disconcerting, though, was that I was not even a jazz critic, but a fan, who happened, on occasion, to write on jazz and variety. The bee stung, and my Hillbrow buzz punctured for ages to come. I turned on my heels and took flight – and forgot about the whole thing until . . . Brandford Marsalis.

That son of a gun – Brandford Marsalis

Episode II

The year is 2006. The season *springs* with new bird sounds and ears and eyes are assaulted by posters and radio jingles, promises of a jazz renaissance – which is nothing but sleek promoters' promises of another jazz gumbo featuring all sorts of acts including rock and kwaito mice disguised as jazz cats.

Nobody cares. Nobody gives a hoot. The music on the streets and the talk in the shebeens and hotel foyers swings to one rhythm and one rhythm only: Brandford . . . Brandford . . . Brandford Marsalis is coming.

First things first: Marsalis, the eldest of the famous family from the root base of jazz, New Orleans; a family that includes the classicist, snobbish jazz musician, brother Wynton, who is possibly this year's festival's big fish, as far as star wattage is concerned.

So, I threw in an inadequate net to catch, only to scratch a sleeping / swimming whale the wrong way – about that later.

A 1990s Brandford fan — even though I still haven't had the hang of what it actually is that he did with Sting — I knew I had to get this interview. So I ring him up in Marseille, France, where he is touring with his family band, and this is the sort of conversation we had. Since you've asked, yes both of us were sober, as far as I could make out:

* * *

Journalist: Hi, can I speak to Brandford . . . Brandford Marsalis, you know, that jazz cat who shocked the charts, played with Sting and dabbled in hip-hop music. Yeah, that one.

Voice: [Brandford, in a New York accent, the result of two decades in the city of sins and promise] Diz iz him, Brandford, man. You speaking to him. How ya doeeng brothaman?

Journalist: Oh, uhm, uhm, excuse me, I mean, this is great. I would like to talk about jazz, seeing that you are headlining the Joy Of Jazz Festival. It's an honour, man — I mean talking to you.

Brandford: Anytime, brothaman.

Journalist: From what I hear, you are the last of the Mohicans. Talk is, American jazz is dead. Is there anything in particular we should anticipate with this festival, with your own gig?

Brandford: What do you mean American Jazz is dead? What are you talking about, man? [Note, brotha was gone.]

Journalist: I mean . . . well, most of American music is dead anyway, and has been dead for some time. 'A mummified art', so say the critics. Nothing new's coming from the sound that gave us Ornette Coleman's *The Shape of Jazz To Come.*

Brandford: Look, I don't know you, brotha. Worse, I don't know what is it you are talking about. First, there's nothing called *American Jazz.* There's only one kinda'f jazz and that is American. Why label it? Have you ever heard of Iceland Jazz or Moroccan Jazz, huh?

70

Journalist: But there's nothing exciting coming out of a music form made significant by giants such as Louis Armstrong, Charlie Mingus, Cecil Taylor, John Coltrane, the Art Ensemble of Chicago . . . I mean, all that's played today is a recitation, and at best, a resuscitation of old glory, and nothing else.

Brandford: Listen and listen very carefully. Jazz, good jazz is the most alive art form today. Good jazz lasts a lifetime. What you hear today is, is . . . look, all those names recorded their best music almost thirty or more years ago. It's still swinging today, do you hear me, brotha?

Journalist: Exactly my point. All we hear is great stuff from old jazz icons. Museum pieces. What about new living jazz, expressive of today's energy and tone? What's young America offering?

In fact, some of the innovative jazz sounds come from Norway and the other Scandanavian countries. What do you think brotha Brandford: Has the music biz killed jazz?

Brandford: Look man, freshness does not come from a country, but people. So what are you telling me? You see most of the musicians playing today have no sense of the bigger world. Just like you critics.

Now you telling me that jazz, black America's music, our forefather's blues, is better played by white boys in Europe, what's that? What sort of reasoning is that, brotha?

Journalist: But really, I can count a handful of innovators in the last few years: Vijay Iyer, Steve Coleman, Terence Blanchard, Roy Hargrove, yourself — but also, you have stopped exploring other genres — and what else do you guys have, Wynton?

I am terribly disappointed at what's coming out of America . . .

Brandford: Oh well, go ahead and get more disappointed, brotha. It's important that we remain steeped in our tradition. You can never advance an art form if you have no sense of its history.

I don't have to listen to you or any of the critics tell me that Europeans play better jazz than black America or American artists. Those people play anything but jazz; they play folk music, whatever, just not jazz.

Journalist: But you guys are not redefining the sound, you are looting the legacy. Well, not you exactly, but . . . [Too late!]

Brandford: How will you know if we are? What have you listened to? What live performances have you seen? Are they representative of the scope and number of live jazz performances happening in America right now? How are you able to tell? What are you basing your critical opinion on, huh, *brotha*?

Journalist: Well, you might be right there.

Brandford: So what are you talking about, if you know nothing?

It went on like that, until the topic touched on Marsalis's now favourite music, classic. At that stage, I clamped up, kept quiet and sat it for a free-rolling lecture in jazz epistemology:

Now listen here, son!

Episode III

Though Brandford — whose latest album, *Footsteps Of Our Forefathers*, is perhaps the most trenchant tribute anyone, including his brother Wynton, has paid to the four jazz masters, Sonny Rollin's 'Freedom Suite', John Coltrane's 'A Love Supreme', Ornette Coleman's 'Giggin'' and John Lewis's 'Concorde' — defends jazz, he goes on to tell me that he is not listening to jazz at all:

'Not these days, man. I listen to a lot of classical music, you see. I have listened to all musics all of my life and there's nothing in jazz that I cannot figure out. That's what I don't want. I want to listen to a music form I can't figure out, and classic does just that.' What do you mean? I asked.

'I find more inspiration in classical music, that's what I am telling you. But not all people listening to, or playing classical music have what it takes.'

He goes on to tear the former Beatles co-composer, Paul McCartney apart, and not because he hates McCartney, or pop, but because, so he says, Mucca [Paul] plays ulcer-inducing music. 'Beyond terrible,' brothaman.

In fact Marsalis loves pop, he tells me, 'unlike my brother Wynton, I love pop. It just so happens that most of what's coming out of it is pure crap. It is all about hits. Do not mistake this. I am not saying all pop music is equal to prostitution. I am just saying it is too simplistic. It is created for today's world, for people who have no deeper sense of the art of music.' There's no culture of appreciating good music, he says. So people accuse jazz and classic of snobbery.

'They do it so they can pull the bar of cultural sophistication down. They want to make all kinds of music accessible, for what? Because that's all radio teaches them – everything deep is irrelevant. People don't want to think. They want to jive and jazz ain't jive music.'

At this stage, I restrain myself from telling Marsalis, if you have problem with other people's crap, better lock yours in, but I let go. Is McCartney that tragic?

'Oh, that?' he says. 'One day this chap says to me, 'Ah, you see Paul McCartney is a serious musician, very dynamic. He used to be a Beatles composer and now he's playing classical music, Bach, Verdi. Ah, McCartney is great', and I said "Whaaat?"

'Please man, McCartney can play Bach all he likes, but McCartney plays crap! Don't tell me he plays great music. Don't tell that to me, no ways.

'People have opinions but no facts to base them on, now we are supposed to hail Paul McCartney as a genius. Who else? Eminem has saved the blues, right?' Marsalis went on to give me a free lecture about the socio-political import of jazz, especially jazz, in its context, as 'a black American art form'.

'It is more than a music form. It is about black aspirations, it is the musical career of our stories. Now people want to topple its heroes and replace them with European heroes. That's sacrilege, brother, that's sacrilege man. I think', he continues, 'you should look at or listen to jazz the way you look at your country, South Africa.

'You see, there should never, ever be a time in South African history or education when apartheid is not taught in the schools, never. You see, people who committed the crime, racists, always speak about the need to move on, the need to create something new, something that has no relevance to the past.

'Yeah, man, it is because they want to erase their crimes. The same thing happens in culture. I am not about to give up jazz, or our forefather's stories. Never.'

This is Brandford Marsalis, who, over a few years ago, was hailed as the freshest voice in jazz, simply because he played with hip-hoppers and recorded a massively popular album called *Buckshot Le Fonque*. These days, he is the guardian of a jazz . . . and never ever say anything bad about it . . . he takes it quite personally.

Now you know. Never believe the critics. Like this one. Thank you, brotha.

Obelix and Asterix

Somregi Ntuli and the Tough Luck Gang

Case Number 300/77, heard at the Springs Supreme Court in May 1977 and presided over by Judge J Curlewis, shed light on the most electrifying gangster tale of its time – the Somregi Ntuli Gang.

Ingredients for a cinematic epic don't come flooding more than this. It started earlier than this 1977 winter of legal and political discontent. Some say it all began in the late 1960s, on the East Rand or Pretoria streets, peaking, ironically, just around the boiling point and cries of *black power . . . black power*! across the Reef's about-to-implode streets, while some point at the nucleus of the then South African Police force – white power.

Ingredients? Two-timing cops. Love, brotherhood and betrayal across the racial divide. Police fraternity gone bust. The underworld versus the legal world. Brains against brawn. Hundreds of thousands of rands . . . moolah galore. Blood on the floor. Blood on the tracks – the gang's and police's even.

Clearly, there was no distinction between cop and cop killer anymore, or between the thug and the law man. A spider web of conceit was unfolding somewhere in South African prisons and the underworld, with the East Rand, Johannesburg and Pretoria as the fuelling tributaries of fire, mafia, greed . . .

In all their glory and sadness, the following characters were all men who loved and hated each other's wits with every last drop of blood in their veins, and perhaps not so bizarre, they all used to be vice-grip chums. Or so it seemed.

Edian Somregi Ntuli, a KwaThema-based crack detective, lived a double life. He was loved by magistrates for cracking the most intriguing cases, yet consorted with the underworld's lynch and kingpins, such as Paul Ramafikeng, Chief Mamashile, and the ultimate Soweto *capo* of all time, Jabu Vilakazi – who, street legend says was mentored and *big brothered* the then up-and-coming Ivan Khoza, which is not to infer any dealings or association, whatsoever, with the Somregi Gang, on the part of the man who'd later be known as the Duke, South Africa's football *el supremo*.

But ahhh . . . such was coterie of guns-for-hire the crack cop swung with in his other life. Ntuli was arrested after he masterminded the dramatic assassination of his right-hand man, Ramafikeng – whom the gang realised was also a police snitch and informer – as well as on charges of more than 25 robberies.

Among these was a daring raid on the Groblersdal Court in KwaNdebele where the gang got away with R40 000; the attempted murder of four policemen on the same day; and the Nigel Standard Bank robbery.

Now, 30 years later, yellowing newspaper reports calculates the total of the Ntuli gang's loot at over half a million rands in a two and a half year crime spree.

Besides the slain Ramafikeng, Ntuli – code-named Obelix in the underworld – was tight friends with an immigrant renegade and streetwise man, going by the name Johannes, or Ionnis, Poulakis pronounced 'Po-u-la-a-a-tjies' by his fellow township rogues who could not pronounce his Athenian moniker, Poulakis.

This was a perfect foil and side B, to computer brained, super cop Ntuli. Poulakis has what is called value-added catchet to his name, something of a premium in the world of crime. Back in his native Greece, Poulakis served in a specialist bomb-making unit of the army, called 'The Lok', before running away and heading down to *darkest* Africa.

Though still under the grip of European powers, Southern Africa, this son of a poor, working-class family thought, was the stairway to heaven (on earth). In short, Poulakis had seen the light.

He first arrived in the port city then known as Lourenzo Marques, capital of Mozambique, before crossing the border and shooting through to inland Johannesburg. Here, Ioriris the lad got himself useful: working as a cash-till operator, and a salesman in a gun shop, loved his Studebaker scooter to bits and set out to start a family.

It wouldn't be long before the white boy got hired by the Reef's super black thugs as a crack bomb-maker and safe-blower. Looking at the racial reality of the time, this was nothing short of race reversal revolution in the making.

So close was he to the 'big man', Ntuli, that his underground nickname became Asterix to Ntuli's Obelix. It was this friendship that was to prove Ntuli's undoing.

The year 1977 will go down as one of the most emotionally draining times in South African history. 'Twas a time when you expected quiet after the storm, yet none was in the offering.

Emotional residues of 1976's bloody, history-making Soweto riots — some believe it to be the genesis of black family life disintergration, the moment of black parental authority loss — were still smoldering, like stubborn coal, in the air. On the streets, an angrier musical expression reflected people's suppressed rage and cynicism towards the status quo.

The Afro-agitative poetry of Ingoapele Madingoana blended with the soul-stirring township rock of The Beaters, as well as the agitative hits from black America's funk-soul acts such as Curtis Mayfield, Marvin Gaye and the rhythm and blues poet Gill Scott-Heron. Across the entire universal black metropolis — from Oakland to Bamako, Johannesburg to the ashes of District Six - no song other than Rare Earth's 'Smiling Faces' captured the rage and cynicism of the time:

> Smiling faces sometimes
> They don't tell the truth
> Beware!
> Beware of the handshake
> There hides a snake

The prevalent township atmosphere was of hate and despair. Public spaces were thick with fear and uncertainty. I was seven years old, and still remember the uncertainty and often helpless, but soul-entrenched community revolutionary repulsion against some intangible monster our parents used to refer to as a-p-a-r-t-*hate*!

Families lost their sons and daughters to the 'bush', as skipping the country was then known. Within such a climate, it made perfect sense for the astute Judge Curlewis to steer Case Number 300/77 from a potential political hot-pot to a strictly criminal case. However, even he could not explain why Edian Somregi Ntuli was held under the dreaded Terrorism Act.

Perhaps later claims by Ntuli's family — during our interview for this essay – that he was neither a 'mere cop' nor 'a thug', but a 'political liberator', influenced the judge — thus, offering an explanation why Curlewis subsequently launched an investigation into a possible political link between crime and politics, with no success.

On the face of it, the case in front of the judge was simple. Ntuli was arrested after a mad crime spree, in which it was alleged he misused his police status to plan missions and hits, as well as subverting police investigations into the broader gangs' activities, thus covering his greasy back.

Believed to have been sold by key gang members, particularly his trusted lieutenant, Poulakis — who, once the light on their lavish lifestyle and ominous dealings had dimmed, and the law's jaws ringed closer to the gang's neck, fled back home to Greece, later to cut a deal with the police, returned, handed himself over at Jan Smuts Airport and was now the State's chief witness — Ntuli was charged with more than 21 cases of armed robbery, attempted murder and murder.

To the police — especially Ntuli's former friend, and partner in crushing crime, Lieutenant Harry Viljoen — the accused's sins exceeded all forms of betrayal. He was a cop who had betrayed his badge, uniform and honour. He should be dealt with the hardest.

During the course of this investigative reconstruction, people close to Ntuli, amongst them old tycoon-thugs who mysteriously beat the trap, as well as his family, believe that same Viljoen was himself a rotten cop out to cover his own blood (letting) on the tracks.

What's left unsaid, perhaps rings a higher volume: Lieutenant Harry Viljoen was in cahoots with Captain Edian Somregi Ntuli! Or at worst, one was beginning to pee on the other's turf. Who could pee the longest? Who could shake off the law? The wildest? Who could shoot with the deftest precision?

How did it all happen? Who is Ntuli what are the earlier traces? Nothing in young Edian's life story suggests that he would become a crack cop — and least of all the mob's top dog.

Edian, grew up the only son of a Mr William and Margaret Ntuli, kicking dust and splashing about in mud with his cousins, the Masemolas from Mamelodi, as well as a man who'd later create his own musical genre, Phillip Molombo Tabane.

'A cordial, charming and extremely generous man, Ntuli joined the police force in 1954 as a 17-year-old teenager from Riverside, a semi-village peri-urban, next to the present-day Eersterust, Mamelodi, east of Pretoria.

'I remember very well the kind of person he was when he arrived in Johannesburg,' veteran journalist Doc Bikitsha, recalled. '*Hy was maar 'n laaitie*. Shy and very respectful. Back then, I thought, *die oukie is maar 'n plaasjapie*. How he got sucked into the world of crime beats me.'

In the force, the young man worked tirelessly around the clock. Almost 20 years later, he had worked himself up the ranks, to be a warrant officer, a position in which he made acute use of the very street smarts he had learned in combating township crooks to outwit and later influence the reigning crime bosses.

Something must have snapped, and snapped darn wrong. Soon, the sleekest crime tracker in the country assumed, unbeknownst to his fellow uniformed officers, the chair and label, *Capo of capos.* Damn right: just like in the movies! *LA Confidential?* No this was the scripting of Johannesburg's underbelly, right on parallel to the white thug cop, Andre Stander's single-minded movie iconoclasm.

It so happened that I got to interview a retired thug, East Rand's club owner, master bootlegger, and one of the underworld's ringleaders who specialised in hitting trucks and signing out hits — Fred Masasanyane, who spun irony on its head when his friends nicknamed him Jesus.

The first time I called him to ask about Ntuli, a clearly disturbed Jesus cried, 'Oh please, you can't do that to me. You can't, *my laaitie.* That man was everything to me. *Wie is jy?* Who sent you here?'

The questions — check out statements, rather — are of course an age-old ruse, aimed at throwing prying outsiders and weaklings off course: *Wie is jy? Wie se laaitjie is jy?*... or as they say in Nigeria: Who's yo' foddah, huh?

It would take a full month before Jesus would climb back from the mountain to speak to me, and of course I would tell him my foddah is of no consequence. At best, a *moegoe, daai ou.* Meeting granted — we drive through screaming traffic to his double storey in Katlehong.

* * *

Long out of the game, Jesus is now reformed, and at his age, his almost biblical knowledge of the world of crime is as crispy as freshly picked cotton from the plantation. Also, Jesus had dealt with both sinners — thug cops ... *Capos of capos* — for he, like Jabu Vilakazi, baptised a lot into the world of crime.

A stout 75-year-old man with a memory like a laser beam, his version of the Ntuli myth is perhaps the most reliable. He was respected by all the players on both sides of the law — yet too oily for the law to ever pin anything on him.

Did the best-known white cop-thug, Stander and the unknown — at least not as hero worshipped, nor later heralded with a Hollywood film with a blazing neon writ over his memory — Edian Ntuli, know each other? Did they hyenas prowl together perhaps?

'I can only say, they certainly *knew* each other. '

'How?'

'Stander used to be a regular visitor to my place, and he was privy to the world of black crime — indeed, we shared tips and other valuables.'

'Like?'

'Just say we were sort-of family? Of course he knew Ntuli, but he did not have any direct dealings with him. All rivers coursed through me.'

Because of his brains, Ntuli's underworld network grew. Its influence spiralled out, from the East Rand, Soweto, Alexandra and Mamelodi to Swaziland, Lesotho and Botswana.

Jesus says he was 'the real tsotsi, which the cops wanted. Not Edian. Edian was not a killer, nor a cheap thug. He was the brains. And all the others were doers.'

As fate would have it, Jesus's father fell ill. He had to decide: quit the thug life and take care of his ailing father or continue to live a life of regret after his father's death. 'Twas a close call.

'I opted out of the mob, but not before appointing my successor. And who better than Edian as the new "chairman" of the gang?'

Jesus says the network consulted him, even when he was on 'leave'.

It's him — he states on record, in this interview — who planned the gang's biggest hit thus far — the Nigel Standard Bank robbery. And it is him who provided the meat of the crime narrative below.

Nigel Standard Bank robbery? 'Oh that?' Jesus wipes his brow. 'Chicken pie.' The story goes that the gang cased the joint and found the bank did not have police or security guards on its premises. A plan — the court later heard was Ntuli's idea — was hatched to plant a bogus policeman, Junior Mnisi — a renowned hit man — in the bank.

With starched uniform, baton and a gun to boot, Junior cut the look. When Fidelity Guards arrived to collect money, they made chums with him, fed him toffee and shared their coffee with him. 'At least,' they thought to themselves, 'we have an armed cop covering us. What a relief.'

On their biggest collection day, the guards were taken by surprise by a gang of robbers — among them their policeman chum, who threatened to blow their brains out. Ntuli and the boys, including Poulakis, snatched R13 500 in cash before dashing away in style.

Three cars bolted out of the scene — a removal truck disguised as, well, a removal truck; a silver-grey Jaguar; and a Valiant Regal stashed with the loot, a variety of submachine guns and disguise gear, and a white man behind the wheel, smiling and whistling a Greek marching band tune: *Peeee, paatha booo bee.*

Although billed as the pinnacle of their success, the mother lode, the hit's aftermath descended into a stinker.

Ramafikeng, one of the top three honchos in the gang and a skilled gunslinger if ever there was one, had disappointed his friends by not participating in the Nigel affair. Nevertheless he approached Ntuli and demanded his share of the loot: 'Equal share or nothing,' said Ramafikeng.

'Nothing,' in gang lore, meant 'something.' A stinking something. Would Ramafikeng — no altar boy himself — open the sewage? Ntuli could not trust fate with that. Taken aback by Ramafikeng's threat, he consulted with the others — especially his trusted right-hand man and explosives expert, Poulakis. In the wink of an eye, the order was issued: 'Let's get Paul, and the stink out of the way.'

The assignment was given to cold-blooded killer Noel Ntonjane — who,

Jesus claims, 'was sprung from jail so he could take care of the nuisance, Paul'. Ntonjane paid a surprise visit to Ramafikeng's Mofolo, Soweto, house where he calmly knocked, greeted his victim, and silently pumped two bullets through the man's stomach and right leg.

The injured gangster — says other gangsters, apparently on authority by Ntonjane himself — attempted to shoot back, but his gun jammed. The assailant fled to a waiting car driven by Ntuli.

Ramafikeng was rushed to Baragwanath Hospital, 'where all of the Reef's detectives rushed to his bedside and he shopped 80 percent of the gang away, to save his skin', Jesus claims. The remaining gang members arranged for a new hit man. 'A very handsome and classicr oke named Chief Mamashile was up for the task', Jesus recalls.

Mamashile put on horn-rimmed glasses, a stethoscope and a doctor's white coat and strolled into Baragwanath's intensive care unit — where he pumped six bullets into the recovering patient, and quickly disappeared into the hospital's wards. Incensed, the police — led by Ntuli's former friend Viljoen — pounced on Ntuli and his remaining henchmen.

'Of all of those gang members, Mamashile was the most hated. He had killed their new turn-coat right under their nose, therein exposing the police's tardy security measures. In short he made them a laughing stock . . . bumbling fucks. So why should we be surprised to learn that he was 'accidentally' killed in prison while awaiting trial? 'It was payback for their dearly beloved Paul.'

It's clear that Jesus did not cough up all the insides of the 'family' in this interview. He also refused to say how one of those associated with the gang, chap going by the name Jessie Ramakatane — now reformed and a multi-millionaire with high government links in Lesotho and South Africa — got himself out of this criminal network to lead a decent life.

If Jesus refuses to go on the cross on some and open the whole dossier, 30 years later, the feisty, Greek grandma, Iris Boulsakis is not so 'chicken pie.'

Back then a head-turning black-haired moll with looks to kill and attitude to die for, if not perhaps a bit of a self-righteous Christian campaigner, Boulsakis was a dyed in the wool liberal fighting for the right cause – the *black cause*. That is how she got to lead a petition to help the trialist Ntuli on his losing battle to beat the noose.

While Jesus tells me: 'Listen here, some of the members of their families are still alive and terribly hurt. I cannot go ahead and smear people's names, simply for nostalgic reasons. C'mon son, go home', Boulsakis, whom I have tracked to Randburg, is full of beans.

She tells me: 'I made friends with Edian when he was on death row. I have spoken with the man for days and days and was there when he converted to become a Christian. At first I was a skeptical, but now I can tell you, the man was sacrificed. Ntuli was the fall man, he never killed anybody. Even the court papers filed no case of murder on him – none.'

Her voice still resonates with self-righteous religious righteousness. So I thoroughly re-read through the court documents. No murder charge against Ntuli, the person. None! That didn't mean a sweat to the police and law system of the time: Ntuli's day of reckoning came, and he was duly executed.

Up to this day, Boulsakis - who is close, by proxy, to the ANC, especially his neighbours, the Walter Sisulu family – is still fighting to clear her friend, Ntuli's name. While Ntuli's closest friend freely admits to the gang's activities, word has it that his family clings to a different version of the 'truth'. One, shared with Boulsakis.

So I voomed off to Mamelodi, known as his 'grounding' place – home. His cousin Sanah Masemola – who, when she was in her 20s, couriered money and coded messages to Ntuli's 'underground business partners' in Swaziland – says its too late to talk about him now. 'But I am certain our brother was not a killer.'

Was he a mastermind criminal, though?

'Not that I know of. The man couldn't hurt a fly.'

Why did his friends testify against him?

'I don't know. Go ask them.'

Others — like his eldest son, Thabo Ntuli, now in his 40s — feels that 'this matter smelt of a *boer* conspiracy from the word go'. Thabo claims his dad was not a thug, but a political liberator. Exactly where his liberation of the black oppressed stopped and the liberation of banks' money took off is all pretty fuzzy, a subject Thabo is not prepared to entertain.

A man of few words, and given to moody, reflective and philosophical indifference to his surroundings, Thabo is a self-confessed 'angry man'.

'Too angry my man. Y'know what I mean? *Gatvol.* That's me. My dad was framed.'

Meaning, he did commit some? 'That can be argued about, but that man used to pour his heart and money into those fleeing youths' 1976 uprisings. So today, you *new* blacks call that sort of a person a thug?'

'New blacks?' Ouch!

'They said my father killed Paul Ramafikeng. That's bollocks.'

'How do you feel right now, Thabo?' I ask him.

'I feel this story must be told. But *eish*, I don't know if big corporate capitalists like newspapers should do it. I'm angry that this government forgave apartheid thugs, but keeps quiet on my dad.'

Thabo's uncle, Densie Masemola, asked, 'Do you really think his underground liberation job was easy? Tell you what, I'll introduce you to somebody who can attest to Edian's political credentials. Come tomorrow.' Enter Julian Bahula, a world famous jazz composer and self-confessed 'freedom artist'.

On a short vacation from his London, UK work and base, Bahula professes intimate knowledge of Ntuli. As young boys they kicked a plastic ragged ball around the neighborhood together, as adults they were comrades in arms.

'I was one of the most wanted activists and artists in Mamelodi, Pretoria', he tells me. 'I was even in the Government Gazette: *Wanted, Dead Or Alive.* Bra Edian organised me a new ID book and helped me escape to Durban, from where I connected to Europe.'

Ntuli's liberation tag kept resurfacing in the course of putting *these* pieces together. So I rang up the legendary advocate George Bizos who had unsuccessfully represented Ntuli in the trail. 'Gee,' he sighed. 'I remember that case, back in 1977. That was one of my failures.'

Still, he livened up when asked about the 'liberation tag'. 'Revolutionary? Where on earth do you get this? I didn't know anything at all about my client working for the liberation movement', Bizos, clearly puzzled, mused. 'There's a tendency to make heroes out of ordinary people. I don't want to be part of that.'

ANC spokesman Smuts Ngonyama does not have a clue who Edian Ntuli was, nor can he attest that the crime boss funnelled some of his loot into the movement. The link with the ANC is not new. For some time, allegations sneerful towards the 'Congress' has always had it that the liberation movement's creaky wheels, has been oiled by nefarious means before.

'Certainly some black policemen would have been on our side, but it was not our strategy nor policy to recruit criminals into our ranks', he said.

Speaking to Ntuli's widow, Violet Ntuli, it felt like I was kicking her wounds open. It hurt for both the inquisitor and the quizzed.

'I can't talk. I have nothing to say. Your story will tear the family apart. Why raise the dead man when he's long gone?' she asked tearfully.

Exactly why am I?

Doc Bikitsha is quick on this score: 'Black South Africans are sleeping tight on their treasure trove of stories. Who knows Edian Somregi Ntuli? Black or white, raise your hands?'

Postscript

Edian Somregi Ntuli was sentenced to death on May 24 1977. Poulakis was indemnified and deported back to Greece. Unable to outwit Caesar (the law) forever, Obelix — betrayed by his chum — dies, while the chum, Asterix, lives on.

Though Johannesburg's underworld was sterner than the comic city of

Gaul, the Ntuli and Poulakis's partnership could not hold on. Greed and betrayal did.

The rest of the ten-member gang — bar Jesus and Jessie Ramakatane, who is alleged to have disappeared out of the country, to be a hard-working and successful millionaire in the mountain Kingdom of Lesotho — met their Creator through the barrel of a gun.

Asterix (Poulakis) might have saved his skin — but his legacy was riddled with bullet holes. Talk is, before Poulakis went back to Greece, he had a young family which he left behind. His offspring all grew into the grimy world of crime in the 1980s Hillbrow and other seedier parts of the Reef.

One day — a culmination of months of backstabbing, the beast eating itself — the children got gripped in territorial turf war and turned on each other in a shooting madness that left blood marks that mysteriously concealed traces of their remaining narrative.

Perhaps propelled by an obsession for a grand finale more than anything else, I have subsequently turned boulders and properties on their heads, talking to figures in the Greek communities and beyond. Perhaps somebody knows someone who knows something?

It turned out to be fruitless five-year search of surviving family members of Ionnis Poulakis, and all I got was *nada*. The safe-blower got done and blew *his-story* away? Who knows?

Amu, hip-hop's warlord

Quick flash, bulletin — the hip-hop and kwaito wars. These have been smouldering for five or so years, with sparks erupting here and there, without igniting any bonfires of the veldfire variety. Also, there have been no direct casualties, other than unverifiable cases of broken noses, and lifting each other by shirt lapels — thank you.

But now, just before the release of his much-anticipated album, *The Rap, Life and Drama*, one of South Africa's most respected — by both the so-called underground set, as well as the pop establishment — Amukelani Tshawane, simply known as 'Amu', is a restless soul. For some time, he has been boiling, and with *Drama*, the man is about to blow the top off.

Ever since its re-emergence on the South African scene in the late 1990s, rap (part of an early 1970s African-American youth cultural expression, referred to as hip-hop, which includes graffiti, deejaying, and turn-tabling, electric locking / break dance) has had running beefs with its unique, South African version — kwaito.

What that means is that local hip-hop MCs (rappers) — initially, most were middle-class kids from BEE-spoke families in the former white suburbia, or township clusters that used to be known as 'buffer zones' — have been pulling their nose up at kwaito rappers, most of which are working-class truants or ex-jail birds to who this township sound is but one of the few options out of poverty.

Musically, artistically and philosophically, both types of music are premised on the young black male-warped sense of macho identities, desperation, peer belonging, and just the playful linguistic banter that has its genesis on street corner jokes, speakeasies' swagger and communal dances, and so forth.

In fact, insofar as expression goes, there's just a few differences between the two, other than class backgrounds and some varying forms of their beats.

Amu — who caught the early hip-hop influences in the United States of America, where he actually did some growing up when his parents lived there, first made his name earlier on, during local hip-hop's third coming, back in the Yeoville streets, as part of a collective called *Tha Mothaload*.

Hip-hop's third coming?

The genre first made its presence known in the mid-1980s, through township bands such as JE Movement, King of Clubs and Senyaka. They came of age when an East Rand, New Jack Swing type of rappers, Karamo and Cape Townians Prophets of Da City 'nationalised' rap, and now, post Mandela's *Long Walk To Freedom*, hip-hop kiddos are back punching and kicking their way back to the centre stage — not always humbly.

Among the present crop –they call themselves MC's, a street abbreviation for microphone controller– are the likes of Amu, Mr Selwyn, H20, Skwatta Kamp, Static Boyz, Waxxy, Naked, Danger, Proverb, Optical Illusion, Hamma (is it any wonder this sounds like the ugly-intimidating bling car of choice of American rap stars?) . . . and some such gadget-like monikers.

Most of them invoke the rough 'n' tumble life of the ghetto streets they really have no experience of, for many were sheltered kids. Leading the charge, amongst these, is King Amu, who, it feels is itching to be the fuse that'll eventually set of the bomb that will, finally, implode kwaito music's dominance of the South African music industry.

Amu and his rap crew would like you to believe they are the messiahs of endangered rap. Mildly talented, but gifted in American linguistics, Amu expresses his hatred of kwaito, a music that resonates with township and rural youth.

It is not a given fact that largely private school-educated youngsters such as Amu are sellouts, simply because they enjoy their parents' suburban bliss.

That's too simplistic.

In fact, a tiny crop of these *nouveau riche* offspring are more sociacly consciouss than the bulk of kwaito stars. They have worked hard to present themselves as South Africa's new radicals, even though some of their radicalism is transmitted via MTV, Rudeboy Paul and Wits University's literature and drama schools.

But you can't take that away from them. Even though if theirs is a consciousness without context, without a sizable constituency, without a clear cultural programme, they are at least one step into the broader church of South Africans who are beginning to question the status quo, be it big business, the government or the recording industry.

You see, if you ignore their copycat beats, slang, macho pasturing and hypocrisy — they rap about equality and proceed to call women ' bitches' and 'hos' — many of them posses a potent lyricism and charisma. It is easy to see that future poets and storytellers of note might emerge from the residue of their art form.

They are brimming with rich potential and street swagger. They question everything and are critical to authority.

Looking beyond their surface bravado, though, beyond their way of walking, beyond their dress style and low-riding parachute jeans and military fatigues, you soon realise that they are indeed radical, as you would expect from youth anywhere.

But there is a difference between rebellion and radicalism. Also a sum variance insofar as commitment, between radicalism and working on a revolution - or being revolutionary.

Most youths in kwaito and hip-hop imagine themselves to be revolutionary, while all they possess is plain youthful rebelliousness, positive but yet not essential to bringing about a revolution. Such desperation, a need for underground appeal and mainstream attention, does more to stoke the fires of black-on-black violence than usher in robust, creative competition.

In his single, 'Attention Attention', Amu and his two obviously talented sidekicks make their dislike of kwaito — basically envy disguised as self-assertion — evident without drawing a drop of blood or negative energy from the kwaito fraternity they so despise.

Now that's a bit rich, coming from mouths that spew made-in-New York slang.

The atmosphere, though not as poisoned or tense as it was in Baghdad, is pretty ugly nonetheless.

Though the battle between South African-brewed hip-hop and kwaito is not yet full blown, it is essential that all who worship at the altar of youth culture — where rap and kwaito stars such as Amu, DJ Blaze, Kabelo, Tokollo and BOP are enshrined as pop culture's high priests — note that the writing is on the wall: '*Mene mene tekele*, hip-hop is lust for blood'.

It may be that at heart, there's no reason to press the alarm buttons, that all there is to these young men is that they are best cases of under-utilised male energy in excess.

In fact, I would even venture that a bit of tension and one-upmanship in any contact, or art, has, in the past, contributed to the development of that art form. Same thing applies in politics, academia and business boardrooms: it's all about male ego tripping crafted to outmaneuver real and imaginary opponents.

There was a time back in the 1970s when music bands were made and broken in the public sphere, through fierce elimination competitions organised by music promoters, who, it should be noted, doubled as boxing, as well as bare-knuckle fighting promoters in the townships.

Youth bands such The Drive, The Movers, The Cannibals and The Beaters, amongst others sweated it out for fans' attention, in the fiercest sound clashes ever experienced *emalokishi.*

Animosity, intra-band squabbles, poaching and all sorts of bad vibes were as much part of the entertainment angle maintained solely for the paying masses' pleasure — but those were all part of the same racket. There was no real threat, no class struggles. There were no guns one finds in hip-hop and township streets today, where kwaito flourishes.

And yet, badly managed, things might fall apart. Examples abound.

We can even stretch it further into the African-literary domain.

In RL Peteni's classical book, *Hill Of Fools*, set in the fictional village of KwaZidenge, on the outlay of the hill of fools, a simple boy-boy (Buqa and Ntabeni) clash over a boy-girl (Buqa and blindingly-beautiful Zuziwe) love affair, ends up consuming an entire district and surrounding villages in one of the most brutal tribal faction-fighting ever set on page.

Initially it was the battle of the wits, the sizing up of each other, as is requisite in any village stick-fighting showmanship or blood letting game between young men battling for a girl's affection.

But when it got out of hand, brother and brother, cousin and cousin, set on each other like wild animals. Though it is fiction, the real, tangible world is full of such tales of young male mayhem: not so long ago, 1995, the media not only observed, but somewhat fuelled, the Tupac-Biggie Smalls / DeathRow-Bad Boy Records internecine wars that killed two of hip-hop culture's most talented street poets, thus setting off a chain of killings no one could account for.

What can South Africa's plastic soldiers, full of bravado, learn from this madhouse of pop? Beware, that's what!

If this hatemongering continues unchecked, things might turn much nastier. Remember the circumstances that led to the premature death of talented kwaito-pantsula singer, Makhendlas? Hatred, guns, suspicions, and offensive lyrics.

Why do I think the situation warrants intervention?

A few reasons suffice. The first is that both kwaito and rap are largely dominated by testosterone-filled young men brimming with misguided macho energy and the desire to provide answers to that perennially entrapping question: *Who's da man?* or, as they say in the streets of Lagos — *who da man is?*!

It turns out that as local hip-hop struggles to define itself beyond its Rosebank-zoned quasi-revolutionary identity, it misses the bare fact the kwaito is not the enemy.

The enemy is the consumerist and imperialist cultural marketplace that feeds this very hip-hop culture. South Africa's rap stars have a tendency to take themselves way too seriously — perhaps just like some of their fickle heroes in the US.

Amu and his ilk — they call these quasi-gang groupings 'crews' — need to do away with their self-hate. They must get rid of their twangs because it will confuse potential fans, such as the youngsters in Ga-Madjadi or Kwa-Qumakala.

Even to some urban youths, Amu sounds more Brooklyn than Wu-Tang Shaolins. More Harlem than Bushbuckridge in Mpumalanga where his roots are.

Secondly, if tough boy Amukelani is so hard pressed to copy the Americans, it would do wonders for his health, spirit and revolution if he were to cull inspiration from American acts such as The Roots, Slum Village and Common rather than Jigga or Tupac-likes such as 50 Cent and Eminem.

Thirdly, instead of spending their talent spewing bile about kwaito, Amu and company should take a leaf from kwaito stars BoogaLove Kabelo and Stoane Seate, two youths whose musical orientation makes them more authentic African rhyme slingers.

No, being overtly American is not a sin, but it is what you chop from the Americans that puts you a cut above your peers.

Now, attention, attention, local hip-hop, 'tis time to grow. It's well past time to keep it real. It's time to live it real — meaning your own reality, not Snoop Dogg's reality.

Reality is that black South Africans have more in common with Zimbabwe and Mozambique than they have with Puffy Combs and X-Zibit, who, realistically speaking, doesn't give a damn about you.

Yo, wise up!

Pop's the New Revolution

Danny Glover

Kicking the revolution at the Hyatt

If you're one of those people who confuses Hollywood make-believe with the real lives of the actors who oil the hype-machine, you would have also experienced anxiety at the idea — just the idea — of having to interview Danny Glover at Rosebank's haute hotel, Park Hyatt.

Why?

Here's the low-down: Since the mid-1980s — long before Denzel Washington played Malcolm X and Will Smith rapped his way to a role as Mohammed Ali (the prettiest and most politically combative pugilist of all time) — Danny Glover has, through films such as *Bopha* and the HBO mini-series *Mandela*, been Hollywood's bona fide radical.

Now, common perception has it that revolutionaries sleep in roach-filled boho-chic lodges, conduct interviews at coffee shops, look terribly unkempt — a terrific fashion statement, I'm told — and, of course, revolutionaries keep a million metres away from marble-gleaming hotels such as the Park Hyatt, the Ritz, the Sheraton . . .

But I soon learn there's either something wrong with Glover or the stereotype of radicals.

Even before I get a chance to check out his struggle cred in person, the six-foot tall Glover radiates me with the kind of energy that says: 'What radical chic? Not for sale. Can't fake funk.'

The more you talk to him, the more his aura (he calls it 'chi'), his passion for life and his humanitarianism gel into one thing: the essence of Danny Glover.

For a start, Glover's acting bona fides cannot be queried.

Time-defying classics such as Steven Spielberg's *The Color Purple*, have placed him alongside great talents such as Morgan Freeman and Washington.

He is a major force in a school of rare black actors regarded as bankable by major studios, critically acclaimed by the agitative left-leaning black culture critics, as well as adored by millions of ordinary movie goers whose buying-power makes or breaks films and, by extension, stars.

But unlike fellow rabble-rousers Tim Robbins and his squeeze Susan Sarandon, and the veteran Ossie Davis, Glover is either brilliant, foolish or risky enough to successfully project opposing screen personas — especially in an industry notorious for typecasting actors, particularly black actors.

On the one hand you have this truly committed actor steeped in black consciousness, artsy, liberatory stories such as *The Color Purple, Beloved* and the South African struggle-classic *Bopha*; and on the other, someone who provides the Hollywood machine with the lubricant it so desperately needs to maintain the box office: cops 'n' thugs shoot 'em ups!

To gazillions of his fans, Glover will remain the whimsical Robert Murtaugh — the black fella 'buffooning it up', whipping baddies alongside Mel Gibson's Martin Riggs in Hollywood's most successful black and white, cops 'n' thugs franchise — the *Lethal Weapon* series.

Not only did this buddy flick of the century popularise Hollywood's version of *simunye* — blurring the racial divide on screen long before Arch Tutu and his SABC congregants patented the local TV version — the film earned Glover the sort of star-gloss that allows him to articulate his left-field beliefs without risking Hollywood's ire.

And boy – I learn soon after meeting him – does he have them!

In my mind, Monday, October 25 at the Park Hyatt was scheduled to be the moment when Hollywood's bling would be tossed out and revolution ushered in.

Tossed? Nah. It turns out to be one of those moments when a seasoned actor and campaigner like Glover uses Hollywood – or the star power that it accords him – to wage his personal revolution.

Also, I learn 'tis quite a demanding revolution, this. And much like George Bush's call, it demands of an interviewer to choose: 'Whose side are you on?'

So, where did it begin – I mean the South African leg of his intifada?

Glover is here to open a Noah (Nurturing Orphans of Aids for Humanity) centre in Olievenhoutbosch, north of Jozi.

As a United Nations Ambassador for Human Rights, the veteran actor has decided to throw his heavyweight celebrity status behind 'worthy development, liberatory, educational and struggle issues'.

And it is to universal human rights – 'more specifically African people's pain', he emphasises – that he dedicates his life.

'I mean, uhm, maaan, I am the child of the Civil Rights, ba-y-bee. Yeah, y'know how it rolls, maaan. Can't pretend shit – I mean mishaps, rape of people's identities, poverty, child and women abuse – ain't 'appenin' in this world.

'The world', he says, ignoring the risk of using a phrase we've all heard a tad, too often, 'is at war': the powerful are at war with the children, at war against African people, brown people, women, all that. What, do they expect me to keep silent, just because I work in Hollywood? Jeee-zus Christ!' he lets rip, the last part of his exasperation sounding like 'Jay-sous Cries'.

'Lordie-eeee!' In urban, slangy Zulu it sounds like this: *Nkosi'yam!*

And true to form, Christ stays with us a while longer. But not in that 'blessed are the meek, for they shall inherit the earth' way. Nix! To Glover, Christ 'was a true revolutionary'.

But the metamorphosis of Glover from internationally-known actor, into radical spokesman for the dispossessed is actually no metamorphosis at all.

'I've been political all my life. I mean, y'know all blacks are political by fate. That's the deal, maaan. You can't escape it.'

Though a committed anti-Aids fighter and activist against pharmaceutical multinationals, Glover's affair with South Africa did not start with the Noah project, his UN human rights ambassadorship nor, contrary to popular belief, with his 1980s introduction to Athol Fugard's work and their subsequent collaboration on the critically acclaimed, *Master Harold ... and the Boys.*

'Of course Fugard's work left a profound imprint on my mind — how I look at and engage with the world. That's the thing: Good theatre should inspire you, great theatre moves you and sublime theatre possesses you, stirs up your spirits, haunts you ... that's what working with Fugard did for me.

'But me and South Africa?' he cackles again. 'I've been one in spirit with this country since the late 1960s, maaan. It all began when I was in college and active in student politics. I remember we used to invite acts such as Hugh Masekela and Letta Mbuli to gig at our campus,' he says in his Southern-meets-West Coast drawl.

'Back in the late 1960s ... no flower power for us: Black power was where it was at.

'As I said, the South African story and the story of African-Americans was always intertwined, maaan — Brotha Malcolm said so and so did Dr King.'

Just as I am about to urge him, 'ride on brotha, ride on,' — in the banshee-shrieking, Afro-gospel way — it dawns on me that we might have become mired in the thick lefty fog that hangs between the 1960s and the 1980s.

"Xcuse me, Mr Glover,' I venture, aiming to sell out, 'aren't we blacks caught in an age-old aria of complaining about whitey? Whitey this, whitey that? Is whitey responsible for Africa's wars? Aren't African-Americans supposed to have been long enfranchised, eligible to run for the American presidency?

'Aren't people like P. Diddy, Russell Simons, Mary J Blige and Bill Clinton's buddy, Vernon Jordan, as well as black America's (un)holy trinity Cornel West, con Reverend Al Sharpton and Spike Lee living it up in the Hamptons ... throwing swanky barbecues down at their Martha's Vineyard villas?'

Of course, I can't resist the urge to mau-mau a brother: 'And while we are at it, say, Mr Glover, don't you own a 40-acre vineyard in California?

'How does all this black achievement tally with the revolution me and you are about to hatch, Mr G?'

Satisfied with the spot my dagger has found, I sink back into what seems like an acre of couch, smirk firmly in place.

'Whaaat?' he feigns betrayal, then, like a seasoned actor he is, let you know the joke, or question, is actually on you: 'Whoaaaar,' he lets out a huge cackle. 'You putting me on or what, huh? Tell me you're joking. Sure you know, the picture of rappers dressed in tuxedos declaring America to be the land of dreams is manufactured fizz, innit?'

Of course I know what he's on about — that P. Diddy's motivations are political is as likely as a merger between the Herstigte Nasionale Party and Azapo — but there's nothing funnier than seeing a black revolutionary reacting to another black person doing what's known as 'Uncle Tomming'.

It's an old trick — the black ultra-anything despises an Uncle Tom more than Uncles Bush sr, Verwoerd, PW and Dubya put together. Still, as any stand-up comedian, especially the sublime Chris Rock, will tell you, there's no funnier way to get a black radical worked up than by wearing an Uncle Tom mask.

But the really tricky thing is that Glover is way too witty and way, way too smart to ever be waylaid.

'You know quite well that in the US, 45 million people are without healthcare. There's no way you can cite P. Diddy or Sharpton as a sign of true, free America. Just no way, brotha.'

There are issues that rile him more than being told to call it a day, pack your bags buddy, da revolution is over. *Never* call him a liberal.

And woe unto you, should you cite the California governorship by Austrian beefcake Arnold Schwarzenegger as proof that the American dream is not a mirage.

'Look maaan,' he told *The Independent*, UK, shortly before his visit to South Africa, 'never ever refer to me as a liberal. I am quite progressive. I question war in Iraq, question globalisation. Liberals don't. The world is just so fine by them. Call me an obnoxious radical if you will. Never a liberal, okay?

'Never!'

The discussion veers from one revolution to another: human rights and black internationalism to pop revolution (to which, it seems, he is not terribly averse). 'Actually,' he puts it, 'you need to know how to play the game, otherwise the game will play you big time.'

For him, playing the game means working with a collective of African artists such as Youssou N'dour, Alpha Blondy and Miriam Makeba, among other pop heavy-hitters, to influence the world in a way that none of them would've dreamt possible, were they not superstars.

Is Glover the new Bono?

'I look at it this way,' he says, a clear 20 minutes after the scheduled interview time has lapsed: 'This is not my fame. It might sound corny, but I stand on the shoulders of spokesmen and women of the race; Harry Belafonte, Nina Simone, ol' man Mandela and Dr Martin Luther King – folks who sacrificed their lives for me and you.'

For a moment I think he is going to name-drop Jesus Christ, as one of the fellas 'who passed the baton and died for us'. But the man is either too smart, or too mean to follow the script and drag 'Jay-sous' into it. And what a sore point for me – I don't think, I will never forgive Danny Glover for denying me a good ol' chuckle, and a career-making headline:

Brotha Jesus, Me and Da Revolution

I will never.

Bantu Biko

Che-rification of the radical sweety

. . . it is not enough to write a revolutionary song. You must fashion the revolution with the people.
Steve Bantu Biko — *I Write What I Like*

Noon time is — as the commodified street argot, has it - 'fly time' in Rosebank. The gloss-dripping shopping complex, The Zone is ablast with the routine lunchtime frenzy. You can buy whatcha want here; from the latest book on horticulture to the latest Afro-hip cred via Y-Fm.

Jo'burg being what it is — what passes for 'alternative' assumes the mainstream tag, just as you sigh — 'ah, now I can read a paper and have coffee without my senses being violated by another celebrity and their train of sidekicks and their sidekicks' looking at us pretending we are not looking at them. No chance.

Time was when Rosebank was a real alternative to super hectic Sandton City and its Mandela Square. Not anymore. That was 2006 BG (before Gautrain). With Gautrain and its Gau-black zillionaires in the wings, bickering or backstabbing each other for what is left of the Gau-shares, Rosebank seems set better placed once to offer a retort to that Ornette Coleman classical album: *Jazz, The Shape Of Things To Come.*

No, I am not talking about the gentrification . . . you see, the place is already self-gentrified, not according to racial strata but class. As they say, Rosebank is now the home of multi-blingualism, but I digress. It is my idol, and quite seriously, philosophical prophet, Bantu Biko — or his face, or spirit — I'm trying to get at, here, in Rosebank of all places.

Like Elvis, Tupac, and the likes, there have been some sightings of him and so my scorpions wasted no chance in alerting me to his said whereabouts. It was while sipping coffee at that honey-bed for the new black 'it' crowd, Primi Piatti, that I caught his rather ethereal look: bearded and ponderous. He was right across from me in the window display of Afro-chic boutique Stoned Cherrie.

And in that look, Steve Biko was 'captured' beautifully, and pasted on the store's latest retro 'icons' T-shirts. So is this what they call a sign o' the times. Lemme outta here!

Bantu Steve Biko, the black consciousness leader, South Africa's own Frantz Fanon via-Xhosa land, an accessible, humble, prophetic, revolutionary spirit of the post Rivonia Trial was now . . . wait a minute: they did that to Che Guevara, Chairman Mao, St Nelson, Jesus Christ even, and now this?

Let's get it clear: So Biko has now joined Nike, MTV, the beatific Argentinian born, Third World revolutionary darling, Ernesto Che Guevara, Jay-Z, P. Diddy, Brad, Angelina and possibly the Dixie Chix, in universal socio-political transactions, a new marketplace where pop passes itself off as the new left, while the old pants after the cookie jar? Is that what is it?

For no reason — other than the fact that I never imagined that Biko, or his version of black consciousness, which, at its basest, is about black folk's psychological and spiritual self-actualisation, was so yesterday, in this age of patriotic looting, I mean, patriotic bourgeoise — it never ever dawned on me that Steve would have his day, too.

It never occurred that like Mandela and Che, Steve would be dolled up for mass consumption — and the fact that I never thought so in the first place, is, as far as paradoxes go, a failure of imagination on my and my ilk's part.

I mean for Steve Biko, who died over 30 years ago, to make any sense to today's youth, dear brother man has to be made accessible and normal to ordinary people, no? Ok, that's too simplistic — for we know that a T-shirt slogan does not necessarily translates into the wearer's beliefs — but still.

Most of us down with the radical programme — note how pretentious this is, for no real radical person ever engages in such hoot blowing — never had an idea how to engage the youth, who, in our own stuffiness, were quite apolitical.

None of us knew how to translate and unpack Biko and his teachings to their most common denominator — and we referred to ourselves as the people's vanguard. Really? Which people? How come everybody sidetracks common sense into the most of the beaten, absurdist tracks in the name of the people, and all this invisible people do is to grin their way to the next episode of *The Bold And The Beautiful*, gossip and non-safe sexual snake dance genocide?

The people?

To Biko: Finally he is on the T-shirt, in varying shades of technicolour. For gents, a black T with your favourite radical, soaked in a burnt orange ochre frame, ah, you all you need is R300 a pop . . . ladies chest-tight, tank top in chocolate hues, get yours now at R250 and get one appreciative nod free.

I have even sighted copycat versions of Biko's image's copycat T-shirt in that black market, down Yeoville's Rockey Street, now derisively known as Brenda Fassie Boulevard. There, Biko flutters in the air side by side with Bob Marley and a whole lot of Rastafarian paraphernalia.

Look, before we get entangled in the collision of the 'Biko preservation camp' — stuffy, old BC ideologues who, as the joke goes, still could not continue to fail to attract even the local church's *umfundisi* to a single church hall-held community rally — versus the in-your-face Afro-hipsters [young dreadlocked kindergarten runaways referring to themselves as poets], there are, it becomes apparent, two main threads here: pop (pomp?) squad and the museum archival squad.

Whichever side you are straddling, soon you'll be faced with the same old question: Is Stoned Cherrie's 'conscientising the popular', as co-owner Zam Nkosi refers to it, in any way disrespectful towards Biko's memory, or are these fashionable T-shirts succeeding in liberating Biko from the mausoleum he has been politically embalmed in for the past three or so decades?

The Steve Biko Foundation, then headed by his son Nkosinathi and self-professed enthusiast, Dr Xolela Mangcu, is bored stiff with this (non) issue. 'Sorry, mate,' Mangcu responded, back when he was with the Foundation, 'there's nothing to say about this matter. Frankly, it's pretty overblown.'

You don't get more bona fida than this: Mangcu, who grew up just a corner away from where Steve Biko grew up and worked — a footnote the wise Mangcu never tires of highlighting, though these days he is on some Nelson Mandela jukebox — was, for some time not only the most articulate voice on Biko, but a Biko populariser of some deftest skill.

An American higher education product of serious academia churning out performance art academics speakers, such as dapper man, preacher man and Rennaisance man, Cornel West, Mangcu came tumbling the public commentary void like a legit, certificated Eugene Nyathi, with the right rolling vowels, and an almost method-like love affair with the telly.

He is bored stiff, here — perhaps rightfully — for, by some weird, political self-entitlement, some organisations have anointed themselves as the custodians of the Steve Biko project — whatever the project is, even if it does not fly as a project.

Yet, though the revolution is known to feed on its children — hence the phrase sacrificial 'lamb' — history does not quite forsake its children. If you apply your mind, you will agree that, historically, they too have a right to guard jealously over Biko's image, for they have sacrificed their lives, keeping his name alive, when it was neither a fly, nor a revolutionary thing to.

Would Bantu have approved? Is it possible that, were he alive, he would have halted or influenced the new street fashion parade of his and other struggle icons images to levels which no side is even brushing the bottom of today? Was it not Biko though, who called for the engagement with the masses all the time?

Would he throw up, seeing the masses giving birth to local councillors with their eyes on the national political cookie jar? What would he say to narrow ethnic-chic such as the '100% ZuluBoy' T-shirts, referring to a 65-year-old granddad?

Possibly, all these are redundant. Steve might not have been such a sexy preposition — a poster boy for the young and terribly hip — had he survived the brutal, 'cold' ordeal at the hands of his killers, the white police force, out-acting the devil himself, supposedly, though it is hard to fathom, on behalf of ordinary white voters.

But could it be that in this age of politically apathetic youth, an age where the ruling party scrambles for votes, black consciousness adherents are missing out on a fab 'n' free marketing opportunity?

Because what's trivial to Mangcu happens to be a major strategic rallying dilemma, rather 'an event not to take too lightly' for the Socialist Party of Azania (Sopa), which, says its leader, Lybon Mabasa, 'devoted a whole weekend, debating and formulating strategies to engage with the pop idolisation of our legends.'

'It's so interesting you're calling about an issue we've been debating,' says Mabasa, a BC stalwart who also, knew Biko personally and feels that 'the T-shirt is a blatant commercialisation' of his image.

But for Stoned Cherrie's Nkosi, the issue is not whether this T-shirt honours the ideals of Biko or not. Nkosi shares the story of his 20-year-old hip-hop-lovin' brother who knew nothing of Che Guevara, Castro, the Bolivian betrayal and Third World struggle.

'Now that he purchased Che's T-shirt he has taken it upon himself to dig beyond the mythology in search of the man.'

For Nkosi, though, 'popular culture' and what Mabasa refers to as 'market forces', 'offer a ripe platform to rescue icons from political snobbery; for the masses those heroes belong to. Biko is alive and belongs to all.'

Remember: for a cool 300 bucks, that is.

For former Azapo executive member Gomolemo Mokae, the T-shirt is a refreshing mobilisation effort. 'In my view, this is pure bliss. Quite a laudable feat these youths are engaging in. One hopes there will be a transition from the imagery of Biko to the content of his writings.'

Hope! That, my friend, should be underlined with the boldest of marking pens. We hope the Rosebank fashionistas will one day get Biko, if they got seShweshwe, they sure would get him, no?

As I sipped my last cup of coffee, wondering, which celeb will come marching across my path today, I could not help but ponder a bit lingeringly:

Who's next? Ayatollah Khomeini?

Goodbye Tata

The young man throws his toys out of the court of public opinion

Dear Tata

Pa, the spirit of the times — this reality TV age, the get rich or die trying era - tempts me to cry out 'wassup ol' timer?' as a form of greeting, but a fraction of what is left of my upbringing prohibits me from such over familiarisation, Tata.

Geewuz, listen to me appropriating you as my father, Tata, but ah, 'tis that small thing about being well bred, or so it seems, for what will I owe this to?

Tata, I, just like the multitudes who still swear by your name, believe that I have earned the right to relate to you as my father — an affair, naturally fraught with expectations, affection and the inevitable blemishes, something you'd be familiar with, since you have your biological offspring and their offspring and their *u khoko* — that's what you are.

It is a right earned through geographical — what is sometimes evoked as the 'national' location — and ethno-traditional deference, not much else come to think of it.

Well, Tata, here we are: 1999. How time flies! Of course, by this time — few days since leaving the government – the media and other related stargazers are flooding technological wire links, elbowing each other out, in the political and celebrity drama of piety, inviting all of as along to appreciate what a saint you are.

It is rather odd, in fact that nobody – none of those oily greedy geeks – has composed a ringtone titled St Madiba. Throw Mzekezeke in there and a hot bass . . . imagine what a hit. Perhaps we are not that bad. National treasures still evoke that aching feeling one develops towards monuments: at best, ignore, at worst, feign an affection for.

I am sorry Tata, I am one of those little dirty bastards, the self-appraised upholders of truth, limited and supple as that moral-laden word might be. Excuse my language Tata, I am the product of 1976, or was it 1984 urban mayhem when guns were as romantic as roses for us, the youth squads – hence my loo-nguage.

Now, timer, it is obvious and confirmed to everyone that right now your beautiful and intelligent wife – aunty Grace, no, that's the boorish, uncle Robert's wife, no? Oh, aunty Graça! – is busy planning a well-deserved mobile phone-proof holiday for you. So you can at last rest your magical old bones, and engage in grandparental essentials like playing with your grand, grand little ones without any intrusive media flashing its cameras at your flash- harassed pupils.

Now I don't mean to spoil your holiday, but I would like you to know my honest feelings about you, I mean, Tata, as your grandson. In fact, one of the millions of grandsons you have in this world, biological and symbolical.

Tata, we both know that every living mortal wants to trip on themselves, trying, as it may, to heap praises on you. Mine, though, dear Wise One, are grudges that I once bottled up, festering in and panging out for you, against you, towards you – they, to be precise, define how I have always felt about you, long before there was a you – I mean you, the flesh-and-blood person we all got to see after your Long Walk To Freedom.

These are badly hurt feelings, which, for some time, for all the time –

time when you were but a figment of our imagination, the soul note in our struggle songs – I kept for the day you come out and lead us to the so-called paradise, and of course that was never going be.

Paradise? Oh, no, this was not even part of the bargain you, your comrades in the 'bushes' or jailers were prepared to deal with. It was just us, the silly masses [who could have done with a little cautionary education on the illusions of icon worship], it is us Tata, who, through no negotiation with you or your family, have elevated you to a transcendental figure. Now look what has become of us.

In your non-denominational religious sainthood, you taught us to love thy neighbour, love one another; the oppressed to kiss the unrepentant oppressor. Like that uncle in a theatrical long purple frock and silver-white hair, you taught us forgiveness without enlightening us as to do with our decades, generations even, doses of anger, sorrow and helplessness.

Forgive, you said, and you will be saved, and so we chorused after you without meaning it, or knowing how to mean it – forgiveness. So it became a national recitation devoid of soul, for what soul can trans-mutate into lightness without first forgiving itself, Tata?

How do we re-grow ourselves if all there is to our beings is hollowness instead of ground to plant the seeds for the tomorrow you are always telling us about, Tata? How were we to forgive others when we could not forgive ourselves? Forgive others for what – if the cold-blooded within us, a nation, cackled with derisive laughter at the sheepish lot, out to engage in a spirit of a type of forgiveness forged in darkness?

About your saintification. I now realise that it is by no selfish act on your part, Tata, that you too lapped it up – the worship, what with all those Hosannas, red-carpeted overseas trips, various charities bearing your name a-flush with large splodges of wonga – in the years after your release.

With initial cobwebs of anger now gone, I too have learned to forgive. Specifically I would like to forgive myself and the masses I danced and plotted with, on the streets and back alleys, in the name of that one thing that got us tripping – the intangible destiny we referred to as freedom. Less did we know.

Less did we know, it too came with a price: a family of eight in a squatter camp – plentiful of those named Mandelaville, or Mandela some such – cannot afford half a loaf of bread, while striped-suited Youth League members and our former neighbours, with pure gold cufflings, fly by in the fast lane, after just another river splash of cognac, bourborn, whiskey, flesh, flash, and flush with recently unbundled mine money.

See, when you were released from your incarceration, you held the hopes of us little ones and our powerless parents on your mortal shoulders.

We saw the Almighty in you. Amongst those of us who had seen a picture of you – who can forget the grey suit, round face with slanted eyes and that furrowed on-the-side hairdo? – had plenty of tales to share. Tales spoken with hush-hush tones, without even a flicker of a lantern light.

The truly gifted within us, spent an inordinate amount of time trying to unpack your numerous speeches – the ultimate cross-nailing one – the Rivonia Trial.

I remember somewhere in the infancy of my own pitiful struggle engagement, that is before the romantic intellectuals of the New Unity Movement drew me moth-like to their waning fire, how I used to feel a hell of a lot like an underground radical, on the frail basis that I had a photocopy of a photocopy of something that used to be a press cutting of your picture.

To land our hands on that image – well, the counterfeit – was ecstacy. Such ecstacy lingered on, perhaps driven by myth more than expectation this time, for you had then been released. Fact is, you were released – a negotiated release, but, such a view was doomed to pee on our parade – no, you were not released, we wanted to believe, you walked out of prison, straight to us, the awaiting masses.

Images don't come as blurry as this: in our heads, the image of you, in your yellow skin, tailor-fitting grey suit, with your then wife Winnie Mandela matching you in step, fist raised high, was not so far-fetched from an image of Christ The Messiah strutting across Galilee towards his disciples.

Imagine then how disappointed we were when you sounded mature, wiser and almost placid. Imagine how you came out too cultivated and too calculating for our liking. Imagine how we felt when you hugged and planted that kiss on ol' Betsie Verwoerd?

All of these, though, should not be blamed on you. Something was amiss from the very day of your release. You see, in the orgy of our celebration, we shoved reality away and cloaked ourselves with fiction. We chose to forget it is the collective leadership of the liberation movements — ANC, PAC, BCMA — and internal organs such as student activism, trade unions, and not you alone, that brought us to the freedom threshhold.

Aikhona! To us Mandela was the man, the deity, the highest living untouchable. It is quite unfortunate that you are still revered in that fashion — how many self-serving books have been published on you and still coming? How many Naomi Campbells and Jay-Z's can you clear up your schedule for?

Within the reverence though, the picture had started looking askance. Our beloved revolutionary was gone and somebody — wide smile and garden-colourful shirts — has clearly stolen into the picture frame. 'Who's that?' we wondered.

Come the mid-90s and you are revered in superlative terms. Your patented grin alone, never mind the religious narratives suggested in your name, has thrust you into that select super team of super-beings, modern saints: Mother Theresa, that Diana damsel, Ayatolla Khomeini and Fidel Castro. A bit higher than Mohammed Ali and, and, of course, eclipsing both dear Martin and Malcolm.

Still Tata, I can't get what is with you and pop celebrities. As we say in the townships — jokes aside — would you care to share what goes on behind your doors when you host such gum-chewing celebs as the Spice Girls?

While we are at it, can you whisper into my ear what those hip-hoppers who are just too grateful to have met 'Mawndelur' say in their privacy with you? I'm sure you exchanged some banter with them, otherwise who can account for their lit-up faces, every time they emerge from a meeting with you?

On a lighter note, tell me ol' timer, what are your after-politics intentions? A career on the circus circuit perhaps? Kids would not want to miss their enchanting super idol with the ready-made smile. Or perhaps you may consider acting. I don't mean political acting but acting yourself in a movie that I have been threatening to write.

In that movie, you are reconciled with Winnie. Then she is the president of the country and the ANC and you, like a true African statesman, are doing a Kaunda dance, coming back to run for the presidency at the age of 100. A humour-stocked flick, I promise. But don't talk to me, talk to my lawyer if you want to feature in that movie.

Perhaps you may consider a career in advertising, or the fashion business, to sell us the Madiba range. Of course, Thabo then would sure be pissed off big-time by all these colourful shirts everywhere. But I would talk to him to focus on his Renaissance dream.

Now my real wish: the wise one, I have never met you. I always missed you when I arrived at functions you graced; never even met you at your famous wedding. So, can we have coffee together in Houghton or even Qunu sometime in the near future?

I mean, like a true pop radical of the times, I am considering running for the 2009 presidency as Winnie's ticket partner. All I am asking for is a few tips: How do I go about befriending old women like Betsie Verwoerd?

Er, er — I thank you!

Your Grandson,
Bongani
Yeoville, 2198

Prof. Malegapuru Makgoba
gaan jou bokkor!

From toddler age, my heroes were always what in reggae / dancehall lingo are known as roughnecks: John Wayne, Clint Eastwood, Tap Tap Makhatini and, of course, Pangaman Sikhapane. Of course the other ones I could not pronounce, much as my uncle tried enticing, but 'Ta—p, Ta—p, Ta—p' and 'Pa-ma-man' oh, did I mouth that off!

Even as I moved into my pre-teens, those — Tap Tap and them - were the *ouens* to watch and witty about, *jy notch?* Not bespectacled *ouens* with soft voices. I would not risk the scary idea of girls laughing at me were they to detect such softness. Worse, my neighbourhood boys would have had me for supper: *Wie se laaitjie is jy, ntwana?*

Later, one has come to appreciate new kinds of warriors, like William Makgoba. We are talking the battle against AIDS, and it's not by happenstance that we find Makgoba at the frontline.

But first, how does the battleground look? The latest report by the Medical

Research Council says AIDS will wipe out at least five million people by the year 2010.

That's roughly the whole of Soweto's population. Imagine then, the whole of Soweto dead, say, in the coming decade.

Against such a grim backdrop, one wonders if Makgoba is committing political suicide in his opposition to Mbeki's views on AIDS, or is he just being true to his character?

But who is the real William Makgoba? Is he a hero or some make-believe? Much has been written about him, yet less is known about his character. What makes him an issue?

Is he riding on the AIDS scare carpet? What exactly lies behind the phenomenon that is Malegapuru William Makgoba?

To get to the bottom of this man, you have to head straight to the 1800s Letaba to understand the legacy of Chief Makgoba, Malegapuru's great-grandfather.

Chief Makgoba fought heroic running battles against the trekking Afrikaner commandos, with their penchant for colonial expansionism that displaced Africans from their land to date.

On 1 March 1894, the Zuid Afrikaanse Republiek issued bullying ultimatums to Chief Makgoba, in an attempt to relocate his subordinates to 'allotted' lands, clearly a precursor to the Verwoerdian madness, homelands.

Like Okonkwo, Chinua Achebe's character in *Things Fall Apart*, Chief Makgoba told the boers where to stuff themselves, a feat later repeated by Chief Malebogo, Queen Modjadji and modern-day revolutionary, Enoch Mgijima.

In his autobiography, *Mokoko*, the present-day Makgoba chronicles how he was inspired by the spirit of this great grand warrior chief in his political battle with the Wits Gang of 13.

Those who have met him have views opposed to those in the media, where he is seen as a troubleseeker and new-age romantic renegade.

But Malegapuru's reputed calculated stubbornness seems out of place in the soul and physical gestures of this man: he is simply too soft-spoken and accessible. His personality brings to mind a blend of both JFK, the inspirational American writer James Baldwin, and a dash of Makana, the renegade Xhosa warrior chief, all rolled into this trouble-prone super intellect.

Upon meeting him, you are struck by this quiet man who carries himself in a casual but subconsciously distant manner, self-effacing without being sheepish.

But Makgoba the man does not perform for the public in his writing as well as his interaction. He is his own man, though many thought he was one of the president's men.

Early in the mid-1990s, his sense of freedom invited both derision and a misguided rebel fan base among the vocally-stunted Wits students and media.

For a man who takes himself a bit seriously sometimes, Makgoba followed hot in Chris Barnard's footprints, outstripping the popular Siamese twin surgeons, the Mokgokong brothers, as a scientist unwillingly thrown into popular culture by his bravery.

Long before we knew Osama bin Laden, Makgoba would be seen bedecked in Arab kaffiyeh, an invitation to racist paranoia, as he was seen by some as a 'terrorist', that new-age romantic figure of destruction adored by CNN.

Though he's terribly soft-spoken, he can be vicious when prompted, especially when he's right. He's use of barbed wire commentary and wit is as biting as it is penetratingly personal. In the aftermath of the Wits furore, the Wits Gang of 13 is looked upon disparagingly.

'Others,' he writes, 'have resigned, while others committed suicide. One is divorced and disappeared from public', while this great-grandson of the warrior chief resigned from Wits University to lead the now famously unpopular Medical Research Council.

Writing in the *Financial Mail* of 21 April 2001, he dispensed with diplomacy in his observation that: 'In the so-called new South Africa, the racialisation of issues has often led to heated furore and a failure to fight for the common good!

Does he mean President Mbeki harbours unproven charlatan sorcery beliefs over AIDS? 'Not quite. The thing is supposed to take place between 'peers' with an equal understanding, but differing views on an issue.'

One cannot fail to observe that this new head-on clash, diplomatic as it is, happens just five years after both men, Makgoba and Mbeki, operated as midwives that ushered in a new Africanist challenge to European convention.

If Dan Akroyd and John Belushi were blues brothers, Steve Biko and Donald Woods 'non-racial' political brothers, then Makgoba and Mbeki's arsenal made them political blood brothers.

The president even contributed an introduction to *Mokoko*.

'It is important that a modern African scientist like William Makgoba is part of a process which will give birth to the African Renaissance,' Mbeki fawned when it was still buttery between 'em.

As far as profiling the soul of any man, never mind a personality bordering on iconoclasm, this article does not even come close to defining who this man is.

I chose not to talk about his lovely kids. I also consciously omitted his colouful red African silk tops, lazy smile and the fact that he is an incurable traditionalist who believes in black magic.

In fact, there's much you have not gleaned from this. Only one man can tell us who Malegapuru Mampokoro Makgoba is. Himself!

Mmmmh . . . say, what's in a name? Does it offer us some inner or fringe insight about any of us?

Born in October 1952 at Jane Furse Hospital, Sekhukhuneland, the bubbly baby would be named Malegapuru, a Sotho variation of an Afrikaner phrase: *'n mal boer*.

His other moniker, Mampokoro, is a slangy translation of an Afrikaner reference: *ek sal jou bokkor*. Can he repeat his great-grandpa's magic? The last I checked he had hopped off onto some new battle altogether.

Prof. Malegapuru Makgoba gaan jou bokkor!

To claim that Makgoba loves race wars as much as that preacher man-hipster academic-rapper Cornel West is an understatement. In fact, he, like his ex-blues brother, Thabo Mbeki, not only loves a good ol' scrap, but in his veneer, is very much the product of his age, and of his native country: After the United States of America, South Africa is perhaps — and correctly so — the most race-wars obsessed country on the face of planet earth.

Knowing him, what better gets his juices flowing than race wars? I was not surprised to see him in the thick of it in the media, after he had suggested in a tad too smartsy-boy essay, intended to shock 'n' awe, that white men's behaviour in post-1994 South Africa is aping that of their not-so-distant cousins, male chimpanzees!

And then, there was his battle with one of the smartest leftist commentators and activist, Ashwin Desai. All those paled in comparison with what a ranting blogger, going by the name 'Acerbic Heckler' referred to as *the sex and rock and roll scandal in academia*, in *blogmark*, in late 2006.

Here are the basic facts: Makgoba, now Vice Chancellor at the University of KwaZulu-Natal, together with the university's council chairman, Dr Vincent Maphai, were accused of soliciting and blackmailing a senior staff member and ex-Head of Management Studies, Professor Pumela Msweni-Mabanga for sex.

Indeed this was rock and roll of the basest kind, as far as academic battles go. It had all the headline-making ingredients: the woman had been incriminated in an earlier scandal, misuse of R80 000 belonging to the university, and of having an affair with a married man, a fellow colleague.

As if that was not spicy enough, the case, like others in that institution, and often in that city — Durban — was entangled with several race and racist finger pointing, backstabbing, name smearing, and just an old battle for survival and supremacy.

In short, a classical, typical KwaZulu-Natal brawl. To those with deep memory vaults, it all reminded us of the Clarence Thomas–Anita Hill case in the US, if not, more crassly: the Tupac Shakur posse case in which the rapper was — back in 1995 — sentenced for taking part in a collective sodomy that involves his trusted thug-friends.

In the US that sort of thing — more than one man doing the nasty with a man — is called, 'running a train'. In many saucy, soft-porn magazines it gets five stars not as an indecent proposal but as an offer for a threesome.

All of these might have made for the sauciest hottest and most scandalous legal case the academia and political scene has seen in recent years, were it not just pure fantasy. Makgoba and Maphai were acquitted and by a commission of enquiry committee headed the retired Minister of Education, Prof Sibusiso Bengu and a leading political voice, Dr Fatima Meer.

Again, Makgoba walked from that scrap without a speckle of dust on his immaculately pressed Mao-styled suits. Though it is quite silly of anybody to say this, one should not be guillotined for asking: When's the next bout happening, Prof?

We are starved of action. C'mon. Kick ass. Please Prof. Kick that ass . . .

Young, Gifted and Whacked

Makhendlas

Menwana Phezulu In Memoriam

A Nile of tears threatens to storm out of my tear sacs, as I hear a replay of a bizarre piece of news clip, I have just heard in my head, on the death of one of kwaito's early super stars — Oupa Makhendlas Mafokate.

Too bloodshot to disguise an outward strength — male machismo ; that alpha bullshit men are supposed to posses as they navigate the jungle of life — and too weak to hold back the swirling tide of emotion, my eyes feel like they are about to dissolve in hot rain of tears. Acid rain, perhaps?

I turn around to whistle a poignant Bob Marley tune, 'Redemption Song' and walk away. To nowhere, in particular. As positive a product of black soul that Marley's classic is, it cannot contain the rage that tornadoes in my mind as I sit iced on a computer word processor asking myself, 'Why?' Why did the young kwaito superstar Oupa Makhendlas Mafokate blow himself away that fateful Saturday?

Makhendlas — township slang for 'fun lover' — is reported to have committed suicide — aged 27! — in the aftermath of a fatal brawl with a stalking less fan. The young star was billed as the top attraction at Saturday night's concert in Tonga, Nelspruit.

You know what they say — fate is a bitch. So, perhaps a bit unscripted and unexpected, Makhendlas got involved in a deadly fracas with a nuisance fan who had reportedly been harassing him and his musical crew all night before he was supposed to take stage.

At some point Makhendlas's emotions replaced his brains and he whipped out his gun and pumped three bullets into the troublesome man.

That is the official story as told by 999 Music, the young Mafokate's label, owned by his older brother, kwaito hotshot, King Arthur the first. But why did Makhendlas have to carry a gun? Was he under some kind of threat? Is a gun an ultimate shield, or is the destroyer of life?

The slain township groovester, says 999, should not be sacrificed furthermore. Especially by the sort of questions they feel dig a bit too close to the matter for their comfort. 'Already he is dead. There is no need to blame a dead man for the sins of an alive world,' says Mpho Makhetha. 'You ask why did Mafokate have a gun on him? How will I know? Can you ask a dead man such a question?

'You know very well that the music industry in this country is in bad shape, insofar as management of the small labels go, which, is rather strange, since they are the money spinners. In some of these shows we have to collect gate share (money) ourselves and even you are aware that the spectre of crime is ever present,' Makhetla puts it. According to his dearly beloved, Makhendlas should not come out as a sore thumb for having a rod with him, in the first place.

'That man was never ever a *skelm* (rubbish). Ever since I began working with him I don't know of anyone who was harassed or threatened by Makhendlas. I don't know him as a gun-blasting sort. He must have snapped horribly, to an extent which I can't measure, for he is nowhere to tell me,' says Makhetha, struggling to keep an ice-cool Clint Eastwood tone of a man hurt but seen to be handling it well.

Makhendlas's road to his destination — if one has to call it thus, though

Makhendlas

I believe dying young robs the dead of the full gallop of the trip — was not quite a route full of roses, neither an act of bravery, however street jesters would like us to believe. It was a brutal, callous even, shortcut, unmediated, hurried checking out by a young man with a bright future, at his own shaking hand, and worse, still smoking, blood seeking pistol.

To many in the townships, his death represents the heightened streak of madness, uncertainty and fear — not only in music — but in the socio-cultural playground in which young black males play and are raised.

History is a classic image of the lives of young black men — more so, the products of 1976. The notion that black men are buffalo soldiers blessed with a natural gift for toughing it out on the rough edges of life has sent young black males into a cyclone of confusion, fear and unending challenges to legitimise their status in this depoliticised, insensitive, indifferent era, where the fruits of the revolution feed on their offspring.

It is unlikely that Makhendlas travelled to Mpumalanga to slaughter someone, least of all himself. That he shot someone was a reactionary act of fear — pure cowardice. His hurried-up self wipe-off from the face of the earth captures the acute social illnesses which face his generation in a South Africa preparing for a post-Mandela era — lack of social, non-celebrity, community, street mentors.

I have met and tried and spent some time trying to dig out some sort of conversation from him — when we both began in kwaito music — he as dancer in his brother's stable, and I as reporter animated by this news — made-in-the township sound, with angry beats and part soaked lyrics.

Kwaito, back then — to pilfer Fred Khumalo's take on its American older cousin, hip-hop — was 'pop music's atomic bomb'. The big bang of party rhymes, gangster boasts, political science, come-ons and the urge to ride in the world's biggest, flashiest Mercedes-Benz.

But also, it's politics were of different stripes altogether. At worst, kwaito — a music with various roots in black ghetto survivalism and reappropriated hip-hop imagery — was a half baked musical attempt by township boys -

mostly boys — at selling never-to-be-realised capitalist dreams.

At best, the technofied, looped electro synthesised, bass anchored sound was an inevitable, cathartic township cry-out. Several fragments of the Kwaito sound were a sonic desire by township, specifically working-class youths to provide their own version of positive template as opposed to the petrol bombed-out surroundings, and worse still, teenagers mutilated self-image and beliefs, a mere five years after children as young as five, witnessed black on black butcherings, and once again, the smell of burning tyre in their neighborhoods.

The kwaito sonic narrative, sought to turn the gory tale of black-on-black violence on its head, to create an escapist world of party-people, thus for the first time urging the poorest of the poor of township teenagers that they too can make it.

Such was the background from whence Makhendlas emerged. Clearly he was a man of contradictions — and perhaps he had a last laugh as it were: what kind of a man is this, who was quiet, so as to border on dullness — stubborn? — and yet, partied and traded the jive-blast-ful footstomping music like his?

Interestingly, I thought he was an utter bore, who could not talk himself out of a corner, but that was not a reflection of his quiet wisdom. Unlike his older and brasher brother, Arthur, Oupa was on the quiet side of quiet — a reflective soul who did his talking onstage.

His story mirrors the daily prison that the music industry has become for young musicians who are huge in the eyes of their fans, and yet remain too inconsequential as bankable artists to receive any protection from music promoters or police.

'If he was an American artist of the same stature,' Makhetha says, 'he would have been provided with extra and even unwanted police protection. But for us such a thing as protection is just but a dream. And if artists do not perform at venues they are billed for, for lack of security, they take the blame for ensuing riots. I mean for an artist to be forced to deal with stalking fans who have crossed security lines is a scary idea.'

As tears of anger at wasted talent begin to dry, I remember Makhendlas's artistic zeal. Quite simply, nothing could steal the limelight from Makhendlas's hit single '*Emenwe (Menwana Phezulu)*' — a simple, mid tempo, soulful piece of dance music, quite popular in the black urban areas and their satellite peripheries.

I cannot *not* remember the song, or Oupa, himself — and it's all based on selfish reasons. Thing is, my unofficial street name is also — don't ask me why — Oupa, and as for the song '*Menwana*' — man, you should have seen what it did to my then three-year-old [step] daughter, Tshenolo. She twisted and contorted herself into a small pack of gum-stretched form, as she moonwalked to it backwards . . . a sight to behold and crack about laughing. Who needs Wacko?

The second-born son of Enos and Grace, Makhendlas was born and reared in Chiawelo. He was a rarity who rose to establish himself as an artist capable of holding his own against the best in kwaito music.

Of course his music, like lots of kwaito, was lyrically deficient, but he was one of the few stars who was in touch with his musical constituency. His second album *Jwaleng* — with the title track '*Otla shwela jwaleng*' (Check out you party animal, lest you drown yourself in a pool of booze), and another 'Jealous' — is as socially relevant as it is packed with infectious grooves.

Oh, *Thixo*! The young, black and talented are again an endangered species under siege from themselves and a society which is not expecting much from them anyway. A chorus from his masterpiece township dance sizzler would do here:

'*Emenwe, menwana, Emenwe, phezulu!*'

While I'm thinking that this life is full of River Phoenix sorts — young shooting stars consumed by all the attendant admiration — I begin to wonder, for Makhendlas's sake, a Pantsula act, through and through — if heaven has a ghetto.

Mandoza

Uzoyi thola ka Njani Impilo

When Musa Sibanyoni and Nobesuthu Tshabalala chanced upon each other in Soweto, a good 30 odd years ago, neither had an inkling they would bless urban South Africa with a child, that would become post-apartheid black rock 'n' roll star – Mduduzi, popularly known as Mandoza.

Rock 'n' roll here connotes a variety of quiz blocks that make up the tricky picture that Mandoza is.

It addresses both the man's (Mduduzi's) heart and the man's (Mandoza's) art. At core, Mandoza is a split spirit living in parallel times with its own doppelganger. The two make up quiz-pieces of a whole, though, they weren't always this way. At the beginning there was only one lad, Mduduzi, your mere edgy township boy, from whose teenage excess and experiences, emerged Mandoza, the rock star.

Millions of fans are always caught in awe, in thrall of, or sometimes dismissive of the musical brashy brat, and yet to make sense of him you have to constantly look at how he emerged out of the dream of the young boy, known as Mduduzi. Parts of the present rock star's music – especially the township-punk metal beats, woven into soulful melody, in earlier works such as '*Ozoyithola Ka Njani*' as well as the racial cross-over '*Nkalakatha*' — weds almost naturally, with the young man's earlier ghetto-triumphant, ghetto *strugglista* and ghetto fabulous narratives.

That and his natural propensity for trouble, fun and rebelliousness, his well reported free-love, free life, free-drugs, rehabs and relapses, renders Mandoza a unique rock'n roll star of his time, perhaps the best of those who slipped off, through the hip and cool man ghetto idol manufacturing factory, that stage manages its product, at least to quote from the bible after one more drug-rehab trip in swanky Houghton.

Mduduzi might have been a pretty impressionable boy, but Mandoza is the most PR-proof rockstar soul, perhaps after Brenda Fassie — South Africa's quintessential rock phenomenom, of our age. Like most of the rock 'n' roll and football stars with a rock affliction — for what could it be? — Mandoza's personality is that of person whose pop shine has not quite succeeded, nor will it ever succeed, in smoothing or dolling up his rough 'n' ready exterior.

The son of Musa and Nobesuthu, Mandoza is plain raw, and at best, a product of his time. In short — at core, he is just plain, Mduduzi. No image stylist can conceal the battle scars he has incurred. Growing up a car-jacking boy and survivor in Zola, perhaps the most notoriously masochistic and trigger-happy part of Soweto, Mduduzi (in his later, rock star incarnation as Mandoza, narrated his life to me in November 2002) internalised the mythological ghetto tales of bravery.

Brave was code word for choosing an easy path of crime and not the supposed nerdy, book-loving sissy boy behavior that was frowned upon in several townships.

A product of a strictly working-class township family, the boy was also a victim-courier of the more established crime syndicates that fed on fellow blacks as well as hard-working white folks' material possessions, in some twisted redress benefitting the syndicate leaders.

It is as a result of these ghetto-scripted midnight raids, gun shoving deep in people's throats and snatching their hard toiled-for wares, that he saw the inside of jail, Sun City, in the early 1990s, hardly out of his teens.

In this notorious Soweto Alcatraz — or blinged out five star, depending on who you are talking to — the young boy was, for the first time, exposed to unacted-out realism. In there, at the coalface of the scary, soul-eroded life of crime behind bars, the young man instinctly knew that this was a world of street dreams — dreams he did no longer want to be part of.

It is out if his experiences with hardened criminals, that upon his release, the young man swore never, ever, to lead a life drawn out of cinematic escapades, and to concentrate on creating a life on the straight and narrow — no crime, no easy loot. He had had enough. Neither gun slinging, nor gang banging would do — stakes were high.

He was not educated, nor possessed any technical education. Moms and Pops were not in line to inherit family-trust *moolah*, nor gemstones, locked in some bank vault or safe. If he had to make it, it was to be through his sweat, or talent, whatever God has blessed him with — luckily, he had one.

Gruffy and grainy, his whiskey-soaked voice was that of a Bobby Womack-meets-Ali Katt of the post petrol bomb generation — but locked in were the pains and hopes of a million boys like him. Rap was the emerging new wave in the townships, early 1990s, and though not a particularly poetic rhyme creator, the man had something to say, something drawn from his personal experiences, which no pop magazine or TV drama can inculcate deeper.

As with numerous township talents then, he did a stint with the kwaito progenitor, Arthur Mafokate — but the latter was not rough, not ghetto enough. Mduduzi and his buddies in Chizkop were hungry for something edgier, immediate, unpolished, explosive: they were simply Soweto's equivalents of the angriest hip-hop outfit on the planet, the Onyx.

They had to move. Soon! They had to get a recording deal, whoever who was going to sign them was onto diamond — but uncut, and possibly, ex-blood diamond!

1995, Kwaito wars — which could be just flimsy, gang star style wars, by two of the most high-profile kwaito gangs in Johannesburg — was at full bloom. Who would sign this rough diamond, ready to explore his working-class tale on CD? Who would take a chance? Who was ready to rock?

* * *

Mandoza's story is that of a young hijacker who discovered music and staked a claim as one of the custodians of the forgotten pantsula subculture. Three of his major albums *Uzoyithola kanjani?*, *Nkalakatha* and *Godoba* have gained him millions of fans on both sides of the colour bar, something that has not been seen since Margaret Singana, Joy and Sipho 'Hotstix' Mabuse ruled the airwaves.

At one point he seems to live in the media headlines, sometimes drug dens, sometime he just looks pretty swell, lending his gruffy soul voice to, say, a Ringo Mandlingozi show.

'Who is Mandoza?' — the rock star, I mean — I wondered . . .

Is his life a constant round of high-voltage music and hanging with the boys, snorting with the hangers, getting down with other pop reculcitrants, in search of a tabloid problem? I ventured forth to discover the unknown side of this self-styled kwaito tough boy, whose voice is a cross between *mbaqanga* groaning of Mahlatini and the kwela growling of Big Voice Jack Lerole.

The day I turned up at his home, a cheerful Mandoza welcomed me, and I have since realised he spends most of his spare time washing his new silver-grey Merc CLK, Crossfire or this or that hot *smovane*.

Mpho Mphuti, his live-in lover and the mother of their son Tokollo, was down with the flu. It dawned on me later that there is a bond between father and son that is rarely seen with young fathers, especially those who are supposedly sex symbols.

I learned from Mandoza that, not only is he a kwaito rapper with rock sensibilities, but also an entrepreneur smart enough to understand the fickle nature of show business. Coming from the streets where he saw his life of crime go up in smoke, he understood that the balloon on which his star-parade is riding, might go bust at any time.

He understands perfectly that a pop tag can be a major brand one day, only to disappear, the next. So, in the current tradition of entertainer going the rag and perfume trade route — Jay-Z, P. Diddy, Damon Dash, and now Jamiroquai — he has created a new clothing range known as Mandoza Wear — swanky, casualwear, based on the Phat Farm cool aesthetics.

'See bhuti (brother)', he says, 'I love sportswear, especially in bright colours. Being a stylish performer with a unique image that my fans love, I have decided to give it to them through a fashion range that signifies that they are young, black and proud. In addition to investing in the rag trade, the 24-year-old Mandoza is a shareholder in In Tyme Management, an artists' management company that guides hot acts such as Mapaputsi and Ernie Smith.

On the face of it, he is just like any other township act, but in reality he is not. Mandoza is probably the busiest single act in South Africa — in the every sense of the word. One moment he is doing Sun City, the next he is performing at the Kora Music Awards, and then he is promoting his new album, on *Selimathunzi* and *Jam Alley* on TV, debuting in a feature-film drama, is seen by hotel staff leaving some all-night fun and drunk binge party, or is working with this or that gospel artist.

Does he understand what family time means? 'Plenty', he quantifies it. 'It's all about planning. Whenever I get the chance, I sleep quite a lot and spend time with my woman, who happens to be my real-life friend, as well as my son.' He also spends time with members of Chizkop, his kwaito group, his mother and two sisters.

'They offer me a kind of emotional support that is different to what the fans offer.

'It's not the same. I love my family. And no, marriage is not part of the equation right now.

'At my age — late 20s — I am still young, and me and my partner are taking things as they come, building trust, bonding and engaging in each others' complex personalities. Yes, I am very complex and so is she!'

Ironically, in person, the gruffy-voiced rapper from a section of Soweto that rides on the myth that it produces 'true ghetto artists', is not quite that tough, himself. He is no different from other successful young black males, such as TKZee, who have suddenly had fame trust on them and are not sure how to deal with it.

True, Mandoza could do with a bit of intellectual, spiritual and emotional charging up, that would just broaden his artistic and personal horizons. He has cast his look back at the journey Mduduzi walked in his quest to become Mandoza.

He has to decide if he wants to develop his art, and not flourish as tabloid fodder — all those are no easy decisions to make in the world where the young, handsome, monied and brash are exempt from taking responsibility for their actions. He has to allow Mandoza to talk to, or, perhaps, finally, merge with the Mduduzi who left the world of crime in Sun City, to recreate his own version of ghetto dreams.

Will he? I asked after a long day listening to him.

'Eish man!' he looked at me, a bit uncertainly.

'God the Almighty knows my destiny,' he says, as we drive towards the SABC for yet another adrenaline-inducing moment — an interview, meeting, autograph, whatever — in the life of South Africa's kwaito-rock king.

Tupac Shakur

Am I my brother's keeper?

It's an eerie Saturday af'noon — one of the last of Jo'burg's extended winter days. The smell of burning tyre underneath the weight of a rickety taxi, bullet speeding to the North West — where I'm off to visit one of Tupac Shakur's jailed fans, my brother Walter — tells you the speed is well over the required 80km/h.

Snaking its way across the notoriously dangerous *coloured* areas, off Newclare main road to Newlands, next to an almost derelict shopping complex full of drunkards, glue sniffers and their Mainstay-sloshed cherries, the four-wheeled horse halts, screeches to a stop and the driver peers out of the window to curse his fellow road user: *Hey, jou poppol!*

But it's not the taxi nor Jozi's ill-famous road rage that would haunt this passenger, off to visit a teenager in the faraway dungeons, but rather a badly-spelt haiku scribbling on the shopping complex's wall:

In Got wet trast / Lard have Macy:
Tupac Shakur will be back
Long lief 2Pac.

The driver, thick with the trademark taxi driver's rawness, curses some more and hot pedals it. *Ride on brother.* It would take a week, no less, before that scribbling became prophetic.

Today, 7 September, marks seven years on the spot, after the rapper, self-confessed *thug lova* — American Vice President candidate Dan Quayle called for this man's 'removal from society' — was mercilessly gunned down in the blazing lights of LA's fabled streets.

All over the country, as it is happens universally — especially in the cyber world of the internet, where you are likely to cull gory details of your favourite dead icon at the click of a mouse — the countdown to post-pop's own scripted Armageddon has begun.

Y-Fm's morning talk show host, DJ Fresh, known as 'DJ Fresh, the *Big Dawg*' and his producer, Thato Molefe, known as the '*Lil' Dawg*' — with the emphasis on the name's reverse spelling — was the first in media to hype the so-said second coming of a rapper whose fans won't just let rest in peace — Amaru Tupac Shakur.

In daily segments, Fresh and co. have an intensely exciting slot, known as the 'seven year, seven day theory', which, according to a Tupac '*fan*'*-atic* website they subscribe to, means Tupac will resurface and come back to this world from the world yonder. Kaput? Perhaps, but then again you got to understand the religious-like myth-belief deeply embedded in the death and significance of Tupac Shakur to fully comprehend the obsession.

Perhaps no other rock star in history — *rock 'n' roll* being the umbrella phrase for existentialist angst and style, the only musical genre other than the blues that served as the sound board for all things primal — has had his life and death wrapped in so many religious references.

'It might sound blasphemous, but you see, Tupac Shakur was a Christ-like figure to his generation,' says poet and author of *Azanian Love Songs*, Don Mattera — a former Sophiatown gang leader himself. Soft, on one hand throwing banter and veering towards the assertive black consciousness' 'memory is the weapon' mould, Mattera carries insight into the subject, because, as he says, he has more than an affinity with Tupac Shakur.

'He was a poet, an activist, an artist, a would-be thug, yes, but also a spokesperson of his people and a fatherless child. I feel for him and his generation now, as I felt when he was alive.'

The Christ-like imagery goes beyond Mattera's poetic licence though. 'It's Tupac, King of the Ghetto, or, Tupac, Lord of the Microphone' — everywhere. According to the website, it was written — no less by Shakur himself, in his *The Don Killuminatti: the Seven Day Theory* — that 'Pac 'will be back'. He's not gone. Never been gone. This is the time for his resurrection.'

To some, the Christ-like references do not carry any weight in themselves, but propelled to pop myth by the rapper's own play-prophesying an expression of fear, rather than brave anticipation of death in his swirling mid-1990's music and public behaviour.

Ever since he co-stared with the young Omar Epps in *Juice*, together with *New Jack City* — as one of the earliest and emotionally disturbing of Hollywood's incorporation of hip-hop in the money culture of pop's big screen commodities — Tupac has had love affair with the concept of 'death.'

In the Ernest Dickerson-directed flick, Tupac plays Bishop, a mean-ass teenage gangster whose greed and blood thirst turns him against his homeboys whom he hunts, all mowed down with his .38 pistol, at each and every turn. The film was, says one of Tupac's biographers, film critic Armond White, 'Hollywood's desperation to catch on rap's cash cow; the mean and dangerous black streets of America.'

But death had caught on. In his 1995 classic, *Me Against the World*, the rappers mixes and sews death and God so many times — *Death Around the Corner, Lord Knows, If I die2Nite, So Many Tears* — and with heartfelt emotion you'd've felt he was a Baptist preacher unleashed to frighten young musical lovers — or someone who knew he was destined to meet his destiny through the barrel of a gun.

It's a theme that would persist throughout his work and through hit-ranting song-poem 'Only God Can Judge Me' from *Makavelli*, the rookie rapper expressed how his pre-celebrity frustration, media meanness, jail spells for sodomy and gun possession are now weighing on him. And that was not the only date with death he had on record — coming more wretched after each and every temporary victory.

In April 1995, he was shot nine times at Times Square, New York City, only to be taken to hospital under police arrest. The event kick-started a deadly play with tragedy between him and Christopher Wallace, also known as 'Poet Laureate' of the streets, Notorious BIG.

Death was his and he belonged to it — only difference is, it was five years before the dark spooky came fully armed to snatch him, riding down California streets. Only one year into the rap and music industry, he made news on 22 August 1992 after a six-year-old boy was shot dead at a benefit party in Marin City. The weapon was traced to Tupac's half-brother Mopreme Harding, who was jailed and released. The boy's family filed a lawsuit against Tupac — and that was just the beginning.

In Texas that spring, writes White in his seminal text, *Rebel Without a Cause* — a 19-year-old Ronald Ray Howard shot a Texas trooper and then later claimed that Tupac's furious debut *2Pacalyse Now* — inspired by Alfred Hitchcock's film and the theory of Armageddon — moved him to commit the deed.

It was not long before America's Vice President Dan Quayle pressurised Shakur's record label to pull the album from the shelves. 'This music has no place in our society,' he fumed hoping to garner votes to stop the swashbuckling governor from the South, William (Bill) Clinton in the next general elections.

While his notoriety rose, so did the calibre of acting talent. A product of Baltimore Arts School, film directors loved his possessed method-acting style — which reflected the pain and sorrow of street life he lived and dined in. John Singleton cast him in *Poetic Justice*, while the Hughes Brothers cast and scratched him from their grimier ghetto nightmare, *Menace II Society*.

'Shockingly handsome,' as *Newsweek* magazine reported after one of his court trials, Tupac did not need the new hip-hop filmmakers to carve him a niche in the film industry. He was, as Michael Jackson had screamed a decade before, really 'baaaad', in both the American dialect that means 'damn good' and 'roguish'. He's life experiences were the subject of courtroom and street drama, so he brilliantly transferred street life to screen life.

Things were on a roll. Hollywood was hungry for new blood — *black* blood. He would soon befriended by Hollywood's notorious famous characters, *9½ Weeks'* bad boy Mickey Rourke, Madonna and her ill-tempered ex-hubby, Sean Penn.

Displaying natural, animated and sterling performances in films such as *Above the Rim*, *Gridlock'd* and the latest, *Gang Related*, as well as turning his rap videos into mini movies of sorts, Tupac had, in street parlance, 'arrived'.

And so was the genesis of a dangerous mix; death, God and superstardom all woven into the soul of a boy hardly out of his teens.

As much as his later songs, such as 'Redemption' and 'I Wonder if Heaven got a Ghetto', continued his theme park, an interplay of death and God, there are two acts in his 200-plus songbook opus that eerily touches on both the absurdity of pop superstardom and reflects the 'ill' genius of pop marketing: a song recorded with his band Thug Life, titled 'How Will They Mourn Me' as well a pledge cryptically scripted on the inside of last of his albums, *R U Still Down*, 'keep faith in me. I will not let you down! Love, 2Pac'.

The album itself is covered back to back with a ghost / spirit / dream-like portraiture of Tupac, eyes at once haunting and lifeless on the front and one of Vincent Van Gogh-like magic realist portrait; swirling purples and blues reflecting the pain in his eyes.

Does this Christ-like figure hold though? Who really was Tupac and why does his supposed resurrection steer the souls of fans, rebels and criminals — from Sierra Leonean diamond-digging rebels, Soweto's gang rapists to Peru's ultra-left guerillas, the Tupac Amaru Rebels — with such ferocity?

While author of *Who's Gonna Take The Weight?*, Kevin Powell — the only journalist the continuing paranoid Tupac ever trusted with his basest feelings, says 'Tupac embodied the struggle and disturbed spirit of young black American better than anyone else did', it is local poet and playwright Duma ka Ndlovu, who remembers where it all began.

While exiled in the US, ka Ndlovu lived some few blocks away in 116 Street, Harlem, where the young Tupac, young brother Mopreme and sister Asantewa were single-handedly raised through hardship by Afeni.

'The whole myth is not an exaggeration', recalls ka Ndlovu. 'I knew that boy as a child. With his positive and disturbed energy you just knew he was destined to die young, leaving a lasting impression. In spirit and behaviour', recalls ka Ndlovu, 'Tupac was child of the Black Panthers through and through. He sucked, ate, breathed, lived and rapped black consciousnesses from conception to death.'

'Unfortunately', Duma puts it, 'America's own social contradictions charmed the young boy into the thug life he so much fantasised about. I remember it too well. When he — Tupac — first bursts into the scene, he wasn't no gangster. He was all about black unity. He was the most significant spirit and symbol of resistance as a musician. Same way Muhammad Ali was; young, gifted and certainly loud mouth number one.'

Both writers, Powell and Duma, agree that 'the reason Tupac's spirit continues to disturb and fascinate boils down to then and now hardships; disease, suicide, economic blues, and self-hate perpetuated by the American political and moneyed class on its black citizens.

'Beyond what Hollywood beams to you on the telly, reality is, there's a riot of a silent type goin' on there. The streets aren't all shining bling-bling. Tupac, who was both a recording artist and activist occupied the void left by the death of black leaders in post Civil Rights America', they chorus. 'From Jesus Christ downwards people have always adored icons. In our silence and isolation, we feel that an icon can save us, speak for us and carry our pain. That just reflects how lost and hopeless people have been made to feel about themselves.'

'Within the multifaceted and multiple black spiritual world, there Tupac represented a two-edged spirit: the warrior and the trickster spirit, Powell told the *Sunday Times* from his apartment in Brooklyn, New York.

For ka Ndlovu, Tupac filled the void left by the assassination of both Malcolm X and Martin Luther King.

'When he came, the whole African population was desperately searching for a universal leader. Nkrumah was gone. So was Malcolm X, Steve Biko, Fanon and Bob Marley. It would take two decades for the black world to really experience the power of a universal leader with the 1991 release of Nelson Mandela from Pollsmoor — silver haired, yellow skinned, fist raised high, the ever-defiant Nomzamo Winnie Mandela on his side — *Aaaamandla!*

Kevin Powell, who later confided to this writer: 'I wrote my last elegy for him in my book, *Who's Gonna Take The Weight?* and I won't write nothing 'bout him no more, feels as much as Tupac was the voice of his generation, 'the whole worship ritual around Tupac is pretty overblown. People must get real. We owe it to Tupac, to further live our lives. 'Pac was an example of what to be and what not to be.'

Still, his much-covered public behaviour doesn't come closer to unmasking the fear and potential of the biggest rock figure to rival Elvis Presley, Princess Diana and Fela Kuti combined.

The story lies with his 'dear momma' Afeni Shakur. Born Alice Faye Williams — named after a 1940s blonde big band singer and movie star — Afeni joined the New York branch of the Black Panthers, by then the chicest, bravest and politically-captivating band of men and women, who wore tight black denims, black polo necks, black leather coats — with men wearing berets while the molls spotted kinky curled Afro-hairdos.

So enchanting, that were an imperiously indifferent Tom Wolfe spoofed, the white liberals who loved them in the classic *Mau-Mauing the Flak Catchers*, whereas Edgar Hoover's FBI played as the third force that would eventually reduce their vision to a rancid plasticine, Panther against the other cat, brother against brother. East Coast against West Coast.

But it was just before Hoover's infiltration that the petite and full-of-fury

22-year-old Afeni — short for ObaFeni, an Africanist name, gave up her 'colonial moniker' — worked hard to rise to become the East Coast secretary to the Bobby Seale and Hey Newton-led party.

It was 1971. The world streets, from Alexandra to Harlem right through the heartland of Black radical street attitude Oakland were held in a political and cultural spell: black is beautiful / black power!'

'The streets', recalls Armond White, 'were abuzz with thick rich soul music notes'. 'Smilin' Faces', which was later given oomph by Norman Whitfield's funksters Rare Earth, was all the rage. With backing vocals asking, 'can you dig it ? preparing for an answer 'Oh Lordy, Oh Lordy', 'Smilin' Faces' became a vestige of negro spirituals that had seeped into R & B's soul.

> Beware!
> Beware of the handshake
> There hides a snake
> Beware! Beware of the pat on the back
> It might hold you back

For Afeni, who had a deep and disturbing love affair with both the Party and some of its leading men, Panther ideology was in her head, in her jail cell and in her bed! Radical mantra was that ' the revolution was an act of love'.

First she dated a man who'd become Tupac's biological father, Billy Garland, then co-habitated with Lumumba Shakur who was briefly married to Afeni when she was in prison and pregnant, and Mutulu Shakur with who she had a child, Tupac's half-brother Mopreme. The Shakurs were all over, leading the party and getting arrested. Others, like Zayd who married a woman called Jo-Anne Chesimad, now one on America's political most-wanted list and in exile in Castro's Cuba, were either killed by other Panthers, the police or languish in jail.

Jail, as it happens is where Afeni nearly gave birth to a bouncy baby boy — but it took four weeks after her release before the struggling woman, then on coke, gave birth to the boy who would later take the world by storm.

A child of the revolution that was never televised, Tupac — which translates as a 'shining sepent', a reference to an Incan warrior — the Arabic name 'Shakur' means ' Thankful to God' — was part of a new generation of children who were given Afrocentric sounding names, challenging them to search deep into the slavery past to make sense of their rot, in New York, Detroit or Birmingham, Alabama.

Now you would understand why, at his prime, he recorded a song regarded by foes and fans alike as the most enchanting, soul composition to posit a son's appreciation for a mother's love where it belongs — in his heart and worn on his shirt and record sleeves. 'Dear Mama' touched where country folk star Merle Haggard touched with 'Mama Tried', his 1972 remake of Dolly Parton's 'Coat of Many Colours' — at the heartstring of emotional boiler rooms.

The rest is pop trivia and the stuff of Hollywood road romance: Think. Think big. Dream. Dream big. Big lights! Big names! Big cars! Big jewellery! Big events! Aaaaaargh.

That's how it felt on the night of September 1996.

The fabled lights of Las Vegas were ablaze in the desert. The much touted Tyson–Seldon Heavyweight Championship fight at the MGM Grand Hotel that lasted all of two minutes in which a multi-million dollar purse was lost and won.

Riding in the passenger seat of a sleek new black BMW sedan, his bearded friend and chief honcho of 'Pac's gangster-glorifying Death Row Records, a mountain of a man simply known as Suge Knight, contemplatively chewing his thick Habana cigar, escorted by an entourage of ten, Tupac might have felt he owned the night.

An indeed he did — his friend and fellow rogue, Mike Tyson, had just disposed of a palooka, Bruce Seldon, in a Heavyweight Championship fight at the MGM Grand Hotel that lasted all of two minutes.

Just then, round midnight, a white Cadillac pulled up beside the BMW sedan at a stop light. Its occupants fired a volley of shots, four of which found their way into Tupac, two of them fatally. He was rushed to LA's Medical University Medical Centre, where doctors attempted to defy nature; putting him through numerous life-saving machines, frantically trying to resurrect the God.

And then Afeni's word finally prevailed: 'It's time to let him go.' There was no public funeral, and to this day his fans are convinced Tupac will make good on his promise in the album *Don Killuminatti*.

Postscript

That rickety made good on its rude driver's promise. It arrives in a record two hours. I met Walter, incarcerated for life at Rooigrond Correctional Centre, just as visiting time was about to lapse.

'Tell me, Walter, why did you love Tupac so much? Were you inspired by his — to quote NWA — 'Gangsta Gangstar' life?'

'No. 'Pac represented life as is.' I remember Walter, voice hoarse and face as sweet as Tupac's, saying.

Life. One gave his up in the rap game. One gave in to the state, where he is serving under a charge: 'mistaken act of murder.' Truth is, my brother killed the likeable family man and teacher in an aggressive act. No, I don't know his motive. Only that he loved Tupac with all his heart.

Life!

Adam Levin's write stuff among the non-believers

'Pon reading Adam Levin's *Aidsafari: A Memoir of My Journey with Aids* — his third book in two and a half years — an overwhelmed literary critic might be gushful with comparisons: 'South Africa's literary blend of *Giovanni's Room, For Whom the Bell Tolls* and a failed hedonist's navel gazing.'

How imprecise that would be! If there's any artistic creation, simple yet large enough to capture the pathos, energy and essence of Levin's book, legendary Latin American poet and lyricist Pablo Neruda's *Los Marineros* — the sailors — would be it:

> *I love the love of sailors who kiss and go /*
> *Leaving a promise / Leaving a promise/*
> *One night they sleep with death /*
> *On the sea bed /*
> *I love the sailors who kiss and go*

Adam Levin

In one breath, this book is about a solo sailor — Aids-suffering Levin — who kisses and goes. The reader is invited along on this trip to watch and listen to him and his deepest yearnings for pleasure on one hand, and join him in excruciating pain as he lay on a potential death bed for the next two years after the worldwide party was over.

The author, as Neruda puts it, slept with death on a sea-bed that life is. And yet, this is neither a gloomy book nor a blues tome for a repentant hedonist. It is about — in both metaphor and sobering directness — a story about a consummate, pleasure-loving exhibitionist, a brave, life-loving but dangerously-living young man in the fast lane.

It is about movement: the author's movement, sometime, to nowhere. A search that takes this man on a journey across the world, seeking — at the deepest core of his spirit — one can deduce, that elusive beast called love.

You realise just then, that Adam Levin's book and the stories it contains, love, lust, selfishness, dreams, desperation and hope are as much about him as they are about all of us. Stripped off its bravado and *sick* humour — the prose heaves with stylistically crafted one-liners pregnant with wit and bursting with self-deprecation — the book asks of its writer and reader: How brave do you suppose you really are?

Though the aim — like all memoirists — is to save one's self or trumpet the subject's triumph, the author's initial independent streak does not really reflect bravery after all, but performs the dualities of expressing and masking fear.

When Levin writes — in a 'round-the-fireside' oral prose — on his gratitude to his parents, particularly his soldiering mom, described here as 'moving from a meal cooking ma, to marijuana / dope collecting mom,' for her addicted son in his deepest pain, you get the stabbing feeling that selfish 'independence' is not quite sustainable after all.

It becomes clear that whatever revolution he waged and won was a purely miscarried revolution. When it was hot and steamy — often in nightclubs — it served none but himself. In *Aidsafari*, the revolutionary freak gives way to the Aids activist, but not before fighting body and soul to save his life.

It is remarkable how a writer as direct and talkative as Levin omits to tell the reader that what he was actually looking for is self-love, something he and billions of us struggle with on a daily basis, often projecting it onto, and expecting it from, others; family, lovers, cheaters, pill-popping friends, whores, one-night stands, literature, music and, or death.

The kisses Levin engages in are no ordinary smooches. They are killer kisses. Fast, lusty, over idealised, romantic, but always the itch to move on would overcome the length of the emotion, kiss, thus propelling him to other destinations . . . Sao Paolo, Bamako, Rio, Jozi, to hell, to heaven and U-turning to hell, and back.

Contrary to what I might have painted, *Aidsafari* is not about disco balls on fire, perverted gay men with omnipresent hard-ons, wrapped in garish rolling pink satin, floating on a river of booze and drugging themselves into stupendous comas.

Though some bingeing — like in a Melville club, where the author was once invited to snort a line of cocaine off a man's penis — does take place, at its basic, this book is about appreciating the complexities of life more.

Having known him — or parts of him, such as the journalist — for over ten years, having read, reviewed his books, disagreed with his takes on the Africa he engaged with in his journeys across the continent, sharing a fanatical love for Senegalese music, and fascinated by what he refers to as his 'Afro-futurist and freakish nature', I felt, still, that I have not a slightest idea as to the inner workings of the man.

An interview was hastily arranged. As in his writing, Levin is an Olympian motor-mouth. An articulate, hilarious and deeply caring creature with a knock-about intellectual and observational eye, no wonder he is perhaps one of the best travel writers to have come out of Africa in a long time.

'The response to the book has started flooding in. Incredible! I had never comprehended the depth of such personal exposure this memoir would draw me to. I do not think I was ready for it. Suddenly, I am forced to deal with this

— Aids and the turn my life took — in public. There is nothing to hide anymore. What's there to hide about Aids? Still I was scared. Confusing emotions.'

'People know me as a writer,' he lights a cigarette — and I cringe — 'cause even in my writing I am quite personal. With this book others would say, 'Ah, it is Adam Levin, that Aids-suffering writer. Did he really live like that?' Aids is such a silenced condition that it really needed opening up.'

While Levin's book's is not the first to plunge into the psycho-challenges and demons of the disease — we are now familiar with Judge Edwin Cameron's *Witness to Aids* and other disparate journalistic by-the-way information leaks and hints — his is a tale deeply entrenched in both the prodigal son's return and a soldier tangoing with death.

It is also neck-deep in what Americans refer to as confessional literature.

Though he loathes reality TV's redemption farce, at its core, his book is part *Oprah-fied* biography, part staggering hero, still holding out after a horrible ambush at the chaptered frontline of man-created malice the world over.

But, death is not his main business in this book, living is. 'After being diagnosed with Aids — and not the beginning stages of HIV — I wallowed in denial, pain, and then arrived at acceptance. I began looking for books to help me cope with where I was clearly going to with this condition, and I found none, thus I began keeping diaries of what I would have loved to read — how to cope with Aids.

'Of course I lived on the razor's edge. My actions might have been of one — one among millions — living in ignorance of it. Perhaps wishing it away and dispensing with precautions. Still, who really wants Aids?' He is candid enough to admit that Aids is, to a large extent, a matter of self-care, self-love and to a bigger and messier extent, a political and commercial ogre.

'You cannot talk about Aids without talking about promiscuity. There is something mysterious and unexplainable about it. An attractive dark hole, perhaps, uncontrolled desire, a monster . . . I don't know.' In a chapter titled 'Whoring' he suggests that promiscuity is a complex demon, impulsive, compelling, mad, irrational, and yet an attractive beast.

If writing about it posed literary and psychological dilemmas — an unspoken literary code is that an Aids carrier is not expected to be too stylish about it — for Levin, living with Aids is a maddening and terrifying project.

'There was a time — and still there is — when my survival was not guaranteed and also, a time — before diagnosis — when it did not cross my mind that I was courting death through my lifestyle. Sure, I have regrets. I wish there was less pain in my life, but fuck it, I am alive.' Nonchalant, or devil-may-care (less)?

'At some point when I thought I was dying, I began bargaining with God in desperation. 'Please Father,' I cried, 'I can't just go, I am not ready, yet.' Corny as it sounds, I found myself turning to God. Of course I was given a longer lease. I am aware it is Him that's saving me.

'Now that I'm feeling like I have a fighting chance against this disease, you cannot expect me to turn around and say faith or any belief sucks. I might not be a church member or card-carrying member of a particular faith, but believe in God, I do. You cannot go through the pain and journey I've had and experience no fundamental change.'

His spirited short verse on God almost prompted me to share with him notes on the use and abuse of remorse, and truth, I had gleaned from the dailies. Rob Matthews, the slain Bond University student Leigh Matthews's dad argued in court that showing remorse, and, or confessing truth after the fact, or 'act' is self-serving, thus essentially dishonest.

Here, Levin is less interested in standing on Mount Kilimanjaro's peak, confessing for all the world to hear, 'Dear Father, you know I am a wastrel, a wench and . . .' but driven to face himself, without a hint of deception or a drop of gloss: Big boy, sorry but you had to grow, and this is the way — fatal as it is — you chose to do the growing in.

If memoirs are the closest to mirroring the author's truths, you can choose to dislike Levin all you like, but you will fall in love with the honesty with which he tackles his demons, wishes, past and his stubborn will to live. Never one to overlook hypocrisy, even in his own life, he reserves his sharpest blade for South Africa's gay fraternity:

'Having not being out in two years since my diagnosis, clearly sick and hardly a picture of a Chippendale or a Cinderella, I went to this a gay club I have been frequenting for years in Melville, Johannesburg. I was aware that my sight repulsed some people in the gay scene, simply because that community is a very big denial trap.

'People in there — the gay world — do not want to be reminded or confronted with Aids in their midst. They wish you would go somewhere, die alone in some far-away rural area, wrapped in a blanket, and of course that's in tune with general silence on Aids.'

Of course — ever the individualist — he is not above an avalanche of self-love, which I suspect is at the root of his survival. Out of the blue he whips up a quote from the surface of his mind: 'A friend, Tracy Rose once said, "Adam, you know you make Aids hip?"'

He recalls a time, about a year and half ago, when everyone around him — and he had shiploads of love and support from his parents and friends, which he names — had written him off as one clearly having reached the end of the road. 'Everyone thought I was about to die. Everyone else, but me.'

Today, looking hip in shine 'n' fade blue denim, black velvet loafers — thanks again to 'dearest mom' — and a pink T-shirt, cutting an image of a hip-hop suburbanite past the heady demands of that culture, the author seems to be at peace with the not-so-peaceful pain of Aids, and not so much living with Aids.

'It is fuckin' painful. Sometime it reduces you to a child. You can't do anything. It can be humiliating.' It surfaces that he has issues with being anybody's burden and yet responsibility is something he concedes he never dealt with, in the way it demanded. Still, there's no shame. He does not even talk about how he got Aids, where and when, and who are journalists to ask?

'I was responsible for exposing myself to risk, but now I have to be responsible for what I'm facing, what I'm living with as it is. This is neither time for regrets or regress.'

He picked up a copy of the book — which the fan in me had prostrated in front of him to autograph — to draw my attention to a passage he feels saliently speaks his truth. I watched as his hands shook and shivered slowly, then steady enough to create a slow rhythm.

Following that motion, I realised my eyes were dancing to his rhythm as I struggled to follow his voice. A million thoughts trafficked and caused a stampede in my mind. My soul took flight.

His last comments filtered through the daylight haze, sounding quite distant, but audible: 'These things — insatiable sex, drugs and life on the groove-lane — drove me wild. Possessed me. This sickness sort of replaced those demons, even though they were its cause. Perversely, it brought peace to my life. Anguished calm but it made things clearer. At the end of it all, I know I'm still fucked. I'm still messy.

'I've had people coming to me with theories about Aids: "It is God's way of solving overpopulation. God's trying to wipe out the Third World." Bull! Aids exists to teach us a very clear lesson about compassion.'

Like its author, *Aidsafari* is at best, the most engaging sermon and redemption song out in secular literature right now.

It is one of those existential, and yet spiritual, journeys without the moral weight of religion. A work of art, and a work straight from the heart, that delivers both the reader and the narrator to their very private mirror moments: you can choose to listen and be confronted with your own worth (lessness), or you can simply shut its emotions out, or choke up.

As the interview wound up, I chose none at that point. Instead, I just went back to my freezing dwelling, where I floated on my tears in the loudest privacy I have experienced in ages . . .

The Wiggah Trilogy

Norman Mailer's
white negro revisited

If Elvis Presley is the King of Rock,
what is Chuck Berry, God?
— Amiri Baraka

The street reference 'wiggah', pronounced 'wee-guh' — not to be confused with its derogatory cousin, 'wigger', often rudely used in reference to the Irish, known as the '*niggras* of Europe' — means, according to hip-hop parlance, a white *niggah*. Note the italics.

In the MTV age — many decades and many memories away from the Civil Rights Struggle and the Black Power radical resurrection in the streets of America, negritude in the mind and coffee shops of Paris and the West Indies, and Pan Africanism brewing in the African sprawls such as Sharpeville — the well-meaning white liberal so lamented in Tom Wolfe's 1960s as part of 'the radical chic' has been replaced by his new, modern and 'hipper' clone — the *wiggah*.

Wiggah is some sort of acceptable, mock and acclaimed reference to those of the white folk or Caucasian species widely accepted, perceived or even dismissed as being *down* with the black programme.

Often, this undeclared but perceived universal black programme manifests itself in both the boardroom and the bedroom, coffee shops and in the modern political firing line.

Often, and without their input — those folks the social and pop cultural theorist Paul Gilroy refers to as 'inhabitants living within The Black Atlantic' — cultural commodities such as jazz, rap, soukous, soul food, slang and pidgin are used as both marketing barometers, religious and economic determinants, or fodder for tourism pamphlets.

In their revenge or playful acceptance of those whites curious enough to be part of some of their glorified vices, such as pimping and gangsta rap, sacred spaces such as *ukuthwasa* and African healing rituals such as *ubungoma* or Candombe in South America or demeaning but commercially packaged Afro-fetishisms such as *Itokoloshe*, Brett Bailey's *Ipi Zombi* or Bertha Egnos's *Ipi Tombi*, black youth managed to hit or feed back the mainstream with a term that is compelling both in its belittling and charming senses: 'wiggah!'

If you follow this pseudo-street *lingua franca* — whether articulated in the slangiest ebonics or pidgin English — you will agree that every generation has had its own kind of wiggah.

A white man rising up through and 'making it' within the world's biggest cultural premium that black popular culture has become — basketball, strumming the blues, walking in a ghetto shuffle while buried in ultra-baggy jeans, fine tuning that salsa fancy footwork, playing mambo, listening to bolero, gyrating to Maskandi and being anointed as the 'white chief' of some obscure African tribe — wiggahs are either in it to up their 'soul quotient' or are just unable to resist that burning anthropological desire to help the natives.

At best — and God have mercy on them — many are simply inspired by age-old missionary ideals of charity and love for the poor.

Not long before his popularity, the beatnik wonder boy, writer Jack Kerouac once said, 'I would have been happiest to have been born black. I love their jazz, spirit, zeal, just being . . . black!'

The famed vagabond went on to achieve fame with *On The Road*, allowing him to trade poetry verses with the best that black America had to offer; LeRoi Jones, Ted Jones, Rob Kauffman and other acts within the Black Arts Movement.

Since Kerouac's deeply expressed wishes, pop culture has seen a groundswell of white artists, either directly feeding on black art, dance movement, swagger or riding on the crest wave created by the mass acceptance of black music, such as soul, mbalax, blues, rhythm and blues.

'The King' himself, Elvis Presley, leapt towards rock's stratosphere on the basis of his association with the blues and soul music royalty, specifically Memphis's biggest black music mogul Sam Phillips, the foundation set by Chuck Berry, the nuances and panache of Little Richard and the jitterburg choreo moves that were part Presley's swagger, part Sammy Davis Jr's genius and overall Ike Turner-esque in essence.

Not to be *out blacked* — which is different from being 'blacked out' like so many jazz stars, from Lionel Hampton to Billie Holiday, were hounded off 'white only' jazz dives in the 1940s in America — the The Rolling Stones' Mick Jagger and Keith Richards found a surrogate creative father in Muddy Waters and Buddy Guy.

We are not that mean: we won't get too deep into the creative debt owed to black music; these things cross-pollinate anyway, as those too precocious to discuss the role of race in cultural economics are apt to say. For that, we should halt the horses here, lest they bolt out and roam into the wild.

We shan't, I promise, go deep into the creative reparation Stevie Ray Vaughan has yet to pay out to the blues giant Albert King or to what extent Led Zeppelin's wizard Jimmy Page has suckled from the metaphoric breast of Howling Wolf rather than that of his mother. We won't.

It wouldn't help, in any case. Ever since the author and controversy-loving polemicist Norman Mailer articulated the origin and reason of his 'existence and borrowed existentialism' in his controversial essay, *The White Negro*, almost half a century ago, the (idea of a) 'white negro' has become serious currency.

Whilst you might wince and recoil at his sight, he has gone on carving a niche for himself — that is, being neither black nor white — while basking in the lustre and lure of being meted the same 'exotic' tag usually reserved to that anthropological census grouping known as 'the indigenous' people. The folk.

As rapsters Eminem and Basement Jaxx, super record producer Lyor Cohen in the US, Johnny 'Le Zoulou' Clegg in South Africa and of late, Germany's reggae superstar Gentleman have shown, is it is possible to reap commercial profits of the 'indigenous' art form without so much as ripping the sacred roots and cultural import of that art form to shreds.

All five acts are today media superstars and with a 'toon superhero's clout and weight, for they know what it means to belong while really not being of the subculture they are interacting with.

Genius as it may seem, that unfortunately is the saddest aspect of global pop culture, especially music and film: smart creatives making profit simply through fitting into cultures deemed 'on the rise' or exotic without really adding anything new or complex, intellectually, artistically or incendiary, to those cultures.

Eminem, though not as radical as the broad church of his media congregants would like us to believe, is a unique case, in that he is a truly gifted comic and comedian in an musical genre that takes itself a tad too serious than it actually is.

In the main, though, the wiggah, like his dumb black opposite in pop culture, the *niggah* will remain a figure known for his derivative genius, the cut-and-paste star, and never as the real article, the real McCoy. In short, while he can fix and change himself to be a *niggah*, he will never be black.

He must give (it) up. The mask!

Gentleman

Reggae superstar — blacker than tar

The midnight breeze from the river Maine coursing through the town of Wurzburg in Germany was enough to reduce a group of teenagers, some standing, some skanking outside Africa Culture Festival's music hall, to snowmen and snow girls.

But that was not to be. The word on the tongues of swathes of congregants in this multi-racial church of reggae lovers is heat.

Inside, the hall is a riot of neon pink, golden blond hair, bunny styled, hose-pipe thick golden hair locks, dots of chicory brown faces and thick Mau-Mau type of locks atop red, yellow and green Rastafarian colours, all mixed with 1970s-type huge disco balls giving those outside the feeling that the house is on fire!

It is the last day and dying hours of a week-long annual culture fest, known as 'Africa Culture Festival: International Afro Music Festival' held in this small town of Wurzburg. Since it took root 17 years ago, the festival, said my host Mr Herold Gaans, 'was intended for Africans living in Deutschland.'

Basically what is fashionably referred to as the 'Afro-diasporians', spread across the breadth and width of Germany and other parts of Europe.

Prior to the main attraction of the festival, every second African I met — that is, excluding thousands of pitch-black Afros I saw pushing nice, little mulatto-looking children with rose cheeks and golden curls in their prams, a European woman on the side — overwhelmed me with complaints about 'when the festival was really for Africans, run by Africans and populated by Africans with dashes of others . . .'

Well, this evening — two hours before the festival's most important artist, Rita Marley takes to the stage 'round midnight — all those Africans, feeling doubly displaced from their original motherlands, were united with the French, Dutch, Swiss and Swedes in a musical ritual — being one in body, spirit and soul with Germany's biggest roots reggae and dance hall star, Otto Tilman, popularly known as Gentleman.

From inside the hall, Gentleman — a 32-year-old lean and fit German attired in regular hip-hop and dance hall duty gear, parachute-sized khaki military shorts clearly three sizes bigger than his, equally bigger brown jersey and fat rubber sneakers — sings, jokes, cajoles, prays, scats and chants in the most mellifluous, most gripping of voices you will ever hear this side of Bob Marley, Anthony B or Wyclef Jean.

He sings, the crowd goes into spiritual seizure, he raps, they rap along, he scats and chants, they urge him on, meanwhile behind him a ten-piece live band gets on with the business of cooking steam hot layers of old reggae sound, mixing and dishing it out with the boom-bam-bap signature sound of a style called dance hall.

Oh Jah Jah I say / hear the words of his son lifting up his voice today /
I know I pray / Never will go astray / me send a prayer to my mama today /
On my knees father I pray / Ina me ganja lee boots and ina me khaki sui /
Yes I'm a soldier and me seeking the truth

How was it? Imagine that scene in *The Matrix Reloaded* where that Martian-like tribe in its faux-Africana gear was enjoined in a metaphysical dance ritual. Disturbing bliss would be the oxymoron best suited to describe the kinetic beauty of it all.

It was in Gentleman's voice, performance, his genuine dedication to a musical art form distinctly black — a music of both international African liberation, a sonic battle call, and a prayer, all bound in its roots' ingredients, drum and bass — that the pain, contrast and cultural confusion with its dualities of identity and tradition of both the festival and its attendants was laid bare.

To visiting American acts such as several American blues musicians, including Corey Harris and Lucky Peterson as well as those interested in the cultural politics of belonging

Those whose dance hall aptitude begins with the mid-1980s Shabba Ranks's multi-syllable ragga chants and ends with Jamaica's MTV star, Sean Paul's made-for-Americans hungry for spicy Jamaica's street — 'Just Gimme the Light, Gimme the Light' as the refrain goes — will find in Gentleman a curious blend of marketing and roots. A cut from an MTV hero you have seen and heard. Ali G he ain't, even though Peter Tosh he will never be.

Yet to adherents of both reggae — that old drum and bass that emanated from the mélange of Jamaican ska and American rhythm and blues — and dance hall — a youth variation that combines brashy, in *yer'* face hip-hop sensibilities, Pan Global Africanism and Jamaica's blinged-out materialist lyrics — the man is a mini-God of sorts.

Not only to those Europe radical chic tribes; wanna be black, pseudo radical, left field Seatlists enviromentalists, skate and surfboard bohemians — but to roots lovers running the gamut of reggae-loving fans, from Cape Town's Gugulethu to the Punjabi dance hall acts in North London.

As displayed during his performance, the man is one of the few in the global dance-orientated music business whose music — not much about lyrics, truth be told, his are pretty much middle-of-the-road lyrics — does not allow a single face to go home dry, after his two-hour outpour of both grief and bravado.

From the piece 'Send a Prayer' to 'Church and State', the scribbling was on the wall: Gentleman is of that rare breed of dance and emoting acts — Haitian Wyclef Jean, South Africa's Simphiwe Dana, the British trio Finlay Quaye, Mali's Lobi Traore, Brazil's Victoria Rodriguez and the American soul queen Mary J Blige.

Artists with an in-built soul antennae that renders them as a very feeling, honest, basic cast of performers who have successfully combined nightclub hedonism with those soul-ripping gospel-tinged vocals.

Unlike UB40 before him, Gentleman is not only white and European — and unlike Koos Kombuis, he can't claim neither Africa as his *vaderland* or Jamaica as *de muthaland* — but an artist known in the reggae musical hierarchy as the 'roots man', roots implying the holy trinity Basic-God-Ethiopia, Gentleman manages to confound cultural purists.

Though he is of pop disposition and like all artists trades in the business of being loved by the fans and the popular media, one word big in that sector you will never hear being said in his presence is *wiggah*.

The man played his heart out and sometimes you forget that the light-skinned dude on the stage beckoning us to a prayer in these voodoo hours in Germany is not actually Jamaican, Ethiopian or Bantu African.

Not that it matters — in fact it does, given a choice between watching a German reggae star and a third-rate minion dragged from the streets of Kingston, Jamaica, many music lovers outside of reggae would opt for the Jamaican palooka — but Gentleman is not your ordinary white act.

It was clear that anyone coming after him would have found him a hard act to surpass, and Rita Marley did not disappoint in that aspect. Tried as she did, with all the choreography and Bob Marley aura swirling around her every move and body sway, the Queen Mudda, failed to match whitey on a roll.

Eminem

Genius, Homo sapiens *or white radical chic?*

Let's get this clear: Like hip jazz cats are fond of saying, dig him or not – you can't escape the rather sordid fact that your children love Slim to bits.

If by now you have made peace with that, I assume then, you realise that this rapper, known as Slim Shady, Marshall Mathers III or Eminem, perhaps together with black ghetto dimwits like 50 Cent and their ilk is shaping your child's cultural and emotional make-up – with or without your collusion in it.

Yep! That super profane verse slinger hailed as a profound white negro in the hip-hop universe – a world in which the stars and their fans are aligned in the cosmos by CD and merchandise sales – is your child's hero, you dig? Bloody scary, no?

Like Superman, Batman and now the larger-than-life Spiderman, Eminem has joined brand names such as Coca-Cola, Nike, Tommy Hilfiger, McDonald's, MTV, Ford and Viacom as one of America's premier brands that shape the way we look at, and react to, life.

He is both your worst nightmare – the scariest since Freddy Kruger's

Nightmare on Elm Street — and the goofiest, most harmless white pop cultural humourist since Woody Allen.

The man's meteoric rise in the multi-billion dollar, but lyrically impoverished, hip-hop universe has recast this otherwise determined and hard-working working-class young man, born in Detroit's trailer park (the closest thing to a squatter camp, as we refer to it down here) as a new creature in pop culture: the anti-celebrity celeb. Oxymoron?

Well, Eminem is the most articulate oxymoron you've ever heard, this side of Jacob Zuma. He claims to be anti-racist, yet he is a homophobe and misogynist par excellence. Listen no further than his sonically catchy album, *The Marshall Mathers Album*, specifically how, in his unwarranted attack on the late Gianni Versace, Slim betrays the core elements of the very culture he's supposed to uphold — hip-hop.

Just like in the streets from which this music derives its raw energy and urgency, it is quite sacrilegious to take a piss on the dead in this culture. Hip-hop respects the dead, and in the streets gangsters do not take pride in annihilating the dead, even if they hated them when they were alive.

Rather weirdly, Em' does not seem too educated in the holy vows of the religion of which he is said to be one of the anointed prophets — the unwritten safety and guide rule number one in the streets is: Take care of yourself and your beloved, while not being too smug about your achievements. Taking pride in easy victories is frowned upon, in case someone faster, hungrier bumps you off, just as you are about to pop a bottle of Cristal to celebrate.

And all those rules can be received free in such hip-hop influencing films such as Francis Ford Coppola's *The Godfather* series. Clearly, hip-hop's supposed cleverest white negro's pop cultural references suck. Or he just finds the dead Versace too limpy, too lifeless, too harmless — unlike Elton John, who he invited to perform on his multiple Grammy winning night a couple of years ago?

I am really not best placed to defend gay folk or any other grouping, for that would assume I understand their complexity. Still, I find passive consumption of a musician's lyrics quite an irresponsible if not dumb manner of spending money, especially if it's hard worked-for cash that your daughter spends to make an already wealthy misogynist and homophobe all the more obnoxious and self-righteous.

In some twisted way the denialist fans and cultural libertarians are right on the money here: Who wouldn't be so self-righteous if the sort of intolerant drivel they scribble swells their bank balances?

As an artist, I love his quirkiness, and yet am all too aware that Em', like the best in the industry he's trying to fool millions into believing he has issues with, is nothing but another product, a self-created product intrinsically wired up to its creator, the hit-making manufacturer.

Were it not for his often heartfelt anti-establishment beliefs, Eminem could easily have entered the product-endorsement spin, hawking his name on tennis shoes, clothing ranges surpassing the one-man global sneaker franchise, Michael Jordan, or Rocawear sneaker-maker, Jay-Z, sometimes known as President Carter.

Like all capitalist innovators with their eyes on the same prize as the rest of the mainstream, Em' — aided by his bona fide working-class resumé — gives off a vibe of a pop antagonist, while playing the rules as a pop protagonist.

Listening to him taking President Bush by the horns, taking white middle America or materialist black celebrities on, *The Marshall Mathers Album*, gives off a rather romantic perception of a man at odds with the industry that pays his bills, while what it boils down to is that Eminem, the rebellious lyrical miner, happens to be quite keen on the gold mine — and there's just no indication that he would be any different were he thrust into the executive seat.

Let's digress and look at Jay-Z himself — the only other street-edgiest, widely popular, smartest, talented and funniest contender to hip-hop's Poet Laureate throne, as well as the CEO of Def Jam, the biggest hip-hop and R & B multinational on the planet, with overheads three times that of a country like Lesotho.

Can we say for certain, that he, or any so-called hip-hop rebel-cum-executive (read, corporate liberator) has done anything to effect the way hip-hop treats women, gays or reacts to the plight of poor black folks hit by Katrina in America, George W Bush's Iraq policies, the war on children and the unborn in the Gaza Strip, Beirut, Darfur or anywhere else?

But then again, Darfur or Gaza does not register on hip-hop's vernac, even though it is an industry with roots based on race (black 1960s Civil Rights) and mutually exploited — by black hip-hop merchants as well as major white capital.

A smart man he is, Em' has succeeded in uprooting race as a political factor in his total artistic and celebrity re-creation. True to America's rooted emphases on individualism, the rapper — and this is easily borne by his work in albums such as *Slim Shady* and *The Eminem Show* — prides himself as being 'the angriest man alive'.

Probably the angriest, since 'Bad-Ass' Mike Tyson graduated from a rapist to Count Dracula, that is after threatening to rip Lennox Lewis' heart out and have his children for dinner. Smart Jack that he is, Em' is quite aware that being 'the angriest anything' has its pegs in America, but his anger is a misnomer. Why? His whiteness, that's why.

See, even though Em' feels he's not white, his whiteness serves his album sales and revs-up his 'peculiarity ratings'. For references of his denial of whiteness, please check one of his most potent lyrical vignettes in *Slim Shady*: '... how can you say I'm white while I don't exist?'

Cleverly omitted, the implication is that America disrespects its poor — both black and white — and that so long as there's human disrespect, Em' has decided to be part of the millions of obscured people: the sick, women, the poor, Africans, Serbs, Palestinians, etc.

Still, being the 'angriest' white rapper hardly does him any favours because 'whiteness' in most nodes of capitalism, is associated with materialism, respect and power. As such, it is rather absurd, that Em' complains, let alone is angry about his whiteness, and he knows it.

Both Eminem and his chosen enemy, Hollywood, are aware that what sells in modern pop — and that includes the media — is the image of the angry black man. What the pop media refers to as 'the crazy negro'.

And, honey, the 'crazy negro' is not in short supply — especially after his death, for in death he is harmless: can't rape, can't lead revolutions and can't complain when he is robbed of his music, land or any of his innovations' royalties.

Among Eminem's peers, packageable black heroes are symbolised by personalities such as the Wu Tang's Ol' Dirty Bastard, the late Tupac Shakur, Reverend Al Sharpton and, of course, 'Bad-Ass' Mike.

It's not difficult to see why anger, craziness and black, as well as working-class pathologies sell the world over. Young brown and black men from the barrios and townships; from Gugulethu, Rio de Janeiro's *favelas*, to Paris's African and Arab *banlieues*, have been sold the image of the outlaw as a hero, the existentialist and the sexiest thing on two legs.

What these criminal cult worshippers aren't too privy to, is the inherent racism lurking beneath the ground occupied by their favourite pop idols. What's not so clearly visible, is that on the flip side of the 'angry negro / hero' icon, lies another kind of creation, or re-creation of black leaders, both radical and reactionary, as buffoons.

To each hero, the Western media get some sense of erotic pleasures in the theatrical deeds of figures such as Mobutu Sese Seko, Idi Amin, Laurent Kabila, Emperor Jean-Bedel Bokassa, as well as political showmen such as Farrakhan and Gaddafi, among others.

Well, do not forget this is supposed to be the Eminem Show. Being born the wrong colour — as any colour and race just won't do for him — what then does our squeaky-voiced urban court jester do? He swiftly and deftly turns the 'angriest' label on its head, opting to sell anti-establishment lyrics back to the establishment that he had us feeling he despises.

And here's the racket: By focusing his arsenal to cheap celebrity and crass consumerism, Hollywood and white middle-class, Em' naturally positions himself on the other side of the demarcation line, an imaginary line that separates the profane from the profound.

His anti-establishment lyrics in turn make him a rapper with a conscience, thereby ushering him into a hotly contested area dominated by self-righteous brothas and sistahs such as Mos Def, Wyclef Jean, Lauryn Hill, Femi Kuti, Talib Kweli, Dead Prez and The Roots, a world he would normally not be associated with, and a world not beyond his biting mockery.

A harder fact to swallow, though, is that as far as creativity goes — and despite his web of childish, cartoonish, often desperate, and aimed-to-shock lyrics, which sadly divest the art of his yearned-for rock rebel spirit — Em' stands head and shoulders above your run-of-the-mill rappers.

In fact, verse for verse, whether involved in battle rap or sick humour , I can't think of many, other than the Afro-rock poet Saul Williams, the said Jay-Z and Nas Jones, who can actually stand in front of Eminem. He sho' will knock the lot of 'em down — a point dramatised in his bio pic, *8 Mile*, the movie.

His epic narrative single 'Dear Stan' was rightfully dubbed by a respectable journal, the *New Statesman* as 'perhaps the cleverest sonic poem'. Sampling a rather obscure techno-folksy vocalist, Dido's mournful song, 'Thank You', and layering with live traffic special effects, that narrates a song as mini-fictional movie, 'Stan' offered rare glimpses into how as an art-form, rap can once again regain its imaginative heart.

Still, with all these accolades, never questioned street credibility and pseudo-revolutionary acclaim, I wonder, is the world media right in their mind to anoint the kid with 'the most radical rapper since the creation of rap' tag?

One case in point here is one Sean O' Hagan, who, in his 12 January 2003 essay, elegy rather, compared Eminem to Bob Dylan. In a provocatively headlined piece 'What's So Fucking Brilliant About Eminem', the literary glossy, *Word Magazine's* Andy Gill goes ballistic, comparing Em' with Kurt Cobain, Bob Dylan and the Olympian Irish wordsmiths, Oscar Wilde and George Bernard Shaw!

Of course, both Gill and O'Hagan cleverly, or foolishly, overlooked the fact Bernard Shaw, upon getting the Nobel Prize for Literature in 1925, the dramatist, Shaw, refused to take the money, but only the honour. How many times, and in how many Grammy Award nights has their favourite plastic-soldier rude boy grabbed the limelight and the resulting loot, every time, he spits 'bitch' every time he beats down the 'faggot'?

How many times has Eminem, the father of a lovely daughter, made records in which he murdered his wife, mother, or some more fags, stuffing them in his fictional car to throw them over a bridge, an act rewarded by his fans keeping the cash tills ringing clink-clankatty-clanks? How many times can a man stoop so low and still be crowned 'the most radical rapper since the creation of rap'?

Is Em' so brilliant, so politically progressive, so creatively charming, so musically transgressive that the Western critics' minds take leave, flight or both when faced with his five album 'oeuvre'?

But the smart chaps at *The Observer*, or those too quick to canonise him into the great English Literary history, are not the only culprits. Two of Britain's smartest black culture critics, Booker Prize winner Zadie Smith and the eminent black sociologist Paul Gilroy, believe 'Eminem is the most insightful voice of youth angst and the most defiant pop star of the times'.

Duh! I mean bah?!

Is Marshall Mathers all that he is cracked up to be? How different is he from other white teens too eager to escape their whiteness and sudden wealth? I would understand his fans follies – I mean, I too, once thought the P-Funk spaceship, jazz music, and later, kwaito would usher in a cultural world order. Insanity runs through true fans' blood.

But for *The Observer* to bestow on him such honours is a reflection of a flight of common sense. It's just like the political analyst Dumisani Hlope's quasi-revolutionary cheap utterance that the kwaito cartoon figure, Mzekezeke will lead South Africa to a true African Renaissance.

It also smacks of selective memory and feeds the age-old argument that the influential white-owned media, and its penny-picked black voices, never accord black artists the due they deserve.

Take the Bob Dylan element: Is this comparison to the folk-rock sage informed by the fact that he, Dylan, and the upstart street poet / rapper — as well as the journalist are both white? Which can be asked: Are O'Hagan's pop sensibilities and sense of history misty blurred by his narrow racial references? Has music criticism wilted into an all-white party bound together by shared pop historical revisionism?

By limiting him to Dylan, the essay is operating within an extremely narrow race-tinted world. Besides, the claim that Em' is the Dylan of the new age is a debatable heresy in itself. The man's subversive comical art tip-toes on the path walked by Richard Pryor and Gil Scott-Heron — or is too much to posit him as the bastard child of black genius and white capital? A beast with two heads?

Those familiar with Scott-Heron are aware that his satirical song-poem, 'Jaws' — a critique of Hollywood's portrayal of black folk — is held up as the most illuminating piece of social satire in contemporary blues and spoken-funk genres.

Worse still, double standards are applied here by Em's sycophants: Does anybody remember the white liberal press and its hip-hop magazines — owned by the Hollywood establishment and aimed at blacks — ever comparing the more talented Tupac Shakur to the street hustling Little Red before he matured into Malcolm X, or even Fela Kuti?

Why aren't African artists accorded the credit that secures them a place in the pantheon of non-racial artistic greatness, a treat seemingly reserved for the likes of Salvador Dali, Picasso, Elvis Presley, James Dean and now Em'?

Why is black genius scale skewed towards the negative; promiscuity and drug addiction and little to do with their artistic output, while white is canonised amongst the greatest?

Also, in all of the media's portrayal of Em' you can trace a sustained aim to disqualify the impact artists such as Rakim, the Last Poets — including white folk poet Leonard Cohen — had on rap by prefixing Em' with the pretentious, liberatory tag 'revolutionary'. Who has he liberated? From what? How?

In one of the most arresting paragraphs in The Observer's epic, O'Hagan unwittingly lets the cat out of the proverbial bag, revealing the truth about the white establishment, be it in the US, Europe or South Africa: that the novice Marshall Mathers was discovered by the super-producer, Dr Dre — yes, that Andre, who, as one third of a trio that referred to itself as Niggaz With Attitude (NWA) wreaked havoc on the establishment's nerves, back in the late 1980s.

In case peeps forget; Dr Dre is black, and just then, there goes the pop out of the fizzle. What it means is that Eminem the artist, has been raised, and artistically fed by a black producer.

Such a visual metaphor brings back a painful chapter in black people's history: that for centuries our mothers have been employed as nannies for white children, sometimes breast-feeding and helping them grow into purposeful citizens while missing out on the time to rear their own offspring and watching helplessly as black families disintegrate.

Are there any lessons to learn in the creative life story of Slim Shady? Perhaps yes, that life is just but a lyric: Eminem is not responsible for your blues.

Divas

Rita Marley

In Bob I trust

Shuffling — crawling rather, since I was wary of disturbing the proceedings — into the conference room at the Park Hyatt Hotel in Rosebank, Johannesburg, I found myself in a full-blown revolution: *womandlaaa!*

I ventured towards the middle of the room where the most famous reggae widow in the world, Rita Marley — along with her fellow I-Threes, songbirds Marcia Griffiths and Judy Mowatt — were holding court at a Women's Month press shindig. Talk ranged from the Caribbean and Africa's shared bonds and roots to women's issues and the like.

Bound by a common spirit, the revolutionaries — Rita and her gang, along with a mix of journalists and Afro-diasporans with syrupy 'Jah-merican' patois — clenched their fists and chanted. Well, the Park Hyatt didn't quite resemble a Black Panthers rally, but you get the point, don'cha?

Her pitch-black dreadlocks half-covered in pre-Erykah Badu headgear — the sort of turban won by women known as 'queen muddas' in the Rasta movement — and her batik dress matching her blue-black skin, beads from the Sahel region in West Africa cascading down her chest, Rita created a very different impression to the one I got when I spoke to her on the phone in the Bahamas a few days earlier.

That Rita had a chirpy naughtiness about her. Cackling with laughter, she kept repeating: 'You see my brethren, after Bob left this world' — icons leave this world, they don't die — 'I told meself one fing: Ah wan' mah total 'appiness. Right now I have my legs up in the air, swinging on a hammock, reading a book and listening to nature's sounds.

'Yee see, ahm at the age — which I won't divulge — I feel good about meself. I feel great, coz ah go to de gym, mon! A lady gotta tone dem muscles, mon. You know . . . look a likkle like a lady; not full-on Hollywood vanity, but I mean, a likkle refreshed, y'know. Ah mean, I have raised all my five children with so much difficulty, all I wan' now is to enjoy meself. Yeah, mon!'

As the head of the Bob Marley Trust — which runs projects in Africa, the Caribbean, the UK and the US to keep the singer's memory alive — Rita was in the Bahamas to supervise a Bob Marley Community Health and Spiritual Centre.

'Anywhere Bob's voice calls me to go, I go', she says.

Listening to her assert herself, her veiled cries for independence, 'looking for a likkle 'appiness in my life' — and counting the huge number of Bob Marley projects she has devoted her life to — it dawned on me how complex, sadder and different the larger-than-life affairs of personalities such as Bob and Rita, Sonny and Cher, Kurt and Courtney must be.

Rita's marriage to Robert Nesta Marley — a young man from Jamaica's rural St Ann parish who would metamorphose into an artist with a pain-soaked voice; a political prophet who would be heard around the world — was as dramatic as one could expect a marriage to a 'messiah' to be.

'I knew', she says, 'that Bob belonged to the world, not me. Also, I knew before we got married — on 10 February 1966, after Bob's twenty-first birthday when I was only 19 — that Bob was on a mission, a higher mission. Still, he was mine! Our spirits were linked . . . there was a natural chemistry, I know.

'Our astrological signs were even right on the ball, him being an Aquarian and me a Leo. We faced each other on the zodiac.'

On a mission perhaps, living with his creative demons and an indisputable gift for weaving and crafting moral tales into incendiary, cutting-edge lyrics. But the later Bob became much more than Rita's zodiac mate. He became an oh-so-cool sex symbol, not in the *People* magazine way, but in the outlaw, don't-give-a-damn manner of Steve Biko, Miles Davis and Che Guevara.

'Oh yeah, Bob was human after all,' she counters — a bit defensively — 'but he loved his children. Still, throughout his love for us, I knew deeply that he was devoted more to his music, his calling, than to me. But he also surrounded himself with an army of strange folks — managers, friends, advisers, people coming in and out of the house that Island Records had bought him in Kingston.

'It was not a home, it was a house. Bob's house. So, the children and I really never lived there.

'He tried telling me: "Rita, this is a big house, mon. This is our first house . . . we never had it so good, Rita. You and dem picknies can come stay 'ere wid me," but there was no way I could've raised children in a house with a constant stream of people. Smoking, cooking, exercising, creating music, loafing . . . what a tribe!'

Our conversation zigged and zagged this way and that, in between my futile attempts to draw her into a conversation about her daughter-in-law, hip-hop icon Lauryn Hill, and her attempts to draw me into her activities in the village of Konkunuru, Ghana, where she has lived for three years. Twenty minutes was hardly enough to go into each of those issues in depth.

'So why can't we reschedule this until I come to Soud Afreeka?' she offered. 'As per your command, your majesty,' I teased her.

Stepping right into the revolution at the Hyatt the week after, I was not fooling myself that we would continue our discussion on either King Bob's prophesies or his widowed queen's beauty and firming-up routine. This was serious stuff.

To anyone who's had the slightest peek at the Rasta philosophy, you know da revolution is stewing hot when you hear converts, fans and journalists peppering their questions with phrases like 'Selassie High', 'give thanks', 'Jah bless' and 'yeah mon!' — right in the Hyatt, Rosebank's haughty bling-bling paradise.

So there was no small talk about why the woman regarded as the 'mother Queen' — even though she has publicly declared she was not a 'practising Rasta' — needed to firm up.

'What about our discussion?' I asked when I managed to corner her as she was leaving.

'Boojah! So 'tis you? Mah dear, Afreeka feels good to me. The sun, the energy, the love, shoo, I feel blessed mon. Blessed! Discussion? Oh, go get the rest in the book, my brethren.'

The book in question is *No Woman No Cry: My Life with Bob Marley*, Rita's autobiography written with Hettie Jones. It would have struck a precise chord were it titled *How I Mothered Bob, Raised his Children and Survived to Tell the Tale*. Staying true to the autobiography genre — particularly the confessional tales of rock superstars and their sidekicks — the story packs it all in: poverty, pride, survival against all odds and numerous near-death experiences; until the final triumph.

It is the tale of Alpharita Anderson, known by her ghetto name, Colitos, and how she grew up as a dark-complexioned young girl, was teased at school for her 'blackness' and later fended for herself among the gamblers, pimps and harlots in Kingston's Trenchtown ghetto — and how she was transformed into Rita Marley, friend, lover and wife of mixed-breed local boy, Nesta. It is told in a chatty, fireside style.

No Woman No Cry reads and feels like a story you have heard a million times before. Often it feels like it's the story of Bob, instead of being Rita's account of her own spirits, dreams and vanities, and why she matters. But that's an unfair accusation, for who would be interested in Rita Marley's story without Bob, or a Winnie Mandela story without Nelson?

Rita Marley

The daughter of Leroy Anderson and Cynthia 'Beda' Jarret, Alpharita remembers how she met Bob and his buddies, Peter McIntosh, Bunny Livingston and Junior Braithwaite — who would make it big as the legendary Wailers — in the sloping streets of Trenchtown.

'My cousin Dream — who would later be renamed 'Vision' by the Wailers — and I were intrigued by these boys who used to pass by my aunty's on the way to their rehearsals at [legendary studio] Sir Coxsone's. I then began axin' dem tings and making friends with dem, particular the skinny, yellow-skinned boy called Robbie.'

She describes how her relationship grew with Marley, son of a retired white naval officer, Captain Norval Marley, three times older than Bob's mother, Cidella Malcolm. Of course it wouldn't be a complete tale were it devoid of sentimental basics — such as how Nesta and Colitos pieced together a life and family in the back shack of her aunty's place.

'They called my aunty 'Vie' and I called her 'Vye Vye' — a proud woman with a red-hot tongue!'

She also writes how Bob and the Wailers stumbled into fame, became the Caribbean version of the Beatles — with a Black Panther essence — and rode the cutting edge of show business before splitting.

There are teary recollections of how their on-off sexual, intellectual, platonic and ultimately tragic relationship affected their children, Ziggy, Cedella, Stephen, Sharon and Stephanie.

Creepingly honest, the book attempts to contrast the earthly with the otherworldly — the spiritual fountain from which Bob derived his somewhat shamanic power — illustrating the extent to which Rita the wife was as electrified by Bob as his fans.

In *No Woman No Cry*, the only woman Bob ever married uses her 'truth' to resculpt aspects of her husband's life. Though she succeeds in sugarcoating 'Bob the philanderer' into 'Robbie, the boy I married', the image of Bob the wastrel remains vivid, alongside that of 'Bob the prophet'.

It is all the more disturbing that she does so at her own expense, for not once did Rita — a woman betrayed in love by a man worshipped by the world — completely shut the doors on Bob.

She once fell in love with a Marley-lookalike soccer star, Owen Stewart, popularly known as 'Tacky'; but the friendship fizzled when Bob's raging jealousy drove him back home to Windsor Lodge, where Rita and the children lived while he had been stirring it up in Kingston.

While not peculiar to her — total devotion is often the weapon of hurt — the book's most poignant moments are not to be found in what Rita says, but in what she omits: that so many women worldwide have had to give up their lives in the hope of making husbands out of their partners.

Part of the book's beauty — if sadness can be described as beauty — lies in the fact that many women can recognise themselves in the story of Rita who, after years of being mistreated as the 'homely child bearer', was always right behind her man.

It was Rita — with Bob's London-based girlfriend, Cindy Breakspeare — who took turns to nurse him when he was first diagnosed with cancer. After Breakspeare got married and cut the hospital visits, it was left to Rita to inspire the sickly, weak and spiritually emaciated reggae king, chanting: 'Bob, don't give the devil your life. No, go to Zion, your God. Oh, don't go, Bob . . .'

This was the same Rita who had earlier revved up the prophet's soul when he was feeling down after a stream of friends, record executives — and countless women — had taken him for a ride.

No woman better understood Bob's cries when he was deep in the creative throes of writing soul-challenging pieces such as 'Redemption Song' and 'Is this Love?' No woman was such a pillar of support when he was driven to take on the social and political illness of his age, crafting compositions such as 'Buffalo Soldier', 'I Shot the Sheriff' and 'Stir it Up'.

It was her girl-next-door arty-tude, her umbilical connection to the scents, scars, fears and grooves of the streets, that inspired Bob and his Wailers to create reggae-rock classics such as 'Jamming' and 'Satisfy My Soul' . . . dance floor killers that rippled out of Jamaica's music halls to the rest of the world.

Rita Marley

It would be easy to sneer at how she had stood behind Bob even when his adulterous lifestyle hurt her the most, forgetting that Rita, an African girl — Jamaica then saw itself as an extension of Africa — was raised in a culture that said: 'Stand behind your man at all times.'

While the general tone of the book is that of forced calmness, it's in those rare moments when she speaks about herself away from the prophet's shadow that Rita the spirit child's life unravels with rollicking wit, lack of self-pity, charm and candour.

Her pain is all the more biting when she gathers herself and looks her present life right in the eye.

'Aha! Here comes menopause! Now I understand,' she says, and you can imagine hearing her chuckling naughtily, "I understand why they call it the 'men-o-pause."

'I fully understand that period really, which puts you on pause where masculine relationships are concerned, y'know. Men really pause. They pause when your hot flashes become miserable and you are not hot no' more, but life continues, mon! Truth is, I still want to be loved. After years of doing this, seeing that, experiencing and experimenting with this, I still have feelings, mon!'

Miss Gay Soweto
Open up darling, that's how we do it!

'W-w-what?' my two fellow travellers in the house music-pumping Maxi night cab chorus in unison, when I carelessly ask if they are a couple.

'We are all gals, sweerrie,' (street slang for 'sweetie-pie') they purr and pout, beginning what will turn out to be a night marathon of pouts and superpouts.

'We are all gals, can'cha see?' Morna and Cassy, two boys, lay it square as the cab driver negotiates through the human maze teeming the street en route to tonight's 'do of all do's' — Miss Gay Soweto 2003.

The event is taking place in downtown Johannesburg. The two 'girls' I'm travelling with are out to make their presence felt. I'm in a privileged position: one of my travel companions, Cassy, a big black man in a military-style khaki miniskirt, see-through top and smokey brown Zsa Zsa Gabor goggles, happens to be Miss Sebokeng 1995 — hence, a grand opportunity for any nosy heterosexual hack to glean the basics.

Cassy's 'girlfriend', Morna, was not to be outdone. Clad in black pants, a pinkish striped shirt and hip dark shades, Morna had it all figured out. He, she, ag, whatever, was out to enjoy the evening.

The show was scheduled to kick off at 7pm on the bullhorn, yet an hour later the city hall is almost empty, save for a trickle of photographers, a TV crew and organisers Letebele Motsuenyane and Kedibotse Mafojane. They're both dashing to and from the backstage where the contestants are pencil-lining their eyelashes and fitting on skimpy and slinky garments.

I'm ushered to the VIP section where there's not even a gatecrasher in sight, let alone a VIP. Discounting the TV crew, I'm almost alone, but not for long. One of the star-spotters is on his way.

'iiiiYo, chomah', he drags the words, almost slurring in a seductive tone. 'I juss wanna ask you to take me photos, so what do you say, hey?'

'I am not a photographer, but don' you worry, I'll arrange with my colleague to snap you up. Deal?'

'Oh, yeah, whateva. Jazz get me in your paper, okay, chomah . . .'

'Mmmh, yeah that's fine. But what makes you interesting, by the way?'

'Oooh me? I am a cabaret star, darling.'

I would later learn every second person here claims to be a 'cabaret star'.

Lazzie, the 'cabaret star' – a dreadlocked young man, attired in a casual white Thelma 'n' Louise Lycra tank top, grey-striped 1970s bell-bottoms, sandals and with lips drenched in blood-red lipstick, is not only a nice 'girl' but a useful pop analyst.

'Darling, you gotta listen here. You straight men always assume gays are all the same. That all there is to us is whining, whingeing and dining. Sorry to burst your bubble, there's more to us,' Lazzie informs me.

More, like?

'Variations swee-Tata, variations d-d-doll,' and so the unsolicited lecture begins. 'Were you aware that there are four types of gay men? You see, we have one, the "active type". This is more the masculine type of man. Most straight men fall into this. They only come out late at night. Remember that movie, "If it's a crime, we all do it after nine?"

'And there's the "passive type". This is the limp-wristed type. The feminine.

There's a difference between the feminine and the effeminate, darliiing.'

By now the auditorium is half full, or half empty, take your pick. The judges are saddled on their seats and munching something. Somebody would later confide, 'they were hungry and could not wait for the late snack dinner, so they gave them half a loaf of brown bread and Red Bull to wash it down with.'

Back to class. 'The third type is interesting. This is the "passive active type". They have both male and female traits. You see, they can fuck and be fucked, hence we call 'em "*Ndiphendule*" [a 1980s Letta Mbuli hit].'

Lastly, my lecturer tells me, there are transsexuals, and 'that's where transvestites and such find a home. Here's where you'll find all sorts of crazy psychos as well as cross-dressers.'

Three hours later than the scheduled time – at 10pm square – the two MCs, Luvuyo Ngqakayi and Aaron Moloisi, materialise amid the smoke machine's relentless perfumed coughs. It feels so 1970s, but the crowd sucks it up.

The 'girls' – urged by a backtrack of Zaiko Langa Langa – peacocked around in a variety of SiSwati, TshiVenda, XiTsonga outfits as well as some Indian saris, with the odd Oriental Plaza price tag still dangling on after the hurried purchase.

Before they came back in swimwear, the crowd were treated to a cabaret performance by Martin Mahlape, otherwise known as 'Unomeva'. Sporting a red hairdo, pink earrings, lime shades, a black polo neck, a slit red skirt and black stilettos, his was potentially the most arresting stage act, were it not for the bad sound engineering.

The 'girl' can damn sing. With a voice sometimes exquisite, sometimes dark, and blessed with a whisperish tenor, Unomeva's vocals and jazz-dipped act would take him places were he to decide on a serious music career.

The judges were getting itchy. The crowd lapped it all up and soon after the contestants did their lacklustre swimsuit parade, Miss Photogenic was chosen: it was number 15, Amici Mathabatha, stylish and looking like comic Martin Lawrence's alter ego, the ultra-camp Sheneneh.

The top six finalists were named and they proceeded to the evening dresses segment. The Queen-crowning moment proved a nail-biter. The crowd became frantic as the judges battled for consensus. Later, after being subjected to the silly but tough query: 'If ignorance is bliss, then why do we seek knowledge?' — it was clear the battle was between number 15 and number 5, Janine Johnson.

Closer to midnight, the winner was announced, and boos, cries, and ululations merged with sneers as the 22-year-old 'girl' from Eesterus, Pretoria, Janine strutted ahead to beat crowd faves, number 15 and the leggy, pitch black-maned number 8, paradoxically named Blondie Winfrey.

'Oh dear, I can't believe it,' Janine simpered. 'I really worked hard y'know. But, I deserve it. I'm so ecstatic, ooooh, *nee. Ek glo nie!*

How apt. Besides his family and chomas, the larger part of the crowd agreed with the winner. They too, did not believe the extent of blindness that afflicted the judges. But then again, somebody once said pageants are not about looks. It's about attitude, babe.

It's way past midnight and the neon lights at a faraway Harrison Street joint dance in blue and pink. Time to vamoose. Has anybody seen my Maxi cab driver?

Makeba

Lunch with Mama

Biography journalism, often passing itself off as profile writing, is a maddening business.

On the surface — what with once-in-a-lifetime opportunities such as asking Michael Jackson, 'Say Mike, is it true that your face has fallen off?' — it is a literary bastion for social aspirants out to rub shoulders with the rich, the vile and the outrageously beautiful.

At its core, it is the province of literary Peeping Toms. There is only a whisker's difference between them and tabloid stalkers.

The difference is, profile writers get to see stars' emotional disintegration or life-turning successes by invitation — spousal abuse scars, emptied booze bottles belonging to an ex-alcoholic on the mend, new sports jalopy for a star on the ascent — and be accompanied by a battalion of PR and family acolytes too ready to vouch for our hero's oh-so-miraculous transformation from life in the gutter to inhabiting the upper social strata.

The game is up for me. I admit to all those charges and more — such as curiosity, unnatural patience, peerless grovelling skills and bootlicking.

Take, for instance, my wait for an interview with the woman who, for decades, attracted leery stares, gangsters' infatuations and police agents' attention — all the while arousing appreciation for the urban African ballad, creating cutting-edge protest pop, and raising defiance the world over: uZenzile, Nut-Brown Baby, Miriam Makeba.

It's a year and some months since I first requested a profile interview with Africa's first Grammy Award winner. At first days turned to nights, which turned into weeks. Yet my desire never waned.

Six weeks ago I sent another SMS request, not expecting the sort of marathon dialogue that would ensue between me and Makeba's 'people'.

Wannabes have hangers on; middle-of-the stream music artists or actors have managers or PR folks. Icons such as Makeba are surrounded and under- served by a whole range of 'people' doing all sorts of chores: making sure performance dates are adhered to; dumping, at the eleventh hour, performance dates booked through crooked promoters; ascertaining which is best, air or sea travel?

These chores might also extend to planning wardrobes and diets — and dealing with annoying necessities such as handling the media. Interviews are initiated, screened, scheduled, cancelled and rescheduled according to the whims and whining of a variety of egos — primarily those of the icon, their managers, or both.

After three weeks of postponements and a gazillion calls to Makeba's people — Gallo Music South Africa, the record company in charge of the artist's 'creative interests' such as her new album, a coffee-table book and a possible Hollywood film — her business affairs manager, Graeme Gilfillan, a stout fella with a rapper's fast tongue and the fighting spirit of buffaloes on the offensive, wired me a curt message: 'Interview at Mama's place. Tomorrow, 11am sharp. Directions in due course.'

Relieved does not quite describe how I felt.

The following morning, an hour before a photographer and I were to leave for Mama's place, another SMS, packed with as much urgency as the first one, rolled in: 'Interview cancelled. Mama not well. Postponed indefinitely'. Or some such.

Sad, I thought, at the age of 72, having played thousands of gigs — from Kofifi's speakeasies to wowing the late JFK at Madison Square Gardens, holding New York's finest with her mournful, African ballads and blues, ducking and diving from South African and US apartheid, being hosted by kings and queens, comrades and com-*tsotsis*, and political allies such as Marlon Brando and Malcolm X — Makeba has every reason to be frail.

And, by the way, this is a great-grandmother and a selfless campaigner for a variety of social issues, chief among which is a teenage girls' welfare organisation. An interview can wait, thank you.

Now, I am something of a veteran of the waiting game — cajoling, blowing empty kisses and doing whatever it takes to get an audience with kings and thugs, crooners and style arbiters. What, I wondered, if this delay takes another year — don't laugh — or so?

I unleashed a barrage of SMSs to whoever I was lied to had Makeba's undivided attention, each time upping the grovelling tone of the previous one:

Wish her a speedy recovery.

MaMakeba d'zevz a break from the rat race.

Hi, will ya pls lemme know soonest of Mazi's recovery? Prpd 2 wait or see her anywhere, anytime any day, soon as she's fully recovered.

Meanwhile I was mad and confused as hell. There's an adage that's more potent in seSotho slang (*ha osena pelo oa shoa*) than in its English version: 'If you can't stand the heat, get out of the kitchen'.

I'd rather roast, I felt. So I'll stay the full course of playing push, wait and see. All along I have been following the advice I had been given — that I should never, ever attempt to call Makeba directly. 'If you do and she turns you down, there's nothing anybody, anywhere can do for you, gettit?' I was told.

Suddenly stories about Makeba began swirling around. More overseas gigs. 'Sorry, Mazi is in Italy, darling. No, Mama is in the Caribbean. She's at the Sheraton Pretoria where she's staying after donating her archives to the Ministry of Arts and Culture.'

For a second I thought I would catch a glimpse of her. The next? Gone!

Headlines moved from the warm 'Mama Afrika donates her personal archives, including her 1975 address to the UN General Assembly, to the national archive' and the tabloidish 'Hugh Masekela reveals Makeba's follies', to the furnace-like 'Makeba refuses to speak to the late Tsietsi Mashinini's family'.

Meanwhile the people in her camp began shooting their mouths off.

'Never, ever mention Hughie [Masekela, her ex-husband] or his autobiography *Still Grazing* to her,' I was cautioned by those who had caught wind that I was angling for an audience with her.

Mazi, they said in hushed tones, was devastated by *Still Grazing* — a rather gauche hedonist's shot at redemption and Hollywood simultaneously, in which the infidelities of both Makeba, the political songbird of the Third World, and her self-destructive, wannabe-hipster husband are recounted with a vengeful frankness that is rare among holier-than-thou returned exiles.

So overwrought was Makeba, I was told, that she had been calling Masekela's sister Barbara — South Africa's ambassador to the US, with whom she shares a tight bond, having foster-mothered the teenage Barbara in the US — in tears, complaining about her 'boyish brother'.

Approached, Hugh Masekela told me: 'Can anyone explain to me what the fuss is all about? You people are reacting to the tip of an iceberg.

'Still,' he added, speaking from a Sandton studio, 'I have strained against reducing the whole thing to a tabloid biography. Yes, Miriam has helped me and a whole lot of others, quite tremendously. Does it mean we should remain forever beholden to her? Does her help accord her a licence to harass me and make my life miserable just because she had helped me?

'There are plenty of people about whom I've reflected a bit longer and sadder. Why a selective noise about her? Is she untouchable? Stranger still is that those patronising her don't know even an ounce about the lady. She can do without their sentimental outpour.

'If I had said the same about a man, nobody would have raised an eyebrow. South Africans need to get rid of their sexist and sycophantic attitudes towards Miriam.'

For a moment, this 'Miriam is livid / Hughie stands his ground' grandstanding seemed to mean no journalist would ever get access to Makeba without her people questioning their motives — until a sycophantic and factually inaccurate cover story in *Y* magazine quoted her responding to Masekela: '*uBra Hugh usile. U bale udoti ngami.* Hugh is a silly old man who wrote a pile of rubbish about me. I regret ever marrying that man. I married him when he was a boy and he has refused to grow up ever since.'

I lost it. Furious, I decided to call her directly.

A sweet, melodic voice answered languidly. My heart skipped and went boom-bap, ta-boom-ta. '*Sa-wuuu-bona mtanami?* Can ah help you, dear?' Is that how the most radical singer of the 20th century sounds off-stage?

'Tell me ba-e-bee, what have I done to you people at the *Sunday Times*? What good have you written about me? Why haven't you treated me well?'

I had heard the same accusations from the battle-ready Gilfillan. Glibly I apologised: 'Please don't ask me 'cause I don't know.' I was conveying deeply-felt apologies — for who I don't know.

It took a few minutes, but finally it seemed my much dreamt-about meeting with Zenzi, Nut-Brown, African Nightingale, was about to gallop into full swing.

At her insistence we met at the Makeba Girls' Home in Midrand — the rehabilitation centre for abused, stray and vulnerable teenage girls funded by Makeba herself.

Seeing Makeba for the first time at such close range — visibly exhausted, exchanging hugs and kisses with the girls while speaking in her dragged, languid voice, her eyes telling the story of a victorious but weather-beaten goddess warrior — well, my journalistically selfish soul ebbed down low. I had to summon my resolve not to disintegrate into sheets of tears.

I can't talk to her in this state, I realised. And just as she finally extended a 'lunch meeting at my place' invitation, a rather strange thing happened: two songs from her blues-soaked 1975 classic *Promise* — a nine-ballad tear-fest that displayed Makeba at her best; Nina Simone meets Janis Joplin in an African church — jostled for what was left of my spirits as they played on the home's sound system.

The Caiphus Semenya-composed title track slowly and calmly reached out and within: *When you are lonely / your dreams will haunt you / you are alone in this world / you just don't belong to / come and give me your love that you're hiding / I will keep your name forever.*

Then came Mama: *Mama, everywhere I've been / I find people so busy / they hardly have the time to be looking my way.*

I felt rivulets of sweat running down my forehead as I recalled her final words: 'Make it around one-ish or two-ish.'

A fresh cocktail of aromas — East African dishes, as it transpires — wafts about the kitchen and into the lounge, where Makeba, in black slacks and orange cashmere, welcomes us.

Like many legendary figures — artists, explorers, healers and poets — much had been documented about Makeba, yet little reported about her life off-stage and outside the concert halls which served as her homes-away-from-home.

I'd heard that she was a great cook, a giving spirit, complex, very basic in her values, temperamental, highly principled, highly unprincipled, easily swayed, bullying, commanding and caring.

But it is her public-relations aptitude that rates as world-class.

We find her, remote control in hand, a DVD of her special performances at the Vatican City in Rome in 1995, 1997 and 1999 ready to go the minute we take our seats.

Standing behind us, she gives us a one-woman commentary in her sing-songy voice; issuing interesting bits and pieces of info — many of them accentuating her stature on the social and pop pantheon of world arts, politics, culture and entertainment.

'There's the great George Makinto on piano,' she says, pointing to the orchestra. Never heard of him, but I nod as if I have. My knowledge of pianists is of kindergarten grade, but Makinto's touch is beautiful.

The MC says something in Italian, turns around and claps fervently as he announces Makeba. The audience roars and shakes in a collective spasm as if propelled by a giant, invisible, magnetic force.

Her running commentary resumes: 'You see, they screened this concert in 75 countries worldwide, but not in my country. Not even once.'

After the Vatican clip, she instructs Chris, an ebony-skinned, affable man of about 20, to 'please put in the other video'. It's her performance at the 2002 concert in Stockholm where she received the Polar Music Prize from King Carl XVI Gustaf of Sweden.

As if by remote control, we are directed back to the screen, where her granddaughter, Zenzi Lee Makeba, is standing in for her the morning after the awards. 'I was sick. I'm diabetic, so my granddaughter did it for me,' she explains.

I am reminded of a news clip that totally bypassed the local media about three months ago. My sources say that at the South African government-sponsored tenth anniversary of democracy celebrations in Dakar, Senegal, where she was billed as the main act, a tipsy-looking Makeba struggled to sing, slipped and fell on the stage.

Sensing trouble, her grandson, Lumumba Lee, who speaks crystal-clear French, addressed the media, telling them his grandmother was sick. Backstage, organisers tried to bundle her to a car to whisk her away, but, my sources tell me, she fought them bitterly.

More than half an hour after our arrival we are invited to help ourselves from a vast array of tongue-whetting dishes: prawns, spinach, rice, beef stew, tomato-and-onion gravy, cassava and other delights.

After a great lunch, and more videos, it becomes clear I am not going to have much time for an interview. So I take a chance and direct our conversation to a question-and-answer routine, which, seeing all niceties have been exhausted, cannot be postponed any longer.

In the book *Burning Hunger: One Family's Struggle Against Apartheid* — a biography of one of the heroes of 16 June 1976, the late Tsietsi Mashinini — author Lynda Schuster alleges that the family refused to discuss the 'circumstances' of their son's death. Makeba was at one time Mashinini's host in Guinea.

The book further alleges that Makeba's last husband — Guinean national, Bageot Bah, who was also Mashinini's caretaker in Conakry — had called and curtly told the family that their son had died of AIDS — a claim not supported, according to the author, by hospital records.

A week before I spoke to Makeba, I rang up Schuster at her place in Florida in the US. 'I am neither implying nor insinuating that Miss Makeba was involved in Tsietsi's death,' she said.

'Still, there are pertinent questions left hanging. Why is her ex-husband giving conflicting reports? Why was Tsietsi's body — if he did die of AIDS — found with one eye gorged out and wounds on his face? Why has Miss Makeba refused to collaborate, answer questions or talk to Tsietsi's family in the 13 years since he died?

'Why,' Schuster asked me to ask Makeba, 'is she so mum about the whole thing?'

Questions that have remained political hot potatoes in South Africa, and questions I was glad to convey to Makeba directly.

At the mere mention of Mashinini, the 72-year-old songstress stands to attention; her eyes, body and everything else suddenly very alert. 'Listen, I have never read that book and I don't intend to. I told you I do not read rubbish. Who the hell is that woman talking rubbish about me?

'She says I refused to talk to her. Precisely! I am not answerable to some little white bitch from God-knows-where! I cannot talk to her without

Mashinini's family authorising me to. She's also lying that I have not spoken to Tsietsi's family. What hogwash.

'I need you to write this'. She livens up. 'When I came back home from exile in 1990, some of the first people I reached out to were the Mashininis. I told them Tsietsi was sick and mentally affected. I also asked them to fetch him from Guinea so they could start healing him here in his home country.

'I spoke to Tsietsi's brother Mpho and his parents. I repeat, that woman is talking rubbish! I was not there when Tsietsi died; I was on tour in Europe. On hearing of his death, I paid for his coffin and his two brothers, who were in England, to come fetch him in Conakry.

'Instead they went to Zimbabwe where they arranged to wait for his coffin before accompanying it to Soweto for the burial. To say Miriam Makeba refuses to speak to that family is pure manure.

'Just a month ago, I called and sent Tsietsi's mother her grandchildren's pictures sent by Tsietsi's ex-wife, Welma. So how can anybody say I have kept mum? Mum about what?

'You see' — she bangs her hand, adorned with silver rings, on the sofa — 'I have no time for these white girls with their ulterior motives.

'The other day, this other one approaches me, claiming she's working on a biography of Nat Nakasa. Now, where does she know Nathaniel from? I buried Nat. We brewed African beer at my place in New York so people could come pay their respects. I was there for Nat, when he was alive and after his death. Still, I am not going to be discussing him with anybody without his family's permission. Tough! I am a very principled person'.

How true then, I carelessly venture, are reports that you have just lost a case involving thousands of dollars brought by your former US lawyer and business manager, Stanford Ross, with whom you apparently had a major fallout and who happens to own one of your old companies, Makeba Music?

'Who told you that? How do you know all that?'

'From my US media sources'. I try to put her at ease.

Makeba

'Sorry, I can't discuss that. It's a pending case and I do not talk about cases like that, if that's that okay by you.' It is, Mama.

Steam out of the way, the discussion settles back on music. She tells me she rates *Welela* and *Promise* as 'my two most accomplished albums' and her late daughter Sibongile — who also passed away in Guinea, 'also mentally affected' — and her former house-mate Caiphus Semenya as 'some of the best composers and writers I have worked with'.

Presently she's listening to Alicia Keys and some of her own recordings she hasn't listened to for 40 years! She shares anecdotes and tidbits about her 'spiritual sister, friend and fellow icon', Nina Simone. 'You know, Nina, was, ahhh, my other half. As it is, I was the only artist at her funeral in Marseilles.

'It so happened that the person who took care of her in her final days refused to tell anybody in the whole world, including Nina's band members in Paris, where the funeral was to be held. Strange, but I boarded a plane in Jo'burg and went straight to her cremation place. Elton John sent 1 000 yellow lilies. It was so surreal and yet so beautiful, if you can refer to a soul buddy's funeral in those terms.

'I feel like she's still alive, sleeping on my bed as she used to do every time she came to Tata Mandela's birthday party. Nina, aahh, we are old, nobody cares. Who knows what will happen to us?' Later, a blanket of sepia begins to cover the clouds and the spring birds in mid-flight.

Faint jackal cries can be heard not too far away as Makeba, clearly exhausted and again the grandmother I met at the girls' home, struggles to get rid of us.

'Will you ever go home *bantwana bam*? I am done with you.'

Just about to, Mama.

Makeba

Even if you were Black Fiend, Mama, you were still a Black Queen, Mama

Photography is a kind of primitive theatre.
A kind of tableau vivant.
– Roland Barthes

As with other key historical figures of the last century — individuals who have influenced the way we live, listen to music, inject ourselves with Botox and participate in politics and religion — Miriam Makeba's image is deeply etched on the universal or African folks' pop psyche.

Like the Winnie Madikizela-Mandela's proto-typical image; clenched fist, shot skywards, defiant grin in place, eyes red puffy with pain or tears, with the daughter Zinzi in tow; images of Makeba seem to be part of a permanent media visual display, and therefore part of international popular cultural memory.

Over the years, we've seen a gallery-worth of them: the sepia-toned period photographs of the fetching Sophiatown damsel singing her lungs out at the Odin, or Back of The Moon. The raw, confident young African woman, addressing heads of state at the United Nations in the 1960s, or a confident, click-clicking full-figured beauty, soaking in to 'em, at some smoky Greenwich Village jazz den, an image flush with postcard romance, defiance and framed by the bohemian spirits of the time.

At any of those dos — be they in South Africa where they referred to her as Nut-Brown Baby, or in Manhattan, New York, where she soon assumed the mantle of an unofficial spokesperson for the liberation of her fellow, dehumanised black folks — somewhere there amidst the smoke would be luminaries such as young Nelson Mandela, Oliver Tambo, on one side of the sea, and ol' Dizzy Gillespie, *über* dandy Miles Dewey Davis and some Black Panther radical chicsters in the crowds.

Of all those snapshot moments of history, one of the most recycled is of Makeba in some Kofifi joint — bow legs slightly apart, yellow tight figure-hugging dress baring her broad ebonied shoulders, microphone stand shooting up from the floor, her face gripped in the pain of the dirge after dirge she was supposedly forced to sing by the slum's gun-toting, music-loving rogues. As far as images goes — nothing is as dangerously sexy as that.

Her story — like that of other magnetic figures such as Elizabeth Taylor, Bob Marley or punk-rock stars The Clash — is intricately interwoven with photography and its potency as a visual art. Dead or alive, these 'icons' are established names whose presence in consumers' collective memory has been permanently fixed through aggressive marketing and merchandising. Thus you listen to your icon's Greatest Hits re-issue on your way to the mall to buy his or her image on a T-shirt, cigarette lighter or arty postcard.

Were it not for the power of photography, all of this icon worshipping — of present-day fast-food celebrities as well as the so-called 'classic' beauties and heroes from yesteryear — the pop industry and our bondage to history would amount to zilch.

Photography's potency goes beyond a creative impact or transformative effect. At best, it instigates — or should — action. At worst, it lulls the viewer to sleep as history rolls by. Click!

HOT TYPE

Think of the famous picture of a nine-year-old Vietnamese girl, Kim Phuc, running naked down a road in agony from napalm burns that had eaten into her flesh. It's an image that defined the tragedy of the Vietnam War.

The story was told. Universal outcry erupted. Hippies and radicals marched in protest. 'Saigon' became part of anti-war cool lingo while the village where the napalm bombing took place, Trang Bang, was put on the map.

Lesson? The photo rules! Still, snap or action, it does indeed say more than a thousand words. And Nick Ut, the photographer who took the picture, went on to collect a Pulitzer Prize.

In our increasingly hi-tech age, photography has sparked revolutions and inspired heartfelt poetry. In fact, at its best, photography itself can be described as tangible poetry.

Photographs convey not only their subject's story but allow you to see your own story within that. They render others' photo stories as part of one's life; a world you weave around yourself. Therein lies the magic of this art form. It has the ability to create a close community of romance and dreams between the viewer and the 'captured' subject. And it is in this space that Makeba's images managed to slot themselves into my life.

Like all city dwellers — especially immigrants to the City of Gold — I have had my share of gypsying around; renting, squatting and being evicted as well as getting sentimental about different 'homes' in various decrepit hovels and skyscrapers in this old mine town, Jozi.

Throughout this life on the go — packing and unpacking boxes of rubbish disguised as 'significant literature', or holding on to a necklace a twice-removed aunt from my thrice-removed cousin bequeathed to my clan — there's one item I've come to guard with my life: Makeba's first US solo album, titled simply *Miriam Makeba*.

I've had it for over 15 years but never came around to listening to all of it in one go, though I have heard all 14 tracks — from the township Afro-spiritual '*Jikele Maweni*' to the hip-shaking '*Iya Guduza*' — as they appear on other releases.

Makeba

The album was released long before the late 1960s when religious mysticism was beginning to influence the cover designs of LP records such as Santana's *Abraxas* and Miles Davis's *Bitches Brew* — and way before spirituality became a component of flower power's heal-the-world escapism.

Miriam Makeba's brown cover with its rustic feel serves as a backdrop to a breathtaking photograph of the artist. With the expression of a woman floating between joy and pain, the picture tells a myriad of stories, though one stands out — passion.

Robed in an ankle-length, royal blue and.jade silk strapless dress that leaves her chocolate-brown shoulders bare but for a long silky scarf thrown over her left shoulder, the photograph makes it clear that Miriam has arrived.

Looking at it on different days, that record cover's tale changes from sensuality, grace, power, determination and simplicity, to the definition of primal sexiness at its pictorial best. The sort of image that makes men young enough to be her grandchildren lose themselves in flighty thoughts of oedipal madness.

Certainly there are more edgy and emotional or even stylistically better images of Makeba on other LP and CD covers. Still, for me this one remains a firecracker and I never thought any other images of her would surpass it or even come near — until the recent release of an autobiographical book, *Makeba, the Miriam Makeba Story*.

Co-authored with first-time writer and filmmaker Nomsa Mwamuka and featuring a black-and-white 1950s cover photograph of Makeba in a cream, strapless dress, her smile wider than the Nile, her gap smack dab in the middle of a snow-white dental set, this 259-page hard-cover book is a visual gift.

It covers Makeba's formative years on the Sophiatown jazz scene, her arrival in America, her bitter departure from there to West Africa with her husband Stokely Carmichael, the most explosively articulate Black Power leader after Malcom X, and her return to South Africa in the 1990s. It delivers everything a 'tribute to' coffee-table book is expected to.

While suckers for style will salivate at Makeba's fashion sense, some photographs will satisfy those still stuck on post-independent Africa's heroic age. The pictures tell her story with a sharp, direct focus. They show how the most enduring gift Makeba gave this country and the rest of Africa is her fashion arty-tude — if not altitude.

In her hands, fashion and style ceased to be mere reasons for glamour magazines' existence, the seasonal change of the models on their covers and debates between pro-fur and pro-faux fur activists.

With her short, corn-rowed hair, dangly seed beads, dresses that highlighted her African contours or decked out in leopard prints and pearls, Makeba — on and off stage — cut an elegant figure at a time when minis were inching their way up women's legs.

Not long after her arrival in the US, the young African woman whose lyrics were unintelligible to her foreign audience, other than the click sounds, which then exoticised her as 'the click-click girl' — showed an acute understanding of fashion as a cultural tool and esteem-builder.

From her hairstyle — curly Afro kinks, styled to give her a dome shape — to her accessories, Makeba's ever-changing style said out loud: 'I am an African and proud.' And this was a generation or two before being African became shopping mall chic and in vogue.

She was bejewelled in gold bangles, a symbol of glam, pride and power in Africa — witness the Ashanti of Ghana, the Masai and Wodaabe tribes' neckwear, the Mandinka hunter-warrior's hat, the ankle-touching Congolese dresses with isiXhosa motifs. The bangles illustrated how Makeba used the influence of a highly visual African aesthetic.

Whether performing for European lefties in Paris or singing Black Power songs for Guinea's peasants, Makeba — eternally stylish and perennially edgy — knew how to carve a niche between counterculture and couture culture.

For her it was, I imagine — as numerous pictures by major lensmen such as Alf Khumalo and William Claxton attest — a matter of saying, 'I am an artist, but if I have to speak for my people, honey, let me do it in style.'

Hence the amount of time and expertise Makeba invested in creating her signature images — layered elaborate African prints, or an elegant, frill-free classic look topped with accessories she collected from all the places she visited on her numerous journeys.

Though she gate-crashed America and the world's popular culture in the early 1960s, her fashion influence, as her music innovation, peaked around the height of the Black Power and flower-power movements.

Soon, soul heavy-hitters such as Aretha Franklin and Nina Simone and actor Cicely Tyson took to this new, breezy, evocative image — the 'African look'. Natural braids, cowrie shells, isiXhosa headgear and the like became a universal Pan-Afro chic look worn by women in New York, London and Lagos.

Her global popularity notwithstanding, it took four decades for Makeba's stylistic influence to be truly appreciated beyond the triumvirate of African liberation, civil rights and soul music — thanks to late1990s hip-hop culture and its musical offshoots in South Africa.

While the 1990s closed with earth *muthas* such as Erykah Badu in flowing batik dresses and queenly headwraps catering for African-Americans' centuries-old yearning for the *muthaland*, Makeba's South African heirs were themselves making a link.

Not content with branding herself 'new African' and, or, red daughter in fashion with her back to rootsy-ness, red being the colour and soul of the soil in some parts of the Eastern Cape where her forebears originate, Bongo Maffin's Thandiswa Mazwai referenced Makeba in songs such as '*I'phindlela*' and 'Makeba', a reprise of the grand dame's own hit, '*Pata Pata*'.

Soon after, Mazwai took to wearing outsized gold bangles, Afro hairdos, flowing long dresses and Vlisco's colourful headwraps. A step ahead of hotair-spitting politicians mouthing off new-Africanisms, the young dame put her money where her pro-Makeba lyrics were — in Africa, albeit a sonically and visually technofied Africa.

The latest in the chain is Simphiwe Dana, a soul singer with an Afro-folksy attitude and an Afro-bohemian image largely based on vintage Makeba. On the cover of her now award winning debut album *Zandisile*, Dana wears a stiff, long hat with a striking resemblance to the one Makeba wore on the cover of her 1970 album *Keep Me In Mind*.

Dana ties her Afro-chic head-wrap in the same shape as the woven straw types (*izicholo*) worn by Zulu women — the same headgear Makeba wore on the cover of her 1987 album *Sangoma*.

The shape of the *isicholo* is similar to that of the Mandinka male warriors hats Makeba popularised during her stay in Guinea, under the patronage of leader, Sékou Touré.

Of all black women, artists and social leaders — Winnie Mandela, Rosa Parks, Gwendolyn Brooks, Toni Morrison, Graça Machel — is one soul, Makeba, who, in her march to personal quest, freedom and musical summit, created a template unto which several generations have and will continue to follow, for as long as pop culture owes currency to *herstory*.

Just the other day, in a chance encounter, I met her and her band crew at the Murtal Muhammed International Airport, in Lagos, Nigeria. The weather was hot, and sticky as hell, the airport a bustling channel of international travelers, tricksters, conmen, military egotists, musicians in transit to obscure parts of the country, dreamers stargazing their way out, and never to come back.

In all that combustion, Makeba, in her old age, as in the book, also as in my dreams, cut a serene yet nerve-dazzling image. Majestic, sensuous . . . indeed style, as an aesthetical expression on your soul — just like beauty — can never be bought.

In her father's tongue, isiXhosa — her mother's tongue is siSwati — a queen or grown-up woman is referred to as *inkosikazi*, a title replete with meaning, implication, symbolism and power — a notch more elegant and potent than the commonly slung around 'diva'.

Dear Soul Sister

I am not feeling you

To hit the vernacular button, and forsake translation — for the essence of the word sheds more 'feeling' than 'meaning' — first thing I want to say is: Dear Simph, *undixolele, nkosazana.*

I possess no special privilege, nor should I abuse any sort of kindness on your part to call you by the name only your beloved folk use: Simph.

Names — as you should know, after you titled your debut album with that of your animated, sweet, little one, Zandisile — are a reflection of intimacy.

In any culture, names — and being on a first-name basis — provide undertones of emotional connection; friendship even. Even if it is only a fleeting encounter, it is through name exchange that dialogue takes root. Hence, by short-circuiting your full name Simphiwe Dana, to Simph, I'm dangerously evoking familiarity and I might be fooling myself in this regard.

It is not even the personal connection that a fan absurdly imagines he shares with the artist. This time around, it is a connection harking back to Yeoville — long before the artist recorded an album, lapped up critical acclaim, toured the world, and had a last laugh at the streets on which she first hustled.

Long before all that I came to know you as that rare breed: an artist with a somewhat edgy approach to art and your public image; a bit conservative, though always an elegant dame to behold.

As for your style, we are both in the loop, knowing that, that other Afro-Space Queen, Erykah Badu, rocked the ankle-length dresses, Nefertiti turbans and Egyptian jewellery long before you arrived. Still, it was quite a marvel seeing you etching your isiXhosa interpretation, quite funkily and sussily, on that EDI (earth diva image) trademark. And, so what? Badu had updated or ripped off Miriam Makeba's daring '60s elegance.

As for that emotion-loaded tenor, sometimes whisperish, often bassy, heaving, vibrating ... Girlfriend, that's not your voice, but an ancestral device, a vocal conduit, a tool to dialogue with the world beyond — a point soulfully played out in Zap Mama's album, *Ancestry in Progress.*

I remember when I first heard that voice. I had met you and Msa, your now ex-partner, ex-manager, the father of your two children, Zandisile and Phalo, in Rosebank in early 2004 or thereabouts.

Finally, after you had worked on your craft, in your home studio, defiant and not keen to hawk your soul to the music biz's highest bidders, you pulled me aside and let it slip that you were looking for a record deal.

All of your energies were focused on it, when not taking care of the newborn Zandi.

Though the home-cooked music was yet to be mixed, mastered and arranged, you had a seed ready to bloom, an artistic grenade ready to go bang with the first touch. You had not, by then, met the man who would provide that crucial touch, Thapelo Khomo, of *Stimela* fame.

All there was to you then was that rawness, determination, stubbornness even. Now in my short life, Simph, I have been lucky to hear artists, as well those not accorded such status; ordinary men and women with rib-cracking and soul-warming voices. Some of those folks' voices were the primal screams, which could chariot a listener closer to God, quicker than a baptismal dip down by the local river.

Dear Soul Sister

Yours was different: natural, slow burning, not quite ominous, even though all the signs were there. One octave lower, or one dark, life-altering experience would have seen that voice on a one-way ticket to Brenda Fassieville, or Nina Simone on her 'Don't Let Me Be Misunderstood' bluest.

Still it was all you had: steeped in the spirits of your foremothers, yet pregnant with possibilities of a new sound, a new era, away from the Dorothy Masuka, Skalites, and '80s black Tin Pan Alley. Yours was at the service of new wars affecting the new generation, in the Thabo Mbeki era. Hence your initial popularity on the mushrooming, live poetry scene.

Believe me, Simph, I have never heard a voice like that. No. Not since Margaret Singana's work on the *Shaka Zulu* film soundtrack, or Dolly Rathebe's work with the Elite Swingsters. Both are now gone the way of all flesh. Your voice, though, is alive, lodged somewhere between their omnipresent energies and this ain't no *New Age* gumpf.

Years later, I heard something akin to that. A voice with an old, grainy, film feel, and rooted, in a way that it could only be a voice from *ezilaleni*, the nucleus of the Eastern Cape hinterlands. A voice, were it not so full of rock-chick falsettos, would have been a voice solely utilised for conversing with the world beyond the tangible. Zolani Mahola's voice.

While hers soars upon the slightest inflection of pain, and paints ghostly, biographical narratives, yours remains the voice of the ghost itself.

Though your CD had that airy, homemade demo touch about it, no one could miss its unmistakable 'Pow!' Particularly, in the title track *'Zandisile'* — your baby girl's name.

While you are a quiet, restrained sort, little Z is a bundle of joyous chaos, a reflection, I have always thought, of something you are holding inside.

I cannot over emphasise the magnetic powers of that song, especially during the spring of 2004. It was almost like an extension of your newborn child, or her, an extension of the song. Unadorned, naked, with no expectation and devoid of anger, the music gave the feeling that you had never had an experience quite like it (giving birth, that is, to either a song or a child).

'*Zandisile*' is a song about a beloved ushered into this life. Any work of art that embellishes, as well as puts a yoke on any child who would grow aware knowing a song bearing their name, should be a result of an exacting creative journey, indeed.

The last time pop gave in to such maternal instincts was in Lauryn Hill's monstrously beautiful self-affirmation, 'To Zion', a song also set to the heartbeat of her first child, Zion Marley Hill.

* * *

We lost touch. You got your deal. Upped your style and, thanks to Gallo Music, had the services of a professional producer.

With his minimalist touch and an acute insight into varying styles, coupled with '70s-styled retro-ghetto hooks to groove up someone as seemingly folksy like you, Thapelo Khomo is a prophet of our age. This is the man who gave *Stimela* its funk, and Jabu Khanyile's *Bayete* its pop back in 1994.

I can't think of anybody else, outside of house and kwaito, nearly as talented — other than Sello 'Chicco' Twala, who produced Brenda Fassie at her best and worst. Khomo is a beast of a producer and it was hardly a surprise that your album went on an ascent.

We did not worry a bit when it did not sell like Thandiswa Mazwai's *Zabalaza*, for album sales are not always a reflection of an artist's craft, nor an audience's taste. We knew that were it thrown into bad hands it would have taken a route planted with disaster.

We also knew there were others. Were it not for people such as Sipho Sithole who launched you, totally wet behind the ears, at Angelique Kidjo's gig on the Urban Voices bill, the fickle music industry would have misunderstood your artistic chakra, doll!

One need not impress upon you the narrowness of South Africa's musical tastes: either you are Sister Bettina, a head-bangingly X-rated kwaito star, with beats to whip up a party; a dance-floor techno-geek like Black Coffee; a pre-packed-tears-and-all Rebecca Malope clone; or a — and this is supposed to offer a radical dimension (though it fails to) — Mafikizolo.

There's not much space for difference. If there is, it is Arno Casterns and Fokofpolisiekar strumming it up in Soweto. And that's a novelty; not the norm. Radio killed variety. Artists are punished at the cash register and not encouraged to seek what is alternative.

Still you made it. Who can forget your history-making debut at the 2005 Cape Town Jazz Festival?

A bit anxious that you were not strictly jazz, the promoter booked you a decent-sized venue at this international jazz peacock display of the best and the simply sublime. Unbeknownst to him, audiences had already connected with your art somewhere on the airwaves. Perhaps radio has its uses after all.

Those inside numbered hundreds, while those outside, even more: a recipe for stampede. People screamed your name: Siiimphiweeeee. . .eee! Quite eerie. Eardrum splitting. A carnage of love. That mad. That touching.

After that performance you were forced to do another show at a much bigger venue to accommodate those who missed out, and a thousand more. From there your career soared you — what is that Santana song? — 'Black Magic Woman'!

It has been almost two years since you hit the scene like a tsunami. But hey, Simph, like most of your fans I have been waiting for your latest release with — this clichéd feeling — bated breath!

You should have seen us media hounds mad-dashing across Newtown so we could be in time for your new album's listening session, at the new Kippies, some couple of weeks ago.

Our mad rush? Just for ye, blessed chile. And that was not even a launch. That was before Gallo wrapped an entire bus with your face and your album cover and sent it roaring along your Jozi's sin streets during peak hour.

Listening session. We waited. Hour gone. Then waited some more. Soon, you rolled in. Bedecked in some oriental silky shawl. Goddess! But I do not recall you apologising to us. How odd. The shape of things to come?

Where's my Simph from Yeoville?

Though you tried to hide it, something clearly got your goat that day. Later, after enduring a very bad sound system — the consequence of a rushed job, and simple disrespect to the media, usually better known for its love of free hooch, perhaps — your record company tried to offer me a five-minute premium interview, since, so went the explanation, 'the queue was long'.

Five minutes? Duh!

Later I was able to piece together a list of things riling you. For instance, I had learned that hardly a few hours before this key listening session, you and the producer of your latest album, *The One Love Movement On Bantu Biko Street*, Bheki Khoza, also known as 'Naganiel Ben Israel', were totally not on speaking terms.

A charged-up meeting, where you had arrived with your lawyers and him with his, was hastily arranged, though there are conflicting tales on this. What is not in dispute is that you and your producer are embroiled in a beast of a fight over the crediting rights of an album hardly 25 days out.

Why?

Up to today, a senior artist-and-repertoire (A & R) manager at Gallo, who worked on your album, tells me, 'the industry has no standards on this. There are just no rules. Nobody really knows where an artist's line stops and a producer takes over in a studio-based creative process'. Perhaps your victory or wound will help provide the industry with the template.

Clearly Simph, what that fight revealed was that a precedent had long been set. It started with Khomo. The reason you axed Khomo is that the two of you are known to have bickered bitterly about the songs' crediting. Same rap with Ben Israel, though this time around one of you is prepared to end up in court — that is, if Gallo does not intervene quickly to avert a PR disaster.

So, how's the album? What do I think about it? How do I feel about it? You must be wondering: There cannot be a separate appreciation of the art without an attempt to make sense of the title, I feel. Some says it's a weird title. I think it is up Simphiwe Boulevard: meanderingly poetic and full of *vooma*!

And that's not even what makes it unique. Only quite alert students of history will dig it is a wicked weaving (dialogue?) between two African visionary icons, who lived in the same age, impacted on the black world with equal force, and then died four years apart without ever meeting: reggae prophet Bob Nesta Marley and the black consciousness prophet Bantu Steve Biko.

Both died in their early 30s, both left lasting impressions on the human psyche and its ability to create resistance against injustice - especially injustice against the poor. Brother Bob and brother Steve never physically met, and yet they loom large in your title: Marley's great song *One Love*, and perhaps your own spirit, gets to take a walk on his not-so-distant brother, Bantu Biko's street.

Can I get a witness? Ahoy, ahoy, *sistren*!

See, the naysayers can bark until they turn blue, but will they ever admit that in an era in which airports, streets and statutes are all named after one party (rewriting a kind of weird factionalist history), the name Steve Bantu Biko is still anathema to the bourgeoise bullies in the commanding kraal?

That you, as a young woman are assertive to the point of tossing off the bling currents and opening yourself to scorn in your quest to create dialogue that goes beyond Luthuli House, tells us more of your will to die. Got my vote there, honey.

The title is not the only kick-asser about this: I am of the school that believes that love is an act of war; protection, bravery, risk. And deep love is an expression of a fighting spirit.

Now, I know you might not be prepared to talk about this (a bad assumption on my part). But, as you artists are want to say, could it be that your very public break-up with your ex-manager and father of your children, Msa, found its way into the lyrics? Is this about him?

Could it be that your song '*Zundiqondisise*' (Understand Here) is a cryptic reference to an art-romance gone sour: Diego Riviera/Frida Kahlo, Hugh Masekela / Miriam Makeba, Lauryn Hill / Wyclef Jean?

You are not my dream come true Understand this

You are not my sustenance Understand this / I've got my own way of coming forth

I've got my own way of soaring
You do not get to decide what I do with my life ...

 And so it goes, with you spitting fire, reminding me of Ms Badu's angriest lyric ever on a pop record, 'Certainly', from her debut, *Baduizm*:

Who gave you permission to rearrange me? Certainly not me
I was not looking for no affair and now you wanna fix me?!

 Fiery sisterhood aside, is the *One Love Movement* as good a work of art, as it socks it out to previously controlling men? Does it rock?

Dear, Simph, I know you are a feeling person, thus I take comfort in talking to you on that level knowing that, my sister, you will surely feel me when I say I am not feeling you. I am not feeling your album, specifically the most important thing about it, the music.

Musically, it doesn't break rules. It does not innovate or risk anything. It lacks the sort of kick and wit that you — a radical sister and an artist with considerable performance presence — carry in your creative foundation. It is musically unadventurous and staid — unlike the sort of caustic political beliefs you are known for.

It's arrangements are quite okay — I mean, it's a so-so affair. But *so-so* has never been good for you. You are not a so-so act. You are a so, so powerful artist and spirit! Which then trips up the alarm bell in me, when, how would you explain this safety net, Simph? Is this what your record company, Gallo expects or chose for you? Is this about retaining old fans — thus making sure there's no commercial loss at the till?

Let's talk sonic art: there's no new or risky drum programming. The string arrangements are staid - without offer possibility of breaking new territory. And of course that talented wordsmith rapper Pro-Kid is reduced to a stroller in there — what was the reason for his inclusion, by the way?

Also, your voice is neither challenged, nor used challengingly. Overall, the sound is quite dated; so 2004. This feels like the material that was left out of your first album, which sounded great when it dropped on the market, but do you have to imitate yourself? What's your name, Tracy Chapman?

See, Simph, I once heard this expression used in some village in the Eastern Cape: 'You are too young to die so young!'

Because you are an intrinsically good artist there will be a gem or so that connects. But it is too little and too far in between. Two pieces in the album tug at my heart strings: *'Ihilihili'* and the sign-out cut, 'The One Love Movement: *Umthandazo Wase Afrika* Part 2 — *Naphakade'*.

Churchy-touchy-feely rituals created outside of pop, or the *pop-con* box that much of popular music is tailored for, they are two lonely standalones. But they are the sort of songs that inspire me to go on bended knees — to pray for the rest of the album.

The other day, out of the blue, I got a call from Thandiswa Mazwai, who, take note, happens to be your big fan and defender, Simph.

'Hey dude,' she cried. 'I just got Simphiwe's latest album,' she began. 'And it is rocking — what's your favourite track?' I kept mum. Am I supposed to love it? I thought.

'I said, which one d'ya love?' Now, artists can be forthright, especially when they are feeling something. This I cannot over emphasise. I am talking to one. So you would understand.

[Cough, cough] Throat clearing. 'What this album does,' I began, a bit feebly, I think 'is make me love the first one, *Zandisile* even deeper,' I said.

'What?' she faded. The line got blurrier. 'Deeper — it makes me dig the first deeper.'

'What?' the fading voice went . . . 'I'm saying d-e-e-p-e-r! Do you feel me?' Thwack! Dead.

We got cut. Just then, I turned around and put on *Zandisile* on the home music player. Oh dear. Oh dear

Jonga'pha, wethu: next time you create something as fearless as that, please give me a call. Meantime, you are free to respond to this. Any time. As for me, I won't be dancing, nor moaning.

Sad. And so is life.

Yours, Bongani PS: *Uyakundixolela, Nkosazana* 17 December, 2006

Dear Soul Brother
The One Love Movement will heal

Thank you so much for your openness and honesty. People like you are what challenge me on my life's journey, making me stay on my toes always. I humbly accept your criticism of this offering and it really is difficult for me to protest as it is your opinion and I am big on respecting people's opinions.

I firstly want to extend my deepest apologies to you and the members of your clan (the media) for coming late to my own listening session. I am glad you got to understand the stress I was under that day. I guess it also is time for me to grow up and understand that people do not live in my head and cannot understand that I always mean well.

I must admit, though, concerning my new work, that you are the first person who has responded to it that way. Most people from all the places in the world I've been to, who have listened to the two albums, seem to really be in love with *The One Love Movement on Bantu Biko Street.*

So I am a bit taken aback, a bit shaken, a bit unsure as to how I should respond. It might be that the others were trying to buy my face, which is a likely possibility in the times we live in, or that you refuse to grow with me: stuck in a time and place that has passed. Refusing to evolve with my melody.

I start to wonder if you ever got me. I totally ripped myself apart to create this new work, with some help from the Divine, though I might not have wanted it, feeling it is quite unfair.

Of course the fact that I went through so much to get to a point where I could create the music does not automatically make it a good offering; far from it. I am my own worst critic, but this time around I find nothing to criticise. I gave it my all, my undivided attention and all the love I could muster.

Now I will stop blowing my own horn and leave it to the peoples of the world to dissect and analyse this offering in the comfort of their homes. But, even if they agree with you, know that I am comfortable in knowing myself and my capabilities. I know that this is my best work so far.

I won't lie to you though. If I have any ego, it has been totally deflated and I really hope that was not your intention. I hope you were just being true to the music. I have met too many journalists filled with self-importance, who make everything about them, not about the work and the people it speaks to; the people they represent.

If you were expecting me to grow out of context to who I really am, it will never happen. That last part was the angry part of me responding.

It maybe that you are misguided, like that time you asked me if I was racist. If you had ever got me you would have known that that was a preposterous question, totally absurd. So, again, I wonder if you ever got me, or if I was just a fashion statement. Fashion changes with the times.

Lastly, *The One Love Movement* understands that we are all victims in this society of ours and, because of that, I can only have love for you. And I do, always.

And no, there is no song about Msa on the album — one more thing about me you did not get.

Love and respect, Simphiwe Dana

FreshlyGroundNut

One love, one voice, one mom

In an attempt to make sense of the magnetic presence of the actor, Samuel L Jackson in the film biz, Jeff Hudson, author of *The Unauthorised Biography of Samuel L Jackson*, observed: 'Defining moments are, ironically, usually indefinable, and never more so than when in relation to a person's career.'

Hudson reasons that 'there is no scientific formula for the circumstances that lead to certain people at certain times attaining a sudden boost, a career elevation, far beyond what others, in the same circumstances, can hope to achieve.'

'All that we know,' he tells us ,'is that it does happen. For some, it takes a moment in the spotlight; for others, a lifetime of immersion in epic artistry to signal their arrival with a bang.'

As recently as 1980, a piano-playing former street urchin with vocal talents many a jazz singer would kill for, shy and bold at the same time, and already possessed by demons, blew onto the charts with a proto-feminist disco cut, 'Weekend Special'. But it was only through her B-side single, the tear-drenched 'Life is Goin' On' that many recognised Brenda Fassie as a child of extraordinary gifts.

It's almost four years since the left-of-centre pop outfit with a kwela flavour, Freshlyground raised its head on the pop and alternative live-music circuit, and yet I do not recall a 'Hail Zolani Mahola' — its lead singer — moment celebrating the group's lead singer.

Alright, alright. Other than the recent national lullaby of choice, 'Doo Be Doo'.

Beyond that, the first thing people remark on is 'that girl's' anti-glossy magazine features and then, as an afterthought, her voice. Even that's hardly registered as a big bang moment.

As is the way with pop and rock, lore has it, Mahola's story is interwoven with that of her chums in Freshlyground. But for the sheer spookiness of her fresh-as-cut-grass voice, it is Mahola, and not the whole seven-piece outfit I've been itching to unmask since that Sunday night, 'round witches hour, when out of the stereo popped '*Nomvula*', a song not only blessed with the memory of township tales, but simultaneously haunting and haunted.

Not since Janis Joplin's Woodstock 1969 'Work Me, Lord' and Mbizo Johnny Dyani's '*Magwaza*' has a piece of music turned my insides upside down like that. I swore not to rest till I could lay my peepers on the spirit behind that voice.

Alas, bad omen was writ large all over the darn thing. First, the *Washington Post*'s foreign correspondent published a page one story on South Africa's racial divisions, referencing a large chunk of a story — on black rock and alternative music — I had written in the *Sunday Times Lifestyle*, as the best example of such divisions.

The original rock piece had a line quoting a young black journalist and part of that scene — dismissing Mahola as a 'brown sugar grain added to (s)punk up the buttermilk'. You didn't have to be a genius to appreciate whom the spear was aimed at. For all its multi-culti cool factor, Freshlyground is still seen, in some quarters as so '90s kitsch - think of Mango Grove - and white, though this is strictly not true - since their sound is more Gugs (Guguletheu) than Camps (Camps Bay).

Soon after the piece appeared in the US, cow dung hit the screens – computer screens – as the band's website exploded with a flood of support, some of their fans casting doubts on this writer's sanity.

The record label, Sony BMG, wasted no time, weighing in, sending a press release celebrating the band's newly certified astronomical sales figures. Indeed, the band's latest album, *Nomvula* has outsold everything outside of the gospel and kwaito market, but that they have achieved double platinum – 110 000 units – and are going for triple, going for 200 000, so it seemed.

Suddenly it felt like the market was experiencing a Freshlyground rapture. Someone pointed out something oddly curious: Freshlyground is the only South African outfit explosively popular within the campus, regional and national radio. Highbrowness be damned! It is currently the only band in South Africa to evoke that line, 'Oh, I hate to love it, but I do (love it) that is.' Well, me, too!

Thus I found myself on Cape Town's streets in pursuit of the voice. Talk here is that the band is something of a local legend, a fact confirmed by a leading electronic music theorist, academic and critic, Julian Jonker. 'From early on, their gigs at the Armchair Theatre in Observatory, which took only a limited – under 100 alternative-culture die-hards – became legend.' And yet, it wasn't always that way.

Prior to meeting the band, Mahola – a budding poet and bath-time vocalist from KwaZakhele, via Port Elizabeth's New Brighton township – was a drama student at the University of Cape Town.

The band, at the core of which were Simon Attwell, Josh Hawks and Aron Turest-Swartz, was then doing the rounds in bars, with no name, no manager and no roadmap to stardom.

Riffing their guitars for supper on the ever-changing Cape Town bar circuit, they couldn't have foreseen what was to hit them, until one night, right in the middle of their routine, a young, pint-sized woman jumped on stage: uninvited, un-pruned, unpretentious.

Mahola's elastic, multi-ranged voice wrapped itself around the song, warmed the microphone, cottoned on to the song at play, built steadily before peaking and then flooded through the speakers; a scene startling and inspiring 'the band' with a gut-kicking impact.

Sevi Spanoudi, Freshlyground's manager, remembers Mahola having a gig at some theatre in Table Bay. 'She had this Ella [Fitzgerald] thing going on, paying tribute to her through haunting cover versions of "Mack the Knife", "Ella Sings The Cole Porter Songbook" and of course that morning dew, "As You Desire Me".

Cooing and blues-ing Fitzgerald's classics went on as a side-gig until her relationship with the bar band — joined by another young dame, violinist Kyla-Rose Smith, fresh from Johannesburg's rock-rap band, Tumi and The Volume — gelled and all members got down to toil for a new baby.

'We didn't have a name then,' violinist Kyla-Rose Smith says. 'All we wanted to do was to create the kind of music we were dying to hear on radio. Music that was in short supply on the live circuit . . . ' she pauses: 'an organic sound.'

Later somebody whipped the name Freshlyground from nowhere, though it never stuck until after they'd used it for their first album, *Jika Jika*, in 2003. As far as album titles go, *Jika Jika* (Nguni slang for going around in circles) was prophetic. Indeed this album went nowhere. Not only was it undone by weak production and, some of the songwriting was of Sunday-school songwriting level, it left listeners with only two worthwhile tracks, the last track '*Nomvula*' and 'Castles in the Sky'.

And it's that very track that would one day rake in critical respect for its composer, singer and the band. As we speak, *Jika Jika* has sold 15 000 units — five G's a year in a market where the worst kwaito outfit or your walk-in-the park jazz band chalks up at least twice that.

But the band's members are not quitters. Nothing, it seems, was going to stand in their way, as they set out to record the follow-up the following year.

Guided by the classically trained jazz and gospel producer Victor Masondo and this other Arthur fella, JB Arthur, Freshlyground's *Nomvula* is a lushly-produced album that blows up a million-gazillion landmines under the notion of music 'genre-fication'.

The album has everything that pleases and displeases the senses. The arrangements and musicianship instrumentation warm the heart, while unleashing musical set pieces as colourful as though Beezy Bailey was their guardian angel.

And that's not all.

Girl-child can sing and swing her vocal chords any which way you want. Rare in a culture as segmented as the music biz, her voice has a fluidity that seeps through sub-genres as diverse as African trance, Soweto jive, the blues, bluegrass, rock and rock as if the Eastern Cape, Memphis and Nashville were only streets apart.

Most astonishingly, though, is the album's emotional elasticity. This is one album as emotionally elastic as Michael Jackson's many surgery faces. You cry in pain and weep for joy all in one package.

Clearly the young woman has some childhood blues to deal with. And she does so with a voice that expresses both real and dramatised emotion acutely. One minute she's whispering amid a bushfire of violins, flutes, harmonicas, electric guitars and weepy slides. The next she's morphed into a hard-done by rock chick barely managing to conceal her rage. She's full of wattage powerful enough to inspire a revolution from Mowbray to Musina.

And yet, instead of choosing the easy and vengeful approach, that of a soul or rock diva with perpetual threats of cutting you — well usually some poor sod of a man — out of her life, she flips the scripts, and asks [in the song, 'I'd Like']:

What would you do if I held your hand and laid it down? Would you find me overly unkind to you? What do I do with all these feelings tearing me up inside? What do I do with all these wasted hours dreaming of you at night?

Cheesy has never sounded so complex, and complex has never felt so accessible. But just who is Zolani Mahola?

Listen no further than the band's most tortured song. The song '*Nomvula*' provides — and that's a spurious claim, for the album is as swampy with what Jonker refers to as *snot en trane* — to have an insight into what makes her who she is, and in that order, who she is. In '*Nomvula*', the poet in Mahola rows the pop boat into autobiographical deep waters, narrating the tale of a young girl raised by a widowed dad, in a voice recalling both Tracy Chapman and Dusty Springfield unplugged:

> *Sondela Mhlobo wam*
> *[Come closer my friend]*
> *Here comes a long tale about where the trouble started*
> *I was raised by my father*
> *Who was bereaved at a young age*
> *by his true darling, my mother*
> *Edith Nomvula Thomas-Mahola*

> * * *

> *There were three of us by my mother,*
> *myself the second ...*
> *Never did my father cry,*
> *when they buried the love of many years*
> *At Don Brosco, we lived in KwaZakhele ...*

> * * *

> *Four rooms with a dining table eBhayi*
> *Small hands throwing dust to dust*
> *not knowing the reason*
> *Tyhini na bethuna!*
> *Sis, No-no has left us.'*

But that's about as deep as she wants you to go, at least lyrically. Somehow though, you can't help thinking: there's more where this bit comes from. Also, there should be a sticker prohibiting listeners from playing songs such as 'I'd Like', 'Nomvula', 'Father Please' and 'Buttercup' any time past midnight.

Disturbed, I tracked her to a one-bedroom flat in Tamboerskloof, a hilly, Victorian-boho section in the Cape Town city bowl.

'I have just moved in here,' she says. 'Say a week or so, and I already feel the place. Dig it.' Though without the requisite accent, her expressions are dipped in hip-hop argot. 'Dudes' and 'Yos' sit snugly with her Xhosa click-clicks.

Other than her sculptural face on the CD cover, I had never seen her anywhere before this very moment.

The first thing I notice are her features. Zolani Mahola is attractive in an awkward way. Something in her — her welcoming girl-next-door attitude — distorts, in a stranger's mind, her height. Suddenly she appears taller than she is as she leads me to the balcony where, to the strains of gospel singer Mavis Staples, we talk like long-lost friends.

'My family moved from KwaZakhele to New Brighton after my mother's death. My whole youth experience was so white. White teachers, friends, music and behaviour, and no I am not complaining. That's how it was. Even now, though I am carving what matters to me, my world is practically white. I guess folks in the townships say, I live white, thus I am white.'

But much as her school life was foreign to her family life, it was quite open to artistic growth.

'The whole thing was surreal to me because at home my father was culturally an Africanist, rearing children single-handedly. He also travelled a lot in those days so he really never shaped how we looked at life. There was always this "let children be" attitude about him.

'At school I lived, thought and acted like other children — white children — and coming back home, I would find an animal, often it would be a goat in one of the rooms or in the yard, readied for some ritual, *Umsebenzi*.'

Ever since her death, when Mahola was six, her mother's 'passing — or living spirit,' as her dad described it the following day, has remained omnipresent within the singer's very being.

An overweight girl with little confidence growing up in New Brighton and composing songs in memory of her mother, as well as the now grown-up-at-

24 star discussing her body politics, Mahola's mother remains central. When she was about 11 all her friends were skinny and beautiful. Not only did that sort of beauty exclude her, but it would elude her forever. 'I could not be that beautiful, therefore much as I wished, I could not be "beautiful" in the way everyone desired. There was no other kind of beauty then, and it's still the same story these days.'

Melancholy threatens. The topic veers into melancholy. The CD is changed. Out goes Mavis Staples, in comes fat, funky Sufi-pop. Above us Table Mountain watches in stone-cold silence. As balls of smoke billow towards its peak, our voices sink a few octaves.

Facing a long bottled youth pain in the company of a stranger can be bruising. Quite calmly she proceeds to blow off the lid of her youth:

'I was a sad little fat girl,' she says. It's tragic, I tell her, being judged on what you can never be, rather than being accepted on who you are. 'It was worse for me,' she says, 'because I did not have a mother who would tell me, "You are beautiful the way you are." I started smoking weed, and I later discovered drama.'

Drama was a way of exploring her identity, or choice of different identities, including some of her true characters she had not, before, come to terms with.

'It was an escape route. There's nothing in this world that accords you an opportunity to inhabit other people's characters like drama. It created an alternative existence for me. So much so that I kept on acting — on and off stage.

'These days, man, I'm really working on that confidence. It is happening . . . I mean . . . it's so great to hear people saying, "I love you. I love what you do." It's cool, but then again, I take it with a pinch of salt.'

Why?

'How can you love me when you don't know me?' she counters, not missing a beat.

'I never proposed,' I retort.

'I mean the fans', she throws that one back, lapsing into sheets of giggles. 'I mean those people always in tears, deep in love with show buzz. That's hectic.'

Though the giggles lift her mood, Mahola — in happiness or sadness — is a serious person. 'Ah, me . . . I live my life. I do not want to get bogged down by being somebody else's hero. Never!'

How does a music star remain calm in the face of multitudes of fans screaming her name and reaching out for a fleeting touch? With all that visually dazzling lighting, and outreached hands from million of strangers screaming their name, how does a star-act remain sane when all she hears is her own voice playback singing her songs — songs she wrote in her deepest privacy — in malls, clubs and supermarkets, day and night?

'It is not always good, I know, but being calm means I can calmly choose not to deal with things I need [not] deal with, when I don't feel like it. It's like . . .' she gestures, 'don't get involved in the heat of things. Never get blinded. It helps me deal with a lot of crap. It's a coping mechanism I can trace back to my childhood.'

Freshlyground drummer Peter Cohen, ex-founding member of both Mango Groove and Bright Blue at various times in the 1990s, tells me the band is built around her. 'She's the glue that binds and the spirit that inspires,' he explained it: 'Every band should have a Zolani Mahola. She's so beautiful. Her mind is so clear. A gorgeous spirit!'

Later in the day, the 'gorgeous spirit' would be tested, right in the presence of a prying scribe.

We feel like a walk. Around the corner from her flat is a joint called Beleza. Though she's new in the area, she's already getting on like a house on fire with the eatery's manager. Nearby, there is a party of five, chatting in various degrees of sloshy-ness. Two women, who just a minute ago were heading to the bathroom, turn around and come to our corner, uninvited.

'*Is jy die meisie wat* "Doo Be Doo be" *sing*?' asks the skinny one, who volunteers her name as Maria Pitso. She introduces her friend with the '70s prom-date hairdo, Dorothy Apollis.

'What band is that by the way?' her friend, Apollis asks. '*Ek weet mos.* Maai hazband loves you, you know. He says you are an overseas artist and I say, *nee man. . .'* And so it goes. The press interview gives way to reality-fan interview. Un-scripted, no pretense: 'Who are you? Fresh girl, *ne*?' one asks. Mahola finally gives in, nods and resumes talking to me. '*Nee, man*! Izit'chu? Really, uhm Fresh girl?'

More questions follow, which she answers with a mixture of boredom and feigned interest. They are not easily shaken off.

'D'ya live in Cape Town?'

'Yes.'

'Where?'

'Here. What, you want to pay me a visit?'

Apollis pushes her friend aside for a slice of action. 'Ahm . . . ahm sooo glad I met you. Please you musn't leave us alone here in Cape Town. We love you.'

Just then the whole party descends on our table. One of them, an elderly oom, Godfrey Philander, asks Mahola to 'please bless me, make it my day'. He thrusts a Lotto ticket in her face. 'Please sign your autograph on my Lotto. I come from a family of songwriters. Good songs we made back then. But I like yours. That one . . . "Doo bee"', he starts crooning. Thixo!

For 35 minutes — a valuable 35 minutes — Mahola calmly tries every trick in the book to win back her privacy. The intrusion leaves me somewhat resentful and nearer to my departure for eBhayi, (formerly Port Elizabeth) a place she sings about with achy-break-mah-heart fondness.

***

It's Sunday afternoon in New Brighton, Port Elizabeth, simply known by its Xhosa moniker, eBhayi. I've missed lunch at the Maholas so I will have to make do with the mountain of cookies and juice obscuring my view on the coffee table.

Opposite where I am seated is Mahola's beaming younger sis', Lukhanyiso. To my right sits her beaming dad, the now famous Doc Nceba Mahola. Dad is still trying to come to terms with his daughter's impact on South African contemporary music.

Like all the Maholas I interviewed, Bra Doc is a man at peace with himself. No, he is not rich. They still live in the four-roomed house his daughter sings about in '*Nomvula*'. But, 'thanks Lord', she has bought him a second-hand Mazda.

'I sent her to university to study drama. The next thing I see this child coming home carrying some worn-out guitar during her mid-term breaks and I thought, what now?'

Whatever it is Zolani Mahola channels as an artist, her father believes, it is the spirit of his late wife, Nomvula. 'Even as a Christian, I believe there's an afterlife. Wherever Nomvula is, I know she's with us all the time.'

Just as his daughter does with a song's structure, Mahola took me through the family narrative, confiding secrets about the short illness and the tragic death of his wife, who was then expecting their fourth child.

'Zo-Zo's mother was highly expectant,' he remembers. 'At some point before she passed away, she had a premonition of sorts, a feeling that she was going to die. Three days after I had left her at the hospital, I got a call informing me that the love of my life was no more.

'I wished the baby had survived, but still it was going to be very tough for us all. The child would have grown up bearing a cross, knowing that she took her mom's life.'

For Lukhanyiso, her sister's triumph beyond the township matchbox, the absence of mother love, and possibly, the triumph of a single man raising girl-children [and a boy not much older], feels like yesterday.

She goes puffy-eyed, merely recalling Freshlyground's storm — the band's first and only performance in its biggest star's own backyard in late December 2005. If Lukhanyiso's reportage is anything to go by, this is clearly a family of gifted narrators.

She tells the story of a family clan packed into three cars before rushing to the University of Port Elizabeth's main hall to welcome the return one of theirs, albeit on stage.

This, according to the tale's linear anecdotes, was a moment of reckoning for all involved; family, fans, the area and the band, and specifically her sister, Zolani.

'Long before the band took the stage, the whole family was in the front row, almost under the stage itself, except my dad. He,' she points mock-accusingly at him, 'arrived late.

'He arrived right at the time the hall was about to burst with the push-and-pull going on in there and, canyoubelievit?, headed for the front row.

'When people saw him,' says Lukhanyiso, standing to demonstrate, 'they started chanting, "*Nomvula, Nomvula.* We want *No-m-vuuula.*" Unbelievable!'

She remembers the band continuing with the song they had just started, but the crowd continued the chanting.

'Zolani stopped right then to explain to the crowd that they had played that song already.' As if they cared.

'*Nom-v-u-u-u-u-lah*! We want *Nomvula*,' continued the cry. The request was granted. 'A few bars into the song, tears started streaming down my father's cheeks, and then he cried. When Zolani saw him, she too cried, and then the whole family started crying.

'The band could not play on. Zolani could not continue with the second verse. She spun around, tried to wipe her tears, and just about then the keyboard player, Aron Turest-Swartz, with whom she composed the song, started crying too. And then some members of the audience could not hold it anymore. They, too, cried.

'It was . . . oh, I can't even explain it to you. The same night, soon after the show, the band' — in a true spirit of an in demand rock 'n' roll troupe — 'rushed to its next performance in the next town, Uitenhage, the younger members of the Mahola family and some parts of the audience in hot pursuit.'

All because of the song '*Nomvula*'. All because of love. All because of longing
. . . the stuff history-altering rock 'n' roll tales are made of – longing.

Were I by any chance present at that now historical show, I too would
have cried. No doubt all five of my siblings would have joined in. As for the
star thing, I too would have galloped behind the band, as their rear lights
disappeared into the dark, too late for their next gig.

I too would be telling this story; Lukhanyiso's, Zolani's, Doc Nceba Mahola's
story. My own flesh-and-blood mother's name was Nomvula. It's over 15
years since she too passed on. Her last child, who was also three at the time
of her death, gave birth to a bouncy boy three years ago.

His favourite song – to quote his exact pronunciation – is 'Doo Be Doo Be'.
When he's too moody they hum it to put him to sleep.

Running with the Wolves:
The Rebel Divas

She

In search of my childhood fantasy

Durban and its sing-songy, Zulu-slangy townships are beyond boiling point this noon as we foot it around KwaMashu's hilly streets in search of a ghost.

We are looking for Linda Mhlongo, and it will be three days before it dawns on me how complex and disturbing her ghost is. This is in contrast to how corporeal and ravishing she was in her flesh-and-blood days – a 'certified' man-eater rivalled only by two other eye-poppingly beautiful she-rascals, the ball-breaker, Dotty Tiyo and the blues crooner, Dolly Rathebe, as various old men keep telling me.

Despite the fact that Mhlongo had been one of the original molls in the international hit musical *King Kong*, she never became a knock-you-down household name like, say, Miriam Makeba. Yet she went on to develop a character that deserved to be writ large in neon – the crime buster 'She' in a 1970s picture book of the same name.

Mhlongo's tale is also the tale of a significant, yet forgotten, chapter in South African pop literature – the reign of those pocket-sized pulp-fiction

227

magazines called 'picture books', popularly known in the townships as 'comics'.

Picture books, as one of the original photographers of the genre, Terry Heywood, recalls, 'were not merely popular, but were the urban underground's Bibles'.

'They were popular from coast to coast,' Heywood tells me, his face brightening at the memory. 'Maaan, I tell you, we lived like stars. Just like in Hollywood — on a minor scale. The girls, the booze, the acclaim. Freedom. Bonhomie. Aah, the time. It was so surreal, so great. I suppose Linda found herself on cloud nine in the black areas, no?'

In the 'locations', as townships were called, *Samson* and *She* were the most popular picture books, while white counterparts such as *Tessa*, *Ruiter in Swart* and *Kid Colt* ruled the roost within both suburbia — *e'ma kitchini* — and townships.

Most of the picture books were created by the Afrikaner-owned Republican Press, based in Mobeni, Durban, in the pre-riot 1960s. Reflective of their age and mores, picture books targeted at whites were known for their Mills & Boon-like love stories — full-figured blondes with pouting lips melting into the arms of rugged, smelly, hairy heroes — while those targeted at urban Africans brimmed with *skop, skiet en donder*.

At their entertaining best, though, several of these magazines, which were targeted at both markets, never meandered too far from the crime-fighting theme. The earlier body of this sub-genre — generally based on a formula derived from the spaghetti Western flicks so popular in the 1960s — showcased black people at their most burlesque. Barbarians such as Chunky Charlie and Batman turfed it out with saviours like Samson, thinning whatever plot there was.

Yet their popularity meant that these magazines, that either sold like hot cakes or like James Hadley Chase literary stick-ups, became the focus of a staggering underground pop literature exchange in the townships. Carrying picture books with their yellowing, dog-eared and beer-stained covers bought you a passport into the world of black hipness and made you something of a bookworm to the non-geeky, streety and dangerous set.

In short, you were the man — but hardly the woman. The only woman of note in these books was the moll, and she was urgently in need of rescuing.

To the mid-1970s black youth — especially boys disinclined to soccer or street-corner dice — these books, and particularly the most popular among them, *She*, was the sanctuary to which we escaped.

Why?

Simply, *She* was da bomb! Besides playing the lead in an aptly self-titled book, the lady was far ahead of the other women of her generation. Her dramatic exploits were heroic. She was smart, and she dispensed witty one-liners as quickly as she demolished her opposition. Of course there was Samson, the beloved kicker, before her; but readers had never seen someone with the lightning speed and sex appeal of She — a woman who had no qualms about smashing men's skulls and punching unreliable women.

Cast in the same mould as Superman and Batman, but without the cape, She was an untypical and fresh crime fighter who delivered equal-gender justice long before it was the norm. She was a captivating and defiant spirit, bringing robust zing to roles mainly thought of as belonging to white men, such as *Kid Colt* and *Ruiter in Swart*.

Legendary 1950s photographers Alf Khumalo and Peter Magubane both remember Mhlongo as a tall, chicory-dark woman with a figure to bring down angels from their celestial compounds.

Well-built with athletic hips, Mhlongo's trademark white bikini top and knickers, matching knee-high boots and magical hunting knife all added to her character's allure.

So popular were the *She* picture books that after Mhlongo left the series, Republican Press tried a variety of actors and models in the role. Unwittingly — probably as a result of its search for a solid replacement for Mhlongo — Republican unleashed something more like female versions of James Bond, what with numerous would-be Shes tripping over themselves to fill

Mhlongo's boots.

Although it lacked the presence and passion of the original, the formula stuck. Issues of *She* such as 'Claws of Horror', 'Death of Fire', 'The Good and The Evil' and 'The Amazon Power' were quickly churned out, all with the hope of emulating the success of earlier classics such as 'Demons of the Dead' and 'Satana'.

The last in the series, 'The Sea Claims She', was published in April 1976. It was wrapped up by She's ultimate assailant, Amazon, saying, 'Trigon, the Goddess of the Seas, I give thee She. Aahh. The sea!' The Shakespeare of the *skop, skiet en donder* genre? If only we knew the meaning of it all . . . And who was Trigon?

In retrospect, though, one could say that She was in the same league as Superman, Batman, Spiderman, Samson and all those other muscular, God-playing men who suffer from an inherent need to rescue endangered children, vulnerable women and frail pensioners — in short, the world.

But the success of *She* didn't mean a triumph for the muted feminism then brewing in black communities. Like any salaried entertainer, Mhlongo was subject to the whims of her creators — who were mostly booze-guzzling, Afrikaans-speaking men. Hence the emphasis on her photogenic body and spectacular kung fu kicks.

In these Missy Elliot days, feminism frowns on gender-reversal stereotypes of egotistical male icons. This is not what women's lib is supposed to entail. Yet the irony is that when She was at her peak, we all loved her. When not wishing for her affection, we hoped — in our little dark corners — for her protection. That simple. The sort of allure that makes for an enduring fictional hero.

For almost five years in the role, Mhlongo carried these expectations gallantly. That is, until the hot fumes of booze, ceaseless public attention and her desire for never-ending fun got to her.

'With all her troubles and passionately detached behaviour, she could have been dead inside for some time,' one of her closet full of ex-lovers would later confide to me. 'But her descent down the celebrity hill went on fast-forward after she stopped playing She.'

Word is, shortly after her celebrity starship arrived ashore wrecked — years of internalising pain, fast life, life of illusions, in which she starred — booze dashed in to claim her life.

But who was she? What do we know of her soul, her beliefs? What happened to her, and why? Well, that's why we are in the lava-hot streets of Durban. Our first stop is E 281 Mnyamana Street, KwaMashu — the home of South Africa's oldest playwrights and theatre couple, Alfred and Patty Nokwe.

'What, She? Ooh, Linda!' Alfred Nokwe exclaims. 'Of course I remember her, like I am certain the sun will rise tomorrow,' he recalls in his showbizzy, impress-the-stranger manner. 'What a looker! Mmmh, yeah. She was beautiful. Had a great smile, which she had a knack of unleashing in a manner that was meant to suggest she was both in control and, depending on who you were, ready for the taking. We also nicknamed her 'shape' — please don't ask me why!

'Our wives felt uncomfortable around her — should I say it on record, Patty? We called her 'Satana', a rather double-edged reference. Satana was the name of one of her picture-book characters, but also, back then, township folk referred to her as *uSatane* — Devil — a street affectionate term similar to the African-American "bad".

Nokwe remembers that Mhlongo drank like a fish and kicked like a mule. 'She misbehaved when in that element and of course men in her life played second fiddle. For some reason she had a thing for timid blokes, but even the bolshiest were soon domesticated by her wild spirit.'

What happened to her?

'Honestly, I never thought of that before you asked. What happened? I don't know. She just left. Nobody seems to remember her at all. Gee, that's strange, huh?'

However, Nokwe could point us to where Mhlongo lived in the 1970s. Number 4463 Ntombela Street, KwaMashu, is your typical township matchbox

— just like Verwoerd had wished the townships would be. A barefoot, yellow-skinned, thick-set woman with bright eyes refused to open the door and instead released a piercing call to her husband.

'Hello, sir. Do you know Linda? Linda Mhlongo? She?'

'I have never heard of her. Who's she?' asked the present owner. It seems Mhlongo had moved out long ago and seven or so families have occupied the house since.

Perhaps one of Mhlongo's old flames would shed some light. Papa Lawrence Mkhonza is initially reluctant to talk; he protests a tad too much. 'No man, she was married to some chap called Sandile Jack. I was only a friend, I mean, you know what that means, just a friend.' After I give him a few reassuring glances and drop a few golden oldies' names he recognises, the old man, now 69, uncoils.

'She was a very independent woman, even back then. I mean, it's been almost 30 years, right? Linda had transcended all the barriers women were subjected to. She was far ahead of her time. Just like women of today. She made lots of money acting in her picture series, but drained it all on the bottle.

'I told her, listen here, this booze will dig your grave, *en sy wou nie luister nie* [and she wouldn't listen]. Cheeky *cherrie, daai*. Still, compared to today's women, say the Boom Shaka girls, Mhlongo was much more decent. Though she radiated confidence, she was not as brash, uncultured and look-at-me arrogant as, what's the other one's name? Brenda Fast. Fassie.'

'She was like a bulb around which men and women mothed. When drunk she would kick the refrigerator's door with her pointed boots, "*a ungi nig'u biya*, sweerie."'

And then? Zip! Mkhonza doesn't have much to say other than that Mhlongo just disappeared out of public life. Was she shot? Stabbed? Did some jealous woman empty a boiling pot on her and drag her into the bushes? 'I just told you, I have no idea. She just vanished,' says Mkhonza. That she's long-dead is generally agreed.

She

But when did she die? Nobody knows. Theories abound. Some say in the 1980s; some say the 1990s; some say back in 1977. However, Sol Rachilo, a 1960s and 1970s man-about-town, record-shop owner and fellow actor, maintains: 'Go to Durban, rake the whole of it and you will find her there.'

In Durban, old men in Havana Stetsons talk in coded tongues, women whisper hish-hushingly. All agree though, that she died in a death befitting the woman of her type — she was driving with another woman's husband. I wish to respect the dead and never speak ill about them — but something tells me she wouldn't have minded tabloiding in that little bit about her final count down. But rumour persists . . . nobody really knows what happened to She.

The fact that nobody seems to know or care what had happened to her adds an air of mystery to the story.

'Oh yeah, I used to love her so much,' says world music star Victoria Busi Mhlongo, no relation. 'She took care of me when I arrived in Johannesburg in the 1960s. She loved fun but she was the most selfless person I met in the big city. She was a talented woman. I don't know what happened to her, but I suspect she went home. Though she was Zulu, Linda was from Joburg. I was young then, but I remember that.'

Mkhonza disagrees. 'Johannesburg? Which Jo'burg? Linda was from Clermont, one of the townships in Durban.'

Not at all, says Nokwe, 'Linda settled in Durban, straight from Johannesburg. I remember she was always anxious and secretive about something. It felt like she ran away from something terrible in Johannesburg after she appeared in *King Kong*. Even with that ocean-wide grin of hers, it was clear she hid secrets.'

Even people once close to her — such as actor Pepsi Nkosi, now 70 — swear by their ancestors that Mhlongo was a Durbanite. 'I can't remember . . .' Nkosi tries to think. 'Possibly Clermont, Durban. What I remember is, she died and was buried in Durban soon after *She* was discontinued.'

And so the yo-yo of Mhlongo's story swings between the sin city,

Johannesburg, and that furnace-like seaside town, Durban.

How old was she when she died? No one is telling. Some resort to clichés and say Mhlongo lived her life like a candle in the wind; that she died young and left a beautiful corpse. Others swear she trotted on till she was in her 50s; until her once-beautiful legs couldn't carry her anymore.

As far as show-business lore goes, Mhlongo's vanishing act is a pretty peculiar affair. Not even the migration of Meadowlands composer Nancy Jacobs in the 1970s from the big city and headlines to a monk's life in the Eastern Cape comes close to Mhlongo's disappearance. She appeared to have simply evaporated, with the only consensus being that she's long-dead. Where and how, you have to crack a rock to get an answer.

How could a woman whose wildly popular picture-book character had both men and women fawning around her pointed boots vanish from public memory so easily, as if She never existed?

I vow to keep a vigil. Perhaps She will turn up tomorrow, just like the King. Or maybe not . . . Surely there must be somebody who can lead me to her grave, where, by luck, one of her lovers would have inscribed: 'She fought like a tiger and made love like a wild spirit. She was a dream. You're looking for a ghost.'

Life is goin' on till when?

Sunninghill Private Clinic, where Brenda Fassie has being fighting for her life and orchestrating — by tabloidished osmosis — a hurricane of media headlines, is abuzz with media hounds, promoters, hangers-on, fans, voyeurs, stargazers and well-wishers as I arrived. Outside Brenda's ward, I'm part of a small band of close-but-not-close-enough friends.

This means I'm allowed onto her floor but not into her ward. An elderly woman I recognise by her lustrous 1960s wig as one of the several 'aunties' Brenda had in Yeoville, sis Yvonne, walks out of the ward — rivulets of tears streaming down her face — to share with us: 'She . . . she moved her fingers!'

Elated, we want to roar with happiness, but 'hey, no party time here, you can't even raise your voice' the security guard reminds us. 'This is the ICU, the closest to where death and angels reside. Please people. Show some respect.'

'Wow!' I think. 'Security guards gripped by poetic seizures?' Only Brenda could get that right.

In the two weeks before she finally dies, Brenda lies motionless in the Sunninghill Hospital. We, participants in her lifelong drama, pace the halls. Any news of her is devoured. Brenda, true to form, slips in and out of death, and in and out of the headlines, with the swiftness we've come to expect from her.

From the minute she is wheeled into the private hospital's Intensive Care Unit to minutes before she dies, Brenda owns the media. Hanging on through the forces of expensive life-support machines, her ancestors' spiritual strength, her family's prayers and her fans' tears, Queen Bee manages to chalk up the most extensive media coverage in the history of South Africa's pop culture.

Of all the well-wishers, the most consistent is Nomzamo Winnie Mandela, who — besides being Brenda's equal in headline hogging — has also been Brenda's foster mother for the past decade. It was Winnie who took the then spiralling-out-of-control young woman into her own malfunctioning but cohesive family home in Orlando, Soweto.

It was she who tutored the delinquent pop star on the joys of motherhood and the dangers of being 'mother of the nation' when one didn't have enough time to mother one's own family. It was she who offered counsel. And it is she who stays, day and night, next to Brenda's deathbed, praying to her ancestors to 'please spare the child, *nina ba ka Dhlomo*'.

After 14 days of high drama, at 4.50pm on Sunday, 9 May 2004, the Queen calls it quits. Her record company of over 20 years, for whom she had recorded over 15 albums, over 150 songs and over 10 000 hours of her childlike, overwrought, drug- and beer-strained voice, issues a statement: 'A hero has fallen.'

A hero? What does that mean?

Brenda Fassie came like a typhoon, and departed like Halley's comet. That natural. That strange. That wild. The first township wonder to defy South Africa's parochialism, Brenda belonged to the constellation of tragic black musical stars immortalised by Billie Holiday, Tupac Shakur and Miles Davis.

Though she evoked the troubled African diva / diviner / perfomer pain, her larger-than-life legacy was not a race thang but a pop thang. Brenda was a troubled spirit, just like Princess Diana, James Dean and Elvis Presley. And like Billie Holiday before her, her lust for life, mood swings, childlike voice, mutually abusive love affairs and financial woes made her an explosive minefield waiting to go bang at any moment.

Publicity was like oxygen to her. At the age of four, Brenda was lead singer and dancer in Tiny Tots, a group who made a big name for themselves in Cape Town under the tutelage of Sarah Fassie, a woman Brenda knew as her mother, but about whom she said, 'There are controversies about whether she was my real mother or not. For the sake of the media records, I will say she was my mom, right?' Right.

'Whatever you wish for, B', I told her. Either way, at the age of 14, Brenda went in search of the greener — albeit neon-lit — pastures of Jo'burg, the Vegas of Africa. Just four years later, her hit 'Weekend Special' made her the first local act ever to make it to Billboard's Top 100.

'Weekend Special' was written by Melvyn Matthews, the key to her success as a hit-maker. I finally corner Melvyn at Brenda's memorial service in Soweto, a week before she is cremated. Matthews has been off the scene for 20 years. Too emotional for comfort, I switch on the tape and let him talk: 'I taught Brenda the lyrics and worked with her, verse for verse.

She had difficulty pronouncing English and cut corners quite a lot. She sang in her Xhosa-lised English, tinged with clicks. But her passion made up for everything. Even at that age [18] she was an emotional artist who would turn any song into a Brenda song. She has feeling, timing, melody, heart and rhythm. She lifted my lyrics to a chaotic beauty I had never imagined.'

The single became a radio and club hit long before it was released as an LP, and Matthews — then just a 17-year-old teenager himself — made sure she had another hit to go with it. 'Life is Goin' On', a gospel-like tune dipped in the blues, is what made Brenda a megastar.

Dragging and slurring her sometimes tenor, sometimes falsetto on 'Life is

Goin' On', Brenda's voice reflected a tortured soul. *The Sowetan's* powerful showbiz editor, Elliot Makhaya, gushed: 'A star has been born.' That song alone elevated Brenda to a select group of the world's most evocative female blues singers — Dolly, Aretha, Billie.

Matthews' songs may have assured her fame, but Brenda's talent had been spotted long before — by Anneline Malebo. Known as Sis' Anneline, Malebo (who died on 20 August 2002, two years after being diagnosed with HIV) was leader of Afro-pop band Joy, when she gave Brenda a kick into the big time. In 1979, Malebo was about to go on maternity leave, so she roped in the 18-year-old girl-child to take her place.

With Brenda, Joy released 'Paradise Road', a sing-along rhythm-and-gospel smasher that topped the charts and instantly transformed Joy into an object of both ridicule and obsessive affection.

Black urban sophisticates adored 'Paradise Road' for its pure soul, yet despised it for sounding so 'un-African', and whites wanted to despise it and couldn't help falling for it. But everyone started wondering, 'Who's that singer?'

Back to 1984, and the release of 'Life is Goin' On'. The year poet Dambudzo Marechera would refer to as the 'mid-point of the scream'. Black consciousness brothers in black berets held the moral ground on the streets, but Brenda was starting to rule the waves.

In the wake of her hit debut album, Brenda and The Big Dudes — comprising of pianist Dumisani Ngobeni (who would father Brenda's only child, Bongani), bassist Sammy Klaas and drummer David Mabaso — set about launching the loudest pop revue of all time. It would last over a decade.

Their work was studded with unforgettable hits, but was also weighed down with mediocre commercial tracks articulating the emptiness of the townships. But when Chicco Twala produced 'Too Late for Mama', an Afro-feminist dance manifesto promoted by a video clip depicting African rural women's struggle and hope, Brenda's mournful chorus moved her to another level.

This song forged a new signature style for her and audiences were introduced to a combative but teary Brenda — a side of the pop star the dives and dodges of Hillbrow were becoming increasingly familiar with.

By 1989, Hillbrow had shed its 1960s white bohemia and 1970s superfly character. Five years after it was declared a 'grey' area, Hillbrow was anything but. A collage of pink, pitch black, yellow and brown people from the Cape to Kuala Lumpur had made it their home. Large residential blocks were taken over by streams of black middle-class people, artists, fashion and hair stylists, fresh-out-of-the-closet black gays and township intellectuals.

Although she owned a mansion in Fleurhof, MaBrrr also owned an apartment in Century Plaza, then one of Hillbrow's most happening spots.

Meanwhile, back in the townships, Brenda's new single, *'Ngiya Kusaba'* ['My Friend U Dangerous'] — a slick rip-off of a US disco hit — beckoned all hedonists and clubbers to come get down. In tacky, groovy, California black polyester bell-bottoms, knee-length boots, a red Afro wig and a rainbow of sequins, Brenda cultivated an empty image consistent with her hot single. On the outside, the party girl was having a blast. She had just left an abusive marriage to Nhlanhla Mbambo, son of a Durban tycoon, and once again she was ready to rock.

Century Plaza was known not only for the musicians who lived there, but also as the epicentre of free expression, style, upward mobility and Jozi's black gays. Jenny Mkhize, now living in Paris, was there at the time: 'It was a combination of 1970s Soweto and designer-obsessed Paris, right in Africa. The exhibitionist gay brigade dripped charm, ruled the style wars, partied hard and ventured deep into the unknown.

'There was a lot of incestuous bonking going on, y'know? Wine, big guys, cross-gender orgies and more orgies. At the same time, there was a beautiful sisterhood there, shared dreams, bashed dreams . . . we were all connected by that inexplicable glue: the artists' desire to live freely, as if every day is the last. Lesbians were bedding gay boys, gay boys were stealing each other's partners. There was a boy called Goofy — he allegedly died of AIDS complications in 2002.'

'Through it all, I remember Fassie as the rock goddess: the loudest and most stylish of the bunch. Even if we didn't see eye to eye, I admired how selfless she was. She was many things in one — a very possessive lover and a giving person. At the time, she was seeing my friend Victoria Sihlahla (Poppy), the most beautiful woman in the gang. Naturally, Queen Bee was jealous as hell.'

'Both women and men vied for Queen Bee's attention,' remembers Oscar Tyumre, a musician and one of Brenda's closest friends. 'Once, while she was dating a woman called Buli Arosi, she was also seeing one of her dancers Ludwe Maki — though not in public. It wasn't that she was promiscuous. She dated Ludwe because her girlfriend had double-crossed her with him. So she says, "Aha? Well, let's play this game. By my rules." She had both of them.'

Though both Mkhize and Tyumre refuse to comment on this, it was also at this time Brenda started serious drugging. By the mid-1990s, the Quirinale Hotel in Hillbrow's Kotze Street was not only the scene of degenerate clubbing, but also a meeting spot for the notorious CBB [Civil Co-operation Bureau] operatives such as Slang Van Zyl, Staal Burger, Ferdie Barnard and co. — which meant drugs, guns, prostitutes and gore galore.

In no time, crack cocaine replaced heroin and dagga as the drug of choice for those who could afford it. Her stream of hits ensured Brenda could definitely afford it. Interestingly, for all their high-flying debauchery, the majority of the gay brigade was not on drugs. In retrospect, Brenda's friends say drugs created a chasm between the Queen and her true friends.

'She had nothing but Poppy and her haunted voice,' says Tyumre. 'She lost weight, lost her friends, lost her money and lost trust. The joy of the late 1980s turned to despair. By 1993 her ship had begun to sink. It's amazing that it took ten years to hit rock bottom. What a pity. What a talent.'

It's 1998, and away from the media spotlight, Brenda has just finished recording a new demo, produced in collaboration with Chicco Twala. The name is not yet finalised: *Vuli Ndlela* or *Memeza*? *Memeza* wins.

She plays me the whole eight-track session over and over again while a group of street kids choreographing performs the kind of energetic, Afro-pelvic moves I haven't seen since Michael Jackson did the Moonwalk.

'So you moonlight as Nureyev when you're not singing?' I tease her. She doesn't know who Rudolf Nureyev is, and doesn't care. The others leave. I go back to listen to the rough tapes again. From the opening cut to the last, her voice leaks emotion. She cries, hums, whispers, screams, moans. I jerk out of my chair, hiding my tears.

'Why do you perform libations for your ancestors on a pop record? And by the way,' I say, 'that's the most beautiful music you have ever sung in one album.' She is so vulnerable.

'Should I release this?' she asks. 'Tell me. Will it sink like *Paparazzi*?' There and then, I feel the risk and rawness that comes with being a hit-maker.

'If South Africa is ready,' I think, 'this will be your biggest album ever.' But I say, 'I dunno, don't ask me.' I can't look at her. How do you tell your childhood star she's on the brink of releasing an album that will either bring the heavens down, or sink her and her 25 years of restless talent?

Three days later, that interview with Brenda was *Sunday Life's* cover story. It said, no flesh-and-blood person can emit such emotion and live her sort of life without a crash landing.

Memeza took off like five boeings all at once, 500 000 units — the biggest and fastest-selling album that year by far. The ANC used the lead hit '*Vuli Ndlela*' as their 1999 general-elections theme song.

Two weeks later, I produced an exclusive hour-long radio documentary on her 25-year career with Metro FM DJ Evidence Kemp. Brenda kept going to the rest room during the interview, each time coming back more animated than the last. But when she wasn't pulling faces at Kemp, or singing, she was sharper than an abattoir's knife.

No question was too heavy or too small. She meditated on some and volunteered on others. She cried when a sobbing fan called in the middle of the interview just to say, 'I love you.' Brenda, live, was explosive.

A year after Memeza adjusted the local pop scene's scales, selling 600 000 albums, Brenda released *Nomakanjani*. It was monotonous and predictable. I'd listened to this woman for over 20 years and with this album I could tell her voice was kaput. Brenda had lost her natural timbre. What she still packed in abundance was that compelling gift for telling stories, a touch for acting, a feel for the absurd and an inherent ability to please. But it was not enough.

It is 5.30am, 16 May 2004, when Fidel Mbhele, a young Mother City-based hack, knocks on Room 718, Victoria Junction Hotel. '*Ndoda* – hey dude – you still dreaming of MaBrrr? She's gone, man, wake up!' It's time to drive to Langa before the funeral traffic jam starts.

At 6am we are on the road to Langa and, as Jack Kerouac said, 'Nothing beats the smell, the junk, the acceleration, the madness of it.' Cape Town is all white, thanks to the morning fog. Mbhele complains, 'It has never been like this before.' We hit the hooter and the lights, and plunge through nonetheless.

The roads and back alley leading to Langa are decorated with posters of MaBrrr. They group, disband and regroup into a continuous collage of her face. number 26 Makana Square in Langa stands out because it's one of those extended face-brick homesteads in a tight chain of township matchbox-dwellings. Today it stands out because its last-born child is back home after a 25-year public journey.

Two hours later, there's nowhere to walk in the small yard. Two priests in their nicely pressed frocks look on in suppressed irritation as a Xhosa poet in Afro-regal attire attempts to steal his two seconds of fame by reciting right into the middle of a prayer. Queen Bee would have been proud.

Back in the early 1980s, far away on the other side of the world, paranoid and cocaine-crazed soul-singer Marvin Gaye asked the question, 'What's Goin' On?' and from Africa Brenda responded, 'Life is Goin' On'.

'Tis.

Mirror mirror on the wall

Over half a century ago, when jazz was as streety as hip-hop and blues as preachy as conscious hip-hop is today, an off-the-beaten-track fanzine, going by a 'made-to-rhyme with hillbilly' pretentious title, *Memphis Blue*, quoted a young bebop enthusiast, who said she'd cried her throat sore 'pon hearing news of bebop king, Charlie 'YardBird' Parker's death'.

Musical genius, Parker, or simply Bird, the epitome of bohemian chic, self-destruction and the spiritual existentialism that blacks are supposed to possess in a high degree had kicked the bucket at 35 – 11 years younger than his huge fan, Jack Kerouac. Both checked out of this world and took their final road trip after relentless substance abuse and wasted genius.

Now our devastated friend here – let's call her Blonde X, the bebop fanatic – had histrionics by the bucket-load.

In addition to her wail fest after Charlie Parker's death, she swore by her ancestors that she'd witnessed this *wunnerful* sight – it rained backwards. Raindrops seemed to be heading skywards while she heard Bird's saxophone burstin' through fro' the back, piercing though the wind that accompanied those light showers.

Not too original this 'fan'-atic. How many stories did we hear of how the weather changed course on the day of Robert Johnson's death? Anyway . . .

. . . Rain. Myths. Tears. Drama. Musical celebrity cult fetish and undertones of sexuality; a young white girl whose emotions were stripped naked by 'promiscuous black jazz infidels'. It's spooky, no?

Well if you're spooked out, then there's a long way you gotta go through, to understand the web-like artery of myth that maketh the world and the underworld of show business, especially as it relates to how you, the fan, relates to it. Tonight, as I am writing, the weather is uncharitable. It's Halloween-dark and, believe it or not, it's raining. Backwards?

Mmhh, 't feels like . . . but y' see, not all us showbiz congregates are into hallucinogens.

Raining downwards or sideways, the atmosphere feels like a dark trance 'n' funk soundtrack, as a variety of the annual, spring-time, Arts Alive Fest' acts annexes downtown Jozi — SA's capital chocolate city's arts district.

History is writing itself at the Turbine Hall — once a colony for the city's subterraneans going by such names as Prince-of-Thugs and Ras-2000, the homeless, ganja dealers and all those who rise to life as the rest of us go to bed.

The Turbine, now a revamped industrial-meets-Afro Renaissance chic space, is hosting Arts Alive's *Tribute to Anneline Malebo*, featuring the haunting and haunted Aura Msimang, young guns such as Gloria Bosman and Miriam Makeba's buddy in the SkyLarks, the 50s blues hipster, Thandi Mpambani (otherwise known as Thandi Klaasen).

Now what has this *Tribute to Anneline* got to do with Brenda Fassie, let alone spooky notions of surrealist rain, musical iconoclasm, overwrought fans and the narrative of drugs, sex and rock 'n' roll? Everything!

Like the well-worn tales of Berry Gordy and Lil' Steveland Morris, Michael Jackson and Diana Ross, Elvis and Sam Cooke, and other long tales of star scouts and their child would-be larger-than-lifes, there cannot be a comprehensive understanding of Brenda Fassie — South Africa and the continent's supreme pop rock star, her ever-childlike dependency traits and the abuse of vulnerability to serve the vulnerable — without mentioning the name Anneline Malebo.

Malebo, who would later be 'Pac's mom, Afeni's and Winnie Mandela's arts-activist buddy, is the glue that binds the Fassie myth and reality into a discernible linear biography in a manner that's easy to miss, but impossible to dismiss. Known as sis' Anneline, Malebo, who passed away the very day this piece was assigned — on 20 August 2002, two years after being diagnosed with HIV — gave Brenda a thrust kick into the big time, when she (Anneline) was leader of Afro-soul and pop band, Joy.

Made up of three supremely talented women: the Indian Mulatto mix-bred Felicia Marion; from Bosmont, the so-called 'Coloured Township' — 'Coloured' in SA is not the same as 'black in the US' — hoarse-voiced Malebo from Gugulethu on the Cape Flats; and Thoko Ndlozi from Dube, Soweto — Joy sat at the top of the country's hit charts and resided in magazine headlines long before the pop machine invented Destiny's Child or the Spice Girls.

Almost perfect products of the American Negro soul music template that produced The Supremes, The Vandellas, The Staple Singers and En Vogue, with lustrous, silky hairdos — like those on 70s earthy sepia-toned hair-straightening cream boxes — sequinned frocks and voices to-die-for, Joy was the outfit both black and white South African urbanites loved to hate, but couldn't switch off the radio.

In the spring of 1979, the group — fresh from a couple of karaoke-kitsch and cabaret performance hits — prepared themselves to launch the most divastating assault on South African show business with the melodically-arresting soul cut 'Paradise Road', penned by Patrieck van Blerck.

Van Blerck — Zomba's multi-millionaire Clive Calder's contemporary and competition in 70s Johannesburg music scene — had earlier played a role in endearing the Afro-wigged Margarett Singana to the white radio listenership, with a series of powerful, but saccharine still, non-black pop ditties.

Not untypical of pattern-loving scouts, dear Van Blerck would not rest till he'd scored another cross-over hit, this time with a sexy trio Joy, devoid of the prevalent late 70s black politics.

'T'was 19 months after 'they' since assassinated Steven Biko in a freak accident preceded by the police's torture and interrogation session.

Out there in the Bantustans, Sin City, err, Sun City had just become deepest Africa's own Las Vegas gambling heaven. Even the temptress, original dirty rapper Millie Jackson, ignored the blues rapper Gil Scott-Heron's 'Ain't No playin' Sun City' call, to scream-out her famous line 'git down on yer' knees and par-tay' — Live in Sun City! before issuing a lame apology for breaking the cultural boycott on South Africa in the early 80s.

It was in this climate that Joy's Malebo — then about to go on maternity leave — roped in a 17-year-old girl-child fresh from bunking school, in the then already star-studded Joy. Veteran impresarios; Gibson Kente, father of township theatre, a quarter of a century before Sarafina, and the Ray Charles' self-styled super scout Koloi Lebona, through whose hands the then still-raw Brenda passed before she aced her way in, have observed: 'that kid's destiny was written long before she arrived at it'.

'South Africa had never seen anything like her before and [has seen] nothing like her since. Brenda was so talented it hurt just to think of the brutalities of the music biz that awaited her in this unforgiving industry,' they reminisced, when asked what attracted them to Brenda Fassie — the then unpruned yet uncontainable and talented voice.

The teen star gave the other band members a run for their money and at the same time captivated soul and pop fans — black and white, young and old.

Recently, Brenda and a fellow band member (drummer David Mabaso) showed me the very spot where she'd auditioned for Joy 25 years ago in Steeldale, Johannesburg, HQ of CCP– Clive Calder Productions!

'I was so scared. But I knew my moment had arrived,' she remembered, flushed with nostalgia.

Journalist, biographer, playwright and 1950s slum cities blues historian

Mothobi Mutloatse remembers her as a 'fat, short and not-too-pretty teenager with pimples and a voice to shake angels from their heavenly comfort zones. Still, there was no mistaking her raw stealth and wretched emotional orientation.'

Joy threw Brenda into showbiz orbit, but you don't become the next biggest thing just by showing up raw and emotionally naked. What happened after Joy depends on who you talk to.

Scout and now Zomba's South African representative, producer Koloi insists that Brenda went solo, while others counter that she hopped off to join *Papa and Blondie*.

Influenced by the androgynous icon; Sylvester's high glamour disco, and emotional rapport with his audience — pre-Wacko Jacko's 'Don't Stop till You Get Enough' era– *Papa and Blondie* was the most popular township revue of it's era, sweeping away its Abba, *Grease* and *Saturday Night Fever* punch-drunk audience.

In a hospital bed two months ago, Brenda herself remembered the time. 'I went into a series of bands, meeting some of the greatest acts, like Harari and Ray Phiri's Cannibals, acts that would define post-World War II South Africa's black urban sound.' She also worked with Blondie's family sidekick project, *Spank* and gigged around with a battery of other 'it bands' — soul and Afro-rock outfits of the time.

Meanwhile, across the North Atlantic, Black America was recovering from late 60s and early 70's assault of soul, doo-wop, electronic jazz-rock hybrid and scattered riots of funk as represented by P-Funk, George Clinton, Sly and The Family Stone, Bootsy and Parliament. Far from the un-holly woods, Pam Grier was still alternating b'tween being *Sheba Baby* and *Foxy Brown* while still kickin' somebody else's son's ass in *Coffy*.

Down southernmost mother Africa, the tail-end of the riot filled early 1980s, presented a ripe opportunity for a new township sound. Characterised by political fear, raw energy and a new self black pride assertion moulded on the African-American (then known as negro) entertainers soul music revolution, the setting providing a perfect canvass for Brenda and her breakaway combo, The Big Dudes — made of pianist keyboardist Dumisani Ngobeni, bassist Sammy Klaasen and drummer Dave Mabaso — to launch about the loudest, most colourful pop revue of all time. It was like George Clinton, Bootsy, Maceo, had teamed with Donna Summer and decamped down south - the muthaland.

The whole music, art, tears, sex, drugs and rock 'n' roll touring and roaring omnibus lasted over a decade, with Queen B in the saddle. But the crown was there for the taking.

Five years after she diced our hearts with her theatrical performances that blurred the line 'tween lust and music, when urban South Africa thought it was shock-proof, what with all the blood flowing in the Reef riots . . . Boom! A starry-eyed, staggeringly beautiful girl from a religious Chiawelo, Soweto, family, Yvonne Machaka rushed on to the scene to give what remains the sexiest, most sexually provocative dance performance of the century, in Regina Mundi, Soweto.

By then known as Chaka-Chaka, after disco-house star, Sharon Red's high hat and percussion-filled music popular in the townships then, young Yvonne was captured in the country's prime national daily *The Sowetan* with only a few centimetres of her upper thighs unexposed — her crotch down lo' — with a life-sized painting of Jesus Christ looking on, unsmiling, from behind.

From then on, though she would have liked us to believe otherwise, the drama shock-queen Her Majesty, was terrified of this new competition. Things were to get quite to dizzying heightened by a young upstart from the Eastern Cape, Mercy Pakela's moves to snatch away the title, 'Queen of Pantsulas'. Business began to heat up from there, turning Brenda into a prowling and nasty cheetah. The rest, as showbiz parlance puts it, is *herstory*.

Brenda and The Big Dudes released their debut album *Weekend Special* in 1982. Besides the title track, a scintillating pop feminist dance hit, it featured probably the most underrated soul classic in modern pop, 'Life Is Goin' On'. Brenda poured her soul with unmitigated hurt into 'Life is Goin' On' draggin' and slurring her sometimes tenor, oft' whisper, muted scream, blended in a neo-pop blues ballad powered by a spiritual nakedness unheard on wax since Hugh Masekela's funereal 'Bo Masekela', 'Aretha Franklin's version of 'Bridge Over Troubled Water', Santana's 'Abraxas', and Righteouss Bros' 'Unchained Melody'.

We are talking long before Mary J Blige, and later Alicia Keys would re-channel something of Brenda's soul fire, in faraway America, 20 years after her debut. No, they didn't know each other: the missing jigsaw puzzle piece that bound the souls of all these women is, and was, the voice.

Fassie's steam train was rolling, and all of you were going to love her or resign yourselves to watching a young woman reshape South Africa's popular music and the overall popular culture, singlehandedly, for the next two decades. At her peak, Brenda released township-slayin songs such as 'Yo! Baby' - long before Jah Rule learned to holler 'Yo, mah niggah' — and 'Zola Budd'.

For the better part of the 80s her work was heavily weighed with mediocre commercial hits, which managed to reflect the townships' emptiness in that decade. It would take a song, 'Too Late for Mama' — a sonic feast of emotions, Afro-communal feminist charter and introspection — to restore her to the top of the charts and ink her name deep in her fans' hearts forever.

Like all the beloved-pop culture icons — Mandela, Muhammad Ali, Fela, Billie Holiday, Winnie Mandela, Aretha, Michael Jackson, Tupac and now Lauryn Hill — Brenda's essence lies in her unguardedness that leaves her both a victim and a conqueror: one of the unlucky, worshipped, surreal yet real flesh-and-blood people.

Those such as *Time* magazine, who will not give up comparing Brenda to Madonna, are annoyingly naive. Of course, like Madonna, Brenda is a magnet for trouble and the media. Both became famous by blending urban recklessness with plastic entertainment and its diet of sex, drugs and rock 'n' roll.

The difference between the two went beyond the difference in style: both clearly were pop tarts, and yet insofar as their choice of lovers, they couldn't have been more chalk and cheese. While Madonna chose the violent but talented Hollywood drunkard Sean Penn as her first husband, Brenda married a terribly handsome young Durban tycoon with Dodi Al Fayed-like insider clout and royal-wannabe sensibilities, Nhlanhla Mbambo.

Mbambo was as striking in looks as he was in his robust and abusive attitude towards his more famous wife, ten years his senior. She appeared on glossy mags' covers with scarves hiding her wounds. They divorced after less than a year — just like Madonna and Penn — and Brenda never married again. Her lesbian trysts are legendary, but the media has been grossly unfair to Brenda as a performer and as a symbol of rebellion.

No doubt, her outlandish open sexuality and sexual expression attracted the attention of African male critics who hated Brenda's hold over their imaginations. In her presence they'd forsaken the art of applying their ears and minds on her art, and instead settled their gaze on her pelvic politics. In that sense she diverted their attention to sex.

Hence, they could not reconcile themselves with their responsibilities to inform, to their averted gaze into the sexual expression of a young black woman whose sexual freedom, pop cultural iconoclasm, outlandish success, meant she was unattainable to them.

To many women journalists, and womenfolk in general, she symbolised both a pop witch and a liberator; the city slicker / voodoo woman dialectic, no decent woman should emulate — yet, also a wayward or warrior sister who voiced and acted out their deepest wishes and dreams. A woman they silently envied and publicly condemned — simply because African patriarchy deemed her behaviour ' . . . a witches and bitches brew'!

Thus, it is no wonder that to the mainstream tribal neo-conservative Africans in the pop media, and the placid, white middle South Africa which never anticipated Africans — especially black women to express themselves out of their assigned boxes — cages? — Brenda became urban South Africa's numero uno 'ho!'

Still, comparing her to Madonna was taking things outa the camp, really. She never copied Madonna nor did she nurse ambitions of being a black

Madonna — though that did not stop comparisons from reaching a sickening if not hilarious peak, when a local magazine plagiarised a Madonna interview from *Newsweek*, replaying the Q & A as a Brenda interview.

The Madonna parallel is so historically problematic and lazy-assed. Rather, Brenda's star quality can be traced to a long line of South African ragtag, jazz and blues divas and anti-divas whose controversial love affairs and stage theatrics would have made her look like, well, maybe not quite a nun . . .

The 50s oh-so-chic model and actress, Dotty Tiyo — who defied the Immorality Act by bedding white film director Bevil John Rudd — as well as South Africa's first black cover gal Dolly Rathebe, were far raunchier and more provocative and street knife fighters to boot.

Sofiatown; South Africa's '50s Bad-Bad Ass' songstresses. Long before Brenda was born and longer still before she would pen her lament 'I'm not a Bad Gal'.

Writing a biographical profile of blues and pop vocally coarse and sexually coarser Dolly Rathebe, *Drum's* New Journalism writer Can Themba captured her essence: 'even then she wanted men at her feel gazing in awed admiration. She wanted the limelight, the spotlight, the searchlight even, so long as she could stand there selling her wares in tuneful magic. She knew she had a husky voice that kindled in men's hearts strange desires.'

And, dear, oh dear, that was in 1953.

'I know I am sexy and realise how beautiful it is to be an African. I am hot, America can't handle me,' Brenda sounded repeatedly to *Time* magazine's Desa Philadelphia in the magazine's international music special issue in December 2001.

But a lot of the time, Brenda couldn't handle it either. The period between between 1989 and 1994 saw her and other '80's pop stars fading away, first caught in the Long Walk to Freedom of Mandela's political relief-victory-hysteria, second, in the new challenges the country had to ponder. Artistic idleness offers a perfect setting for drugs.

Lately, she has lapsed again into self-destruction, to the apparent satisfaction of her manager — 80s pop friend, father figure and self-styled saviour, Sello

'Chicco' Twala– who invited the media to witnesses him carrying, like a baby, a teary Brenda to a rehabilitation centre.

They lapped it up, except for supermarket tabloid- *Sunday World's* leading bull terrier Charles Molele.

In a piece titled 'Run Too Fast, Fly Too High', he chastised Twala for behaving like 'a saviour'. Like his *Sunday Times* predecessor 20 years previously, Janie Allen (she who found Brenda talentless, with a face 'as ugly as a horse'), Molele wrote that "Weekend Special" was not only the making of Brenda but the breaking other as well.

'She stole her friend Deborah Fraser's voice, abused herself thinking we will spend our pity on her.

'I have no time for this weakling. Her manager has to baby her until she is 60! I really feel sad for her son, the Little Lord Fauntleroy, Bongani, who has grown up under all her siege. It's terrible.'

Ouch.

Brenda's close friend and sometimes-mentor, jazz musician and show promoter Fitzroy Ngcukane shared a sad story about her rehab blues as well as her abusively dependent relationship with Twala: 'That man is not good for her,' he wasted no time telling me.

'It's sad, even Hugh Masekela's rehab centre turned her down, citing her bad reputation. Hugh told me, he wants nothing to do with her. She seems to have made a mockery of the word "rehab".'

To the prophet, seer and African scientist Credo Mutwa, 'Brenda is just a victim of a hugely terrible show business industry that reduced black talent to waste. What's the use of a Western rehab? Brenda needs love and strength to pull herself out. It's a pity that we reduce our icons to nothing in times they need us most.'

Something weird happened a week before the press wrote that Brenda was to get a break from the Kempton Park Recovery Centre, in transit after all, to Hugh Masekela's heralded clinic.

* * *

Boogawoo! Slap bang in the middle of Yeoville's Rockey Street, there she was, looking fresh and sober, eyes covered with her signature Diana Ross-style Wayfarer goggles and flanked by both of her lovers — 18-year-old Lumka and the trouble-prone Sindiwe Nkhambule whose beauty makes her a spitting replica of Queen B's late lover, Poppie Sihlahla. Brenda brushed right past me, as if I existed not.

Was this the woman who'd cried in my arms when she felt robbed at the SAMA awards? Wasn't she the star who'd unfolded her emotions to me, just two months before, about her cousin's suicide in jail? The friend with whom I'd prayed in hospital when she was admitted for a troublesome knee?

But nobody can accuse Brenda of putting on airs. She remains one of the few truly giving, honest icons, known to have treated the media and fans as if they were her aunts, cousins or even big brothers. I made a point of catching up with her at Jozi's own Time Square, Yeoville's gangsters and gay chic paradise, where you are likely to sight Brenda at her elemental best, fuelled by her shrilly joy luck club of gay buddies, giving her fans a free concert, backed only by an acoustic guitarist or some dreaded electric bass player. Y' thought Jimi Hendrix was dead? Head towards Yeoville, where he plays with this electric lady.

Friends might tell you that she's doing a Women's Day gig in the North West, but a Times Square regular will prod you to wait: 'She might turn up anytime. She lives here.'

At her new Sunninghill Mansion, Brenda's older sister, ex-musician Lindi, plays the role of bodyguard.

Brenda the headline fodder — I would learn amid caustic gushes of sobs and verbal assaults — causes her family pain. Yet they love her madly. Believe you me, this is not choreographed affection, I mean, they're not the Jackson Five family.

'Enough is enough', Lindi says. 'All of you should leave Brenda alone. How will she heal while you demonise her? Ag maaan, even if she's a star, Brenda is still human, my brutha, please understand! Oh Lawd of the high heavens: I am torn. Her big sister's appeal gets all too disturbing. I feel I should shoulder my fellow news-hounds' bloodlust.

But the family should know by now they won't get no *mea culpa* from the media. 'She's invited all this on herself, just like manipulative Princess Diana.' says one, while sis' Lindi's words drill a hole in me:

'See, Brenda has feelings too. How would you like it if your life was reported like this, day and night for 20 years? Tell me. . . tell me. . .'– unable to hold back her tears.

As for me, an outside observer, who fell for Brenda as a 14 year ol' — a one-night stand of musical revelation, Brenda's long countrywide small towns' schedule, when she appeared on the local townhall, clad in snow-white fur, knee-length boots, white tank top, hot-pants, and white pimp straw hat big as Cab Calloway's, eyes glazed red and voice soul-aching like a priest who has seen duty in Cambodia — she cooed, rocked, screamed, lullabied, and dared the men within the audience to get down on their knees with her on stage. 1984!

What did George Orwell say about this year? . . . Aas I wuz sayin', as an outside observer, who fell for Brenda almost two decades ago, I have no reason to doubt Brenda's recovery. Earlier in the year, when the state's PBS SABC 1's prime-time 7'o'clock Arts news anchor asked what I thought of her, I responded with a metaphor:

'She is South Africa's mirror, her constant rehab trips reflect our pathology. When she is in deep trouble, we share her pain. By baring her soul in public, she reassures us that we are not all that badly off. She reassures our frail ego and emotions that our families' blacksheeps; junkie pop and drama mommas, thug sons, rapist uncles, white-collar criminal accountants, the promiscuous pastor . . . the works - are not so bad, compared to this public villain, star and self-destructive icon.

'When she releases, once more another hit, like she did with 'Too Late for Mama', '*Memeza*' and '*Nomakanjani*'? and now her spiritually-laden latest festive scorcher '*Myekeleni*' — that translates into: Lever her damn alone! - we march en masse to the music bars to purchase the gospel according to Queen B.'

She is us, we are her . . . thing is this, our very mirror is foggy, we can't see ourselves in her, now can we?

Ain't no sunshine
when she's gone

'Over the years,' pop critic and Brenda Fassie enthusiast Charl Blignaut observed, 'I have come to realise that there is no way to write a Brenda interview without it being personal. That's because there is really no such thing as a "Brenda interview."'

You don't interview Brenda, Blignaut explained. 'You experience her. You could be the recipient of her venom or of her devoted attention. Most likely it'll be both.'

The words zig-zagged strangely down my spine: 'You could be the recipient of her devoted attention . . .' Some people are lucky. At least, however brief it may have been, they happened to be recipients of an icon's devoted attention.

Gazing back, my introduction to Brenda Fassie was wrought with admiration for her vocal power — the sort of spiritual admiration one reserved for gospel hymns — as well as troubling boyhood affections for the star.

It's the sort of affection all normal pre-teens and teenagers at one time or the other have harboured for, say, Elvis, Ali, Jimmy Dean and now Britney, Justin Timberlake, Mandoza and Thembi Seete's boobs.

It's in such innocent affection that the roots of my interest in Brenda the artist were planted.

This is — for me — how the 'Brenda experience' that Blignaut refers to panned out. Back in the summer of 1982 in Temba township, north of Pretoria, a big, black and beautiful woman with a township sex-symbol front-tooth gap, and a dark mole on her left cheek, eyes as alert and wide as a lion's, yet with a lazy leopard gait, was not only my mom's friend but her confidante. Her name was Ous Lizbeth.

The luxuriously furnished tin shack in which she lived with her husband, a dice gambler, Bra Phil, was a mini-cinema by night and a gambling den by day.

Besides the fact that Ous Lizbeth and hubby had the largest collection of blues and pop LPs, they also happened to be proud owners of the township's — well part of my township's — one and only TV set. A black and white 37cm Phillips beauty, around which a whole village — as large as the shack could accommodate — converged every Friday night.

It was on one of those nights of super-kitsch, urban black TV programming that I came into contact with Brenda, on *Lapologa*, a music and variety show on the then TV1. The show was loved for its jive-talking anchors — a big curvaceous woman with Ruby Turner lips and a squeaky voice known as 'The Mary's', and a portly man, Letsoalela Mothiba, whom I now suspect was thrown in to neutralise the great femme fatale.

One of those evenings the producers messed with the show's pacy format by airing a video clip of a totally unknown musician with a thick, teary, spooky, throaty and mournful voice.

Wearing a shoulder-exposing patch dress, a thick punk-rocker style belt and knee-length black boots, the young woman — she could have been 20 and me, well, 13 — had unusually ugly and fascinating features. She had a deep coffee hue, a pronounced forehead, wide flat nose and eyes like a cheetah's.

Crouched over a Fender Rhodes piano — on which she worked with subtle intensity, as if enveloped in a trance — she went on to sing a dark but tuneful piece titled 'Life is Goin' On'.

With her voice tucking both male and female feelings at one moment and prodding her audience's tears the next, the artist sung with such subtle yet gospel-powered emotion, my tearful mom would later confess: 'Only Nina Simone's "My Baby Just Cares for Me" and news of Steve Biko's death has had such effect on me, dear'.

That was my introduction to Brenda. The beginning of the 'experience'. Three years later, when I was about 15, sans my baby fat, the 'experience' would move from the goggle box to the real thing — Brenda in the flesh!

Billed to perform at the local community hall, Kudu Cinema, as Brenda and The Big Dudes Live, slap-bang in the middle of 1984's winter, this was a show to die for. As luck had it, I earned the trip to go and see Brenda through nefarious means, masterminded by a character called Bra Frank.

Bra Frank was a soccer star known for his bullet-speed goals and magical left foot on the pitch, but he was a loser and flop with women.

He would come to my mom's shack, lying that he was taking me to practise football with the crowd favourites Topio All Stars, while in reality he had turned me into a courier boy and pimp, delivering letters to Suzan, a young, round woman with a slow rhythmic walk that seemed to be choreographed from her hips.

She probably succumbed to a rush of his decoratively styled letters for, soon after one of my postman duties, Frank came over to our house to ask my mom if he could take me to a Brenda and the Big Dudes show.

The big night. The hall was full of dandyish men in Viyella shirts and jazzy Harlem Nights caps tipped over one eye, and big-hipped women in their multi-pleated skirts and fashionable shoes known as 'BootJoyces'. Men were referred to as 'Bra' so-and-so and their chicks were 'Ous' this and that. Like Bra Frank, they were resplendent in their finest Pantsula and Ivy fashion.

The Brenda Fassie Trilogy

After what felt like three or so hours of waiting, the hall came close to caving in or exploding as the ululating voices from the audience filled the air, just after the scented smoke came billowing on stage and the disco ball lights turned a seductively dirty orange and red.

Cutting through the frenzy, a voice cracked in that old-style showbiz MC tone: 'Iyyyyebo. Yebo. Ladies and gents: Brrrrrrenda and the Big Dudes! Sho' your love, ladies and gents.'

I was wet with tears then. Happy, scared, confused and, well, just crying. Everybody did. Especially the women.

The Big Dudes' bassist Sammy Klaasen, drummer David Mabaso and keyboardist Dumisani Ngobeni – who would later father Brenda's only child Bongani – strutted onto the stage with that 1980s showbiz swashbuckling 'I am a celebrity therefore I'm closest to God' veneer, obviously stoned on something. Perhaps the audience's shrieks.

After, say, three minutes of the bass guitar's frenetic riffing and boom-bam-bap hard drumming, cushioned by soft synthesisers – I remember vividly, 'twas an instrumental cover of Donna Summer's 'Bad Boys' – that young woman who had reduced my mother to tears came thundering onto the stage.

This time fuller, rounder, fitter and clad in white body-hugging, sequined hotpants and silver skimpy vest, hair and knee-length boots studded with crystals, that young woman who sang the blues had transformed into a disco and punk freak act number 1. Move over Donna Summer.

By the time the band hit their anthem, 'Weekend Special', the women in the audience were out-shrieking each other.

How does one explain the whole performance? The music, the madness, the love, the pelvic grinding? Beautiful debauchery. That's how.

Twenty years later, Brenda Fassie had grown to be Queen of South African Pop, headline fodder, mother, one-woman freak-revue and a star with a sharp political sentiment, especially heard on three of her most political pieces: 'Black President', 'Boipatong' and the smash hit 'Too Late for Mama'.

259

Unconfirmed industry investigations by one media lawyer, quoted in a local tabloid, suggest Brenda had generated more than R25-million for her record label CCP/EMI.

Friends, hangers-on and media reports — a fact she confirmed to me — say she has lived in and messed up more than 20 houses and apartments, made love to countless celebrities and nobodies, gold diggers, gays, lesbians and straights in the last 20 years at the top of South Africa's fast food pop industry.

Three years ago, she told the then *City Press* showbiz editor Vukile Pokwana: 'You see, you don't understand. I am like Marilyn Monroe. I am a big star. The world, black and white, is fascinated, disturbed and curious about me. Madonna is only big within white pop. I am beyond pop. I am life. I am Brenda Fassie.'

Tomorrow, Brenda is turning 40, an event she's celebrating with the release of the album *Mali*.

Will she begin a new life at 40? Will she get married for the third time? Will she stop drinking and join the Jehovah's Witnesses?

The media critics, gossip hacks and stargazers have their different takes on where she is right now. But for me, it is not where she is that invites scrutiny, but what led her to where she is.

'The turning point,' Brenda confessed to me at The Market Theatre's Couch restaurant, where we had lunch with singer and friend Patricia Majalisa, 'was the death of Anneline Malebo.'

See, 10 years before Chicco Twala's affair with Brenda, Anneline Malebo was the shoulder onto which the young Brenda would cry and confess. There cannot be a comprehensive understanding of Brenda Fassie the rock star phenomenon, without mentioning the name Anneline Malebo.

She is the glue that binds the Fassie myth and reality in a manner that's easy to miss but impossible to dismiss.

Known as Sis, Anneline, the late Malebo gave Brenda a kick into the big time, back in 1980, when Anneline was leader of Afro-soul and pop band Joy.

The Brenda Fassie Trilogy

Joy were the perfect replicas of the US negro soul acts with big hairdos, big attitudes and voices to die for. In the spring of 1979, the group prepared to launch the most diva-stating assault on South African showbusiness with the arresting soul piece 'Paradise Road'.

Joy's Malebo — then about to go on maternity leave — roped in the 18-year-old Brenda, fresh from bunking school (Soweto's Phefeni High). The teenager captivated soul and pop fans with her emotion-filled voice.

'I was so scared, but I knew my moment had arrived,' she recalled.

Journalist-turned-playwright Mothubi Mutloatse remembers her as a 'fat, short and not so pretty teenager with pimples and a voice to shake angels from their heavenly sleep'.

What happened after Joy depends on who you talk to. Talent scout and producer Bra Koloi Lebona says that Brenda went solo, while others counter that she joined *Papa and Blondie* and *Spank*.

Talking to her, mid last year, at a hospital bed in Alberton where she was recovering from an old knee injury, it became clear Brenda herself has blurred memories of her post Joy days.

'Mmhhh, it happened so quick. I went into a series of bands, meeting some of the most talented and biggest stars of the time. It was so hectic. A typical rock 'n' roll life with The Big Dudes, ahh, The Big Dudes.'

But just before the end of The Big Dudes, the writing was already on the wall for Brenda.

It was obvious the Queen's crown was no longer that safe when a staggeringly beautiful teenager, Yvonne Chaka Machaka, exploded on the scene to give what remains the raunchiest performance of the century in Regina Mundi Church, Soweto.

She was photographed by *The Sowetan's* Mbuzeni Zulu in a wide-legged squat, with only a few centimetres of her upper thighs unexposed, her crotch down low, while a life-sized sculpture of Jesus Christ watched, sadly, from behind.

It would take a song like 'Too Late for Mama' — a subtle political manifesto for rural women — to restore Brenda to the top of the charts.

Fast forward to 2001. Attention moved to newer and sexier kids on the block — Thandiswa Mazwai, Lebo Mathosa, Mafikozolo's Nhlanhla Mafu and TV presenter Modjadji.

Still, there was only one Queen.

Early this year she got into a huge fight with her manager Chicco Sello Twala, who got into a fight with her record company CCP, which itself was involved in a contractual dispute with the Queen of Pop.

The script included record executives buying and reclaiming mansions from her, alcohol abuse — which had replaced her cocaine addiction — and the future and behaviour of her musician son, Bongani, referred to as 'Little Lord Fauntleroy' by the then most articulate of the sneering hacks, Charles Molele.

And if you were a caring and present parent — which Brenda is not — you'd appreciate why 'Little Lord Fauntleroy' really needed checking up on. Among other shockers, his mom's lover, Sindisiwe Khambule, was reported to have seduced the boy into an orgy of sex, booze and manipulation.

By earlier this year, it felt like 'Brenda the myth' and the cash cow had finally exploded.

But Elliot Makhaya, the journalist who discovered Brenda in 1979, once advised me, 'be careful, never rush anybody's epitaph, especially not Brenda's. She's going to outlive all of us.'

Makhaya died last October and Brenda has proven him right.

Mid this year, her record label apparently gave her R1 million cash to sign a new deal. She bought a house in Sandton's popular suburb, Buccleuch, furnished it and called a huge press thanksgiving party for her ancestors.

Besides gallivanting around town and giving riveting performances at Melrose Arch's haven for posers, Club Kilimanjaro, close friends say she's been holed up in studios, writing and perfecting her pitch, toiling hard for an album that seem set to materialise into her third biggest since *Weekend Special* and the anthemic *Iphin Ndlela*.

In Zulu, *Iphindlela* means 'where's the way?' As far as her life goes, only the Queen knows her way. She just ain't telling.

Tomorrow it's her fortieth birthday and 37 years after her first public performance with The Tiny Tots in Elsies River, Cape Town.

Also, it's 21 years since I first laid my eyes on her and, believe it or not, I'm still stalking the Queen.

Life is a funk

Busi Mhlongo says, 'I can retire anytime I want!' Not

Cold facts first: one of the truly gifted singers, and ritualistic performers of our age, the subversive torchbearer of contemporary black, female pop, Victoria Busi Mhlongo is suffering from breast cancer.

It's supposed to be a hot newsflash, but it isn't. The African telegraph to the sky — to pilfer jazz poet, Sandile Dikeni's lyric — has been riding a whirlwind of rumour for months running. But then again, who has seen proof? Rumour mongers?

Over her dead body! And that's just a figure of speech.

Inasmuch as it's hosting a deathly illness — hers is a body quite alive, and yet, at peace with its own fragility. Even as write this, I am uncertain as to how the negative phrasing *suffering from breast cancer* best expresses how she feels about herself at this very moment. Thus, long after the interview I rang her up, to ask: How are you feeling?

She's quite adept at the question-deflecting game. Months before the interview and days after she would ignore it, at best, or, at worst, opt to tell me about everybody else's life, but hers.

One day, just after her initial chemotherapy, and on the eve of a major concert she was billed to star in, the façade could hold no longer. With her voice lowered conspiratorially, she dropped the mask and broke down — 'oh *bandla*, oh *baba*, I am very sick. I am in pain. My feet are yellowing underneath, the pain in my nails is excruciating. Sometimes the headache just won't go away.'

It's around this time that her older sister — and her boulder to lean on, at her Morningside, Durban, home — Mam' Beauty, told me: 'she's sometimes vomiting and sleeps quite a lot.' And yet, days are not the same. If you are lucky, you'll catch her and her three-year-old niece, little Andiswa, getting down to Fela Kuti's and — yes — Jimi Hendrix records at home — that's only if you have her house number. If you don't, tough.

Her home is located in a block of flats impossible to access. You cannot even pass the foyer gate without somebody coming down to escort you. Even then, you'll have to explain how you made it past the remote-controlled main entrance gate.

Like most artists worth their salt, Busi Mhlongo is a fiercely private soul. Yet, still — based on an assumed closeness, a closeness forged on such arbitrary mutual pastimes, such as a shared love of Taiwa Moses Molelekwa's, Prince's and Bob Dylan's music — I miscalculated.

I had thought she would be tripping over herself to unburden herself, as she had previously done about other things. Weeks morphed into months while all she could ever utter was 'I am very sick', without a thread of a clue as to what was going on.

By the time she eventually spoke to me, I suspect she had known about her condition for months prior to the official diagnosis. And that like all of us, she was just afraid of checking with the doctors, in case she got more than she bargained for.

Like all consummate artists, blinded by an inner, obligatory sense to serve others, whatever it is that's eating her could wait. She has fans to satisfy, and a forever beckoning stage to continue her live rituals on, in the full glare of photographers.

Still, the questions persisted: Who is Busi Mhlongo? How sick is she? How does she deal with cancer, or any other malady? If the cat's out of the bag and the rumour mill has spun out of control, how long does she intend to hold out?

* * *

The danger with writers being too close to their subjects – especially enigmatic souls like Busi Mhlongo, whose swell of dedicated fans often assumes they know her – is that you end up blurring that sacred line between art, artist and the watcher.

Though most hardened scribes will lie about this, for a real fan – and that includes critics, folks the masses (mis)trust for critical arbitration – watching, meeting, or being in the personal or creative orbit of an artist with abilities to transport them beyond their bodily limitations, is, my friend, akin to falling in love.

Being a fan is, at best, an infantile project. Like a child, you throw your trust unto someone who has never asked for it. At its most honest, fan-dom differs not from any religious belief.

The fan undertakes a personal oath, an article of faith – just as long as your desired artist continues delivering what you like, or creating artwork that opens up channels for escape, or reconnection with the self. Thus, every time a true fan meets the artist, it feels like falling in love for the first time.

Attending a countless number of Busi Mhlongo's gigs – over fifty, at the last count; from her Civic Center launch, where audiences witnessed Hugh Masekela and Bheki Mseleku bowing before throwing notes into an on-stage hat, to the Union Buildings Millennium Festival show, in which the heavens opened up to release shit loads of rain in the middle of her grand finale, the then unknown songstress TK, vice-clinging my hand, tears, sweat and rain soaking up her oversized top — I have seen Mhlongo's art, breaking and reconfiguring people to their core.

Not so long ago, at the Urban Voices Festival held at Bassline, Newtown, her third show that I attended in a month, I marvelled at individuals rushing the stage, dancing trippy-ly, mad swaying of dreadlocks, and karaokitschly attempting to sing, note for note, with the master shaman on stage.

My eyes followed the movements of a young man who'd pushed his way right to the front of the stage, upper body shaking in a robot-type dance, as though dismembering his own body parts, and then jumping one beat a second for a good 30 minutes. This was a man evidently lost in a charged-up atmosphere akin to religious surrender, water baptism, sexual release, a mind trip and meditated loss of personal sense, for the sake of being in a shared communion with the artist on stage or with the gods and demons this artist provoked in him.

Later, I would understand why audiences react this way, after driving with a friend for six hours from Johannesburg to Durban, through unforgiving darkness, to attend a Woman's Month gig which she co-led with Mahotella Queens at the legendary Bat Centre. 'This is where I first played when I returned home after 20 years in foreign lands. And this is,' I remember her pausing, to let it sink in, 'where I will retire.'

For days preceding that show, we have been in a marathon exchange of telephonic chats. Again, she has not being feeling well, and for somebody who once 'interviewed' her, in which she only uttered three words, on the eve of the launch of *Urban Zulu*, and another, four years later, in which she spoke right up to 4 am — I was kinda'f attuned to her unstated pain by now.

Showtime! The Durban dockside-located Bat Centre is packed like sardines the ocean it harbors has long ceased throwing down the beach. Near the entrance, a push-and-shove show takes place, government types and the holloi-polloi, angle for better seating inside the dance hall.

Busi Mhlongo takes the stage after an impressive all-women Zulu dance and song troupe set the audience on high alert. What ensued, I don't think the audience was prepared for.

In my daily hustle — in the name of work — scavenging shows locally and around the world, from rock band Skunk Anansie at Madiba's eightieth birthday bash, to 1997's Fugees *Live at The Brixton Academy*, backed by The Wailers, to Salif Keita live at Vista Soweto Campus, add Boom Shaka's all-time edgy, experimental at the Rosebank Fire station, circa 1996 — I make for a pretty jaded live music fan.

Yet Busi Mhlongo's show conveyed the message with hard-hitting beauty: Blessed are the jaded, for they, too — 'pon experiencing a musical baptism of this nature — shall inherit the earth, or the grooves, or both.

The band was on a deep funk and gospel-meets-lounge music element. Syrupy bass, sparse, spaced-out keyboards that out bass'ed the bass, and the guitars wailing in tandem with the drummer, who seemed to be keeping the center holding, but was not in fact. Though the intent was noble, there was something annoying about the sound. People didn't seem to notice though, or care.

Ever alert, Mhlongo's body language conveyed a bit of displeasure but the problem persisted, at which point something other than her mere self took over as the band settled onto the third track. She took control. Her usually shriek-ful vocals blended, and then rose a whisper above the guitars.

She stood there, dead still, heat, make-up, sweat and the reddish lighting giving her face a bloodied Aztec or West African mask resemblance, and with all the power she could summon from her belly, and every pore in her body the artist let rip into '*uMethisi*', from her debut album *Bhabemu*, in the most beautiful voice I have ever heard sung live.

Her repertoire and choreography, halted only with occasional, teary announcements — 'I love you, let's appreciate love, what God gave us' — was of an initiate performing an *abangoma* ritual, a passage into the world of healers and marabouts. The audience was there but not aware of her; she belonged to some other time.

Busi Mhlongo the wailer gave way to the balladeer, the artist gave way to the healer, the healer beckoned the priest, who led us to a brothel, where body and soul merges, even if it's for a five-minute duration of the rhythmic snake dance, back to the stage where the tame Zulu woman about to celebrate her sixtieth birthday, gave way to a rock-star chic, an Afro-alien funk Goddess on a futuristic mission to convert the non-believers.

How then should an objective writer extract himself from (such) an artist's creative grip? How are you expected to separate that piercing note, that uplifting piano mastery, that magical body contortion, that poetic verse, that blinding energy that blurs the person (artist) from the personality (fans' objects of creative desire)? Just how?

Rightly or misguided, I do not posses the requisite skills to separate a writer's professional objectivity, and the art-induced affection, whenever the fan is summoned to their hero's inner walls of solitude, even the most ardent fans are barred from.

For, you see, danger lurks round the shadows here. At worst, such access can unwittingly reveal your hero's viciousness — their true self, or their otherness. And yet, sometimes it can be an ironical, perhaps, ethically un-allowed blessing. I mean, how does a warder fall in love with a prisoner? *Oi,* *Oi* 'tis pushing it too far.

* * *

Wednesday 6th September. The weather is sulky as a bitch, and the phone cling-clacked for my attention. It's Busi Mhlongo. She's speaking shotgun rattle like: 'You know, I have been sick. Been wanting, to talk to you. Well. It's time. They found breast cancer. It is spreading. I am afraid. They might remove my breast. Do you hear me?'

'I do.'

'I need you to come, and talk — perhaps you can touch my left breast before it goes, if it does.' Touch it? I freaked out and froze attentively, feeling waves of confusion and honour lifting me up and splashing me in more emotional waters.

'Please make it tomorrow', she pleaded.

I realised, as soon as I arrived in Durban, that Mhlongo had more than cancer to get out of her system. Most pertinent in her battle with it, she has a powerful reservoir to draw strength from — herself. This, it turns out, is not the first time she has had cancer.

'The first time — 30 years ago — was cervical cancer and I was living and working in America back then. I was quite young and full of fire. I am still passionate about life, but back then I was naive and looked forward to my old age and not early death.' She had a hysterectomy; hence, 'I could not give birth anymore after that.'

This time around, she felt something was amiss when she was in a bath tub last year. 'I felt this lump, and immediately painful shoulders.' Still, she ignored it and undertook a three-month tour in Holland, her spiritual home in Europe.

'Ag, so I told myself that this lump would pass. Nothing serious. And now just see where I am — it's so painful. Clearly, even if I were able to, I would not have stopped cancer from attacking my breast or any part of my body — I think, though it sounds terrible, it was coming.'

'I am not making excuses for it, but I am quite bad with absorbing death, particularly accepting other people's deaths.' In the last three years, six of her closest band members and other collaborators' musicians, all guitarists, died.

Nobody mentions the disease. Nobody asks. Business as usual, only that she made it hers, to shelve those musicians memories in her soul, and she takes it personally.

'Why', she once asked — rhetorically — in one night's telephone chat: 'Why . . . why them?' Since I had no answer then — and do not promise one now, or tomorrow — my immediate reaction was to wonder, what type of a person Busi Mhlongo is, really?

Those keen on the biography of her pain have to scramble for clues in her music. Like Bob Dylan, Busi Mhlongo's blood is splashed on the tracks she's done, particularly her late work, *Urban Zulu*, and her collaboration with the Swiss harpist, Max Lasser, on the meditative release, *Between*.

Buried somewhere there in her voice, and not the lyrics, lies a confessional, festooned with tell-tale signs of a woman, and an artist's life, lived on the fast lane to Painsville.

The story of Mhlongo's life journey has a familiar, if not discordant ring: Some time back in the 1970s, after her big pop smash single 'My Boy Lollipop', Busi Mhlongo infamously left her daughter, Mpumi, barely eight, with her then husband and musical collaborator, Early Mabuza, to ply her talent overseas.

'I still cannot explain it, but I knew I wanted to leave this country. It was, like, a voice instructing me to', she says. Ever since then, Mhlongo's affair — or non-affair — with her only daughter has never really been the same, and perhaps there's nothing such as 'the same', for the ties of mother-daughter had been dealt a blow, first by her departure, and then upon her return, decades of denial, overcompensation, regret and guilt.

Mpumi is now a woman of 40 and a married mother, based in the United States. Once every week, her five-year-old daughter, Zowie, and Zowie's three-year-old sister, Suraya, call from their parents place in Palm Beach, West Coast, to sing Mhlongo's songs back to the granny they have never really met. Eery? Their granny sees it as a karmic connection. 'Ahh, they are so, sooo sweet. I love them', she tells me. 'I lurrrve them'.

'... But I don't think I've forgiven myself for leaving Mpumi back then. It hurts. I was not there for her when she had first periods, nowhere to offer that motherly affection. Looking at it now, I do not think I will ever forgive myself, never!'

Why not?

'See, I do not understand what people mean by "forgive". I will always feel that way. How are you able to bond with your grandchildren if you have unfinished business with their mother?

'The first time their mother phoned, I was afraid. I asked myself, "Vicky, how are you going to deal with this?" but when I heard their voices, I felt a flood of reassuring feeling washing through me'. Still, she lays her unresolved knot with her daughter as the root cause of the tension, anger and confusion she's carrying in her body for ages past.

'I am not surprised I have cancer. It reflects an unfulfilled care. My breast is telling me: If I am symbol of affection, then you have not loved me for a long time, mate', and as she says it, I realise a faraway gaze in her eye. 'That means', she pauses as though in dialogue with herself, 'I have not loved myself for a long, long time. It all piles up'.

So where to? Will she become the new poster celeb for cancer?

'I have had three chemotherapy injections thus far, and hear it from me: It is hell! You know, I am not hiding anything. But I cannot be a campaign symbol, as I am loath to take too much responsibility for others. The only responsibility I embrace is singing. I am not a talker. I do not want to talk in case I hurt some people's feelings'.

And yet, she is bothered by the language that caring friends, the medical industrial complex and religious well-wishers use: fight.

'They tell you, "Vicky you must fight, Busi you must be strong, you must fight for your life," and I'm like fight for whaaaaat!?', she hits a high pitch. 'Tell me, did great people like Shaka Zulu or Mother Theresa fight for their lives, huh? I do not imply I am in their league, but you see, even the greatest perish'.

And, what was that, that retirement talk about? 'Weee- gi-gi-gi', she laughs, heartily. 'Oh, you see, I meant it then, when I told you I was retiring. Didn't last long did it? I informed you before my first chemo, simply because I was afraid. I did not know what to expect'.

She lets out a huge crackling giggle and — for the first time in weeks — I too feel a sense of relief, for what I don't know, and she turns to face me: 'Ok, this pain is a *mutha* but, I cannot imagine myself not creating music. Think about it: What will I do if I ever stop singing?'

Where's Diego Garcia?

Barefoot Indian Ocean's diva's blues

Who says platitudes are meaningless? Consider this: 'My existence is tied to the life and collective breath of my people — children of the high seas, rock people. For that, I pledge to live and die for them.'

Mmm. Poetic nonsense?

And who is this beautiful nonsense attributed to? Self-righteous Ayatollah Khomeini, pretty-faced Muhammad Ali, saintly Nelson Mandela, Mickey Mouse?

Nix.

No, the person behind this poetic fury is Charlesia Alexis, the folk lyricist-cum-activist from the island of Diego Garcia in the Indian Ocean; the most famous granny you have never heard of.

Usually known by her stage name, Charlesia (pronounced Shah-lay-zia) is a stocky, chocolate-dark 72-year-old woman with silky silver curly hair, slanted reddish eyes and a voice that cracks, croaks and occasionally lapses into yodelling — especially when she is at her most nostalgic.

My meeting with Charlesia was pure happenstance, thanks to David

Constantin — a young film director from Mauritius I had met in La Possession, on Réunion. He had made a provocative documentary on the little-known Chagos Islands, which include Diego Garcia.

Usually a man of few words, Constantin, possibly high on coffee, became very excited whenever he spoke about his home country. 'The very idea of Mauritius sucks', he told me.

'The image of Mauritius is the greatest con in the world, or at least in the Indian Ocean. Mauritius is the most beautiful lie to have been sold to the gullible world of tourism. There are two countries in one — the postcard picturesque Mauritius, and the Mauritius you won't see on TV.'

Tell me something I don't know, I blurted out. And that's how the interview with the grand mama of Diego Garcia — who, as fate would have it, was due to perform on Réunion on the day of my departure — was hastily arranged. 'It's 12.30pm on the needle', Constantin instructed me. 'Hotel Central in the belly of [Réunion's capital city] Saint-Denis.'

Cometh the hour. The paint is peeling off Saint-Denis and the rest of the island is cooking itself to a stew. It's 40°C and there's no sign of either Constantin or the 'miracle' I am supposed to interview.

The Creole Chinese lady at the hotel's reception tells me: 'Oi, non, monsieur. Non madame Charlesia here. Non, monsieur, non.'

I am outside the foyer, lunching on takeaway pizza, Coke and badly burnt chips, waiting for the goddess. After what seems like a century, a small truck full of hunky Rastafarian musicians — the sort of fellas whose tropical images are usually seen in tourist brochures — arrive.

One by one, the Rasta hunks file out and hug and kiss an old, slightly limping woman in a heavily embroidered white country-style dress. Untangling herself, she heads straight for me. 'Monsieur — ahh — Afrique du Sud, a-i-a joernaliese?'

'Yes ma'am, joernaliese.' My eyes nearly pop out of their sockets. 'You must be Charlesia, non?'

'No', she jokes, and requests that I return a little later.

Where's Diego Garcia?

Meanwhile, I learn from the translated sleeve of her debut album *Charlesia la voix des Chagos*, released this year, that she is revered by the people of her country as the very embodiment of Chagos's soul.

'Where is Chagos and why should we care?' an impudent South African writer, unable to disguise her sarcasm ('Aagh, you and your explorer's fascination with native things!') would later ask while laying out a giant map on the floor.

Triumphantly, she burst out: 'Hoaaar, it's not even on the damn map! Cha-what? Oh, please.'

Well, the Chagos Islands might not be on some maps, but exist they do. They lie in the middle of the Indian Ocean, about 2 200 kilometres east of Kenya, a little over 1 000 kilometres south-west of the southern tip of India, and about 1 000 kilometres east of the Seychelles.

In short, they're not far from Mauritius but far enough to have survived for centuries as a semi-independent island group. Initially a French colony, they became part of the British Empire in 1814 in terms of the Treaty of Paris.

The group, which includes Diego Garcia, the largest island; the Salomon Islands; Peros Banhos; and a number of smaller islands; has its own unique cultural mores.

The islands' economy consisted mainly of the production of coconut oil from large coconut plantations. The plantations were freehold but during the nineteenth century they passed into the hands of private companies.

All that changed in the early 1960s when the islands' population — less than 5 000 people — began to decline as low wages, monotonous work, lack of facilities and the great distance from Mauritius and the Seychelles discouraged recruitment and made it difficult to retain labourers. A number of islanders had left in search of work opportunities and medical facilities.

Meanwhile, the US military had earmarked Diego Garcia as an ideal place to build an air-force base, its location making it perfect for launching attacks on countries such as Afghanistan, Iraq. . .

In the late 1960s, the British government struck a secret deal with the US whereby the islands' population would be evacuated so that a military base could be built.

As an excuse for exiling the people of Chagos, the British claimed that the coconut plantations had suffered from a lack of investment. Thus followed the forced removal of around 2 000 islanders between 1967 and 1973. And those islanders who had left to look for jobs or medical facilities were not allowed to return.

The Americans duly built their base on Diego Garcia — their largest in the Indian Ocean area — and used it in the 1990 Gulf War and the wars in Afghanistan in 2001 and Iraq in 2003.

The exiled islanders and their descendants, meanwhile, have been living in slum conditions in Mauritius. They have suffered high unemployment and endured racist treatment from the indigenous Mauritians.

'The saddest thing,' Charlesia would later tell me, 'is that, in Mauritius, the Chagossians had considerably less clout than the giant tortoises and seagulls they had left back home.'

The seemingly irreversible displacement created a culture of permanent longing as the Chagossians lived with their fading hope for an unreachable home. But instead of crushing their soul, their nostalgia has been responsible for other Indian Ocean nations developing a grudging respect for the Chagossians — hence the often back-handed appreciation: 'Aah, the Chagossians, a people full of passion.'

From a young age, Charlesia saw her country being passed like a hot potato between the world's superpowers and their sidekicks.

Back at the hotel I found Charlesia, this time with Constantin and Radio France International correspondent Vincent Garrigues, who had also gotten wind that there was a new musical sensation and fighter for Chagossians' sovereignty: le Mama, Charlesia.

'I was one of those who came to Mauritius with my family in 1967,' Charlesia recalls, tears reddening her eyes, which are already swollen from cigarette smoke and emotion.

'Each family was given — well, it's not like we had a choice, now did we? — 36 000 rupees to make way for the Americans and their huge ships.'

Back in Chagos, music and fish was all Charlesia and her folk had — and this they lived on, day in and day out. 'It is not like Chagos was some terribly picturesque land, rich in minerals or anything like that. But it's my home. It's our country. We loved it then and we still dream about it today.

'We sang at church, we sang when we performed rituals, we sang when we met our mates, when we went to the sea to catch fish, when we drank and when we made love. Music was always with us. We are its troubled blues rhythm.'

She speaks without regret about the time she was jailed in Mauritius for being one of the 'voices' — with other family members, including her sister Marie Therese Mein and her niece Jeanette — of an ill-fated campaign to have the people returned to their island.

'Both the British and their Mauritian sidekicks had never seen a resistance led by women, but we did it. We might not have made an international noise like in South Africa,' she remembers with fondness and hurt, 'but we fought so much in the market square, in the city centre, in the villages.'

Charlesia's struggle journey, though waged on a very small scale for an almost invisible island, mirrored the life and times of several other troubled blues spirits — Nina Simone, Miriam Makeba, Janis Joplin, Aretha Franklin — all great voices, aware of their power.

As Charlesia speaks in long, meandering sentences, joking and asking us to light her fourth fag in an hour, it becomes clear that after 30 years in exile the idea of home has become an ideal; a dream rather than a feasibility.

'Deep down we are still fighting to go back home but the thing is, home has become a mirage. I become quite sad when my grandchildren ask me about "this home you are always singing about". But of course I perform my grandmotherly duties, entertaining them with folk stories about a home they might never ever touch. Thing is, there is no longer a home.'

Her album — recorded when she was 70, on a moonlit night around a huge fire — was not a labour of love; rather proof that you don't need fancy studio machinery to make a record.

'I have been singing for ages but never thought about recording. Not at all. So one day these young folk, a community organisation from Réunion that preserves traditional folk poetry and music, approached me to put my gifts on a record.

'I knew the time had come for the world to hear Chagos's spirits on a record. Aah, my children . . .' She jerks her head sideways and releases a soft cry mixed with laughter. Emotions, in the form of two rivulets of tears, cascade down her well-worn face.

Her 11-track album does not differ stylistically from thousands of Creole folk recordings made all over the world, from the Indian Ocean to the Caribbean Islands. What sets it apart from other such recordings — like those of Cape Verdean folk superstars Cesaria Évora, Dulce Matias and Tito Paris, and the silky smooth vocals of St Dominican music — is its lack of revelry (carnivale).

Charlesia's deep voice — a blend of raw emotion, anger and longing — is more coarse and rough at the edges than similar voices heard in Cajun, soudade, morna and other Creole varieties sung on Réunion and various Atlantic Ocean islands.

Her music is mostly led and held together by her voice, the chief instrument. Yet this voice is remarkable for its lack of clutter and dripping emotions.

Her songs, such as '*La Zirodo*', '*Naisa Mama Poul*' and '*Papiyone dor'e*', are true Indian Ocean blues. They could be rich material for the funky tribal dance, Cuban salsa mixes and trance dance tracks presently in vogue in Europe.

Three weeks after the interview, a call wakes me up at home. It's Charlesia's grandson, calling from south-east London where the majority of Chagossians have settled.

'Mama said to pass her regards. She has finally moved to London, but she's not well after falling from a bed in a hotel. But she's happy . . . London might be the home she never had. But then, what does home mean?'

Two pop hits have tried to answer this question. While Paul Young tells us that wherever he lays his hat is his home, Hugh Masekela tells us that home is where music is.

In Charlesia's case, she is music and the troubling rhythm of it. Will she hit fame in her mid-70s?

It depends on whether hip music clubs — such as London's Ronnie Scott's, the Jazz Café and the Barbican, and the blues clubs of Paris — are willing to discover another chain-smoking diva.

If not, Charlesia might have to pray to her Indian Ocean gods to bring that rock explorer with a touch of gold, Ry Cooder, down her street — or wherever it is that her home might be at that moment.

The Queen and I

Naomi Campbell and
La Dolce Vita *Brigade*

Act 1
The icon as photo *artefact*

In pop-culture — that includes popular political imagination — timage construction can make or break you. Think of one that has permeated our collective consciousness, with or without our approval: Jacob Zuma doing the rat-a-tat, rat-a-tat (sound of the machine gun) choreo-dance: *Mshini wa'm*!

What a man. What a sight . . . political burlesque — or, as the saying goes, 'the theatre of the absurd' - has never looked so photogenic, so photo inviting, photo baiting, and plain prostrating itself to the omnipresent media lenses .

Clearly, modern politics have waken to the fact that, complaining about the media's 'one-sided aggressive approach, being quoted out of context' and all other kindergarten excuses, is illogical in the face of the very same media's cameras — the true eyes of the people, thus, the politician's audiences.

Cue: there just no substitute for effective photography, a point even the usually sedate President Thabo Mbeki belatedly woke to, on the day the ANC held its ninety-fifth birthday bash in Witbank.

Almost without irony or shame — or playing the irony out - the President was captured jumping mid-air in a ZCC mkhukhu remixed indlamu dance act, next to the grinning Zuma, (who's glee, calls upon an image of a school principal called to approve his students' homework). High marks, Mr. President! More pointedly: Power to the power of the image maker!

Be it a supermodel ramping it down at a top Milan Fashion Week shindig, a boxer smashing his opponent against canvass — like that famous Muhammad Ali-'Sonny Liston, Get Up You Sucker!' photo in which Ali cuts a menacingly lofty image as he lords it over the fallen Liston - nothing possesses effective emotional power like a picture.

So much the better if it's a work of a master, in whatever genre: Patrick Demarchelier, Guy Tillim, Santu Mofokeng, Bruce Webber, Lord Snowdown or a Koto Bolofo, etc. Great photography equals great art — period. One of my favourite pop culture art pieces is that of the brash iron Mike Tyson — round about early 1990s - and his then squeeze, the supermodel, Naomi Campbell.

Beaming with confidence, shoulders lifted up, and muscles rippling through his black skin-tight top, King Mike was snapped with his then not-so-iron, 'Lady' Campbell, about to make a dash into a waiting limo.

Both the King and the Queen were bedecked in black — as though Johnny Cash was their guru. Black linen pants, tight turtle-neck top and black brogues for the King, and an ankle-length black cashmere coat, knee-length boots and skin-tight pedal pushers for the Queen.

In the only way that only 'Lady Campbell' could pull, she topped the whole darn thing with her science-fiction flick, space-styled dark goggles, like her name was Obi-Wan Kenobi, or the incurably camp, Neo of the *Matrix* serial yarn. As far as pop goes, this was as surreal, as gothic-bling, and as close to a Renaissance-mood painting, as a celebrity picture could aspire to.

Here were two young black folks — one an orphan from Brooklyn, New York streets, one raised by a single mom in the backwoods of a British monarchy, brought together by fame, power, and as the author Toby Young is fond of saying, driven by a simple urge to take on Manhattan.

Ten years later one fell from grace, started chomping on his opponents body parts, did a stint in wrestling, and finally retired from boxing, a sad shadow of his ferociously fascinating younger self, while the other — the Lady, herein sometimes referred as the Queen — has taken up boxing, kick boxing, cat clawing, mobile phone head bashing, and other physical conducts in addition to her still oh-so glam career as a model.

Still, ladies and gentleman, Naomi Campbell is still the best cat on the ramp. Nobody moves, pout and prowls like her. Nobody attracts so much heat and screams to be loved — as expressed by her ferocious temper and now legendary court cases — like her.

And so it was a foregone thought that I would lose myself, upon receiving an invitation to come just a screaming distance away from Lady Campbell. For the record, I lost myself when that invitation finally arrived, courtesy of the Milan-based Pirelli Tyre company — about that later.

And yes — I cannot concur less — this sort of celebrity devotion sucks, and sucks worse when you know that Naomi Campbell is one of those models constantly pointed out by activists for promoting fur, and is always reported to be prostrating herself in front of numerous, dirt-wealthy Mediterranean billionaires old enough to be her grandpa.

Also, the woman seems to need a PhD in anger management. Say, how many of her personal assistants and 'domestic executives' heads has she bashed against some hotel walls? Yuk-yukky, this Naomi *innit*?

Well — she is, and so are all of us media hounds, keeping tabs on her minute-by-minute movements, documenting the rise and fall of her well-known temper, as though Campbell's antics are as significant as North Korea's threat to nuclear-bomb us to stone age.

Act 2
La Dolce Vita: The Devil wears stilettos in Rome

Pirelli's South African marketing division's Daniel Cartha arranged for the two of us — the other, a fetching magazine scribe with a Greek moniker, Aspasia Karas — to come see their latest film, *The Call*. Need I say Cartha threw in that magical cherry on top, 'and talk to Naomi Campbell herself' as a bait?

Just under a day we were zooming off, crossing the Med, air leaping into Rome — ah the city of God, art, and history, and *conquistadores*! Campbell and Malkovich's film shindig, as well as Naomi sighting, is set to take place at the historical Diocletian Baths — a retro place where ancient Rome's great warriors used to dip in to destress.

The part of town we arrive at, Largo Argentina — with its lived in exterior and street pizzerias — is charming in its ordinariness. What better location than an accommodation a whisker's distance from the 1970s Cinecitta studios, Roma's once glorified laboratory of big dreams and big stars, where Federico Fellini created the now highly romanticised *La Dolce Vita*?

The whole town is on high alert, back alleys buzzing. Journalists, media spinners, advertising types, from different parts of the stiletto-shaped country and the spread of the European Union are all here.

Rome is thick with accents. The streets are a permanent art-deco display of fashion, style and swagger, and yet it feels welcoming. Is it because Rome is the most religious big brothel on planet earth, or the most religious shopping compound for style slaves? I could not bother: it's Lady Campbell I came here for.

The day the film is launched . . . well, let's speak a bit about the film. Scripted by the Leo Burnett Italia's chief creative director, Sergio Rodriguez, directed by an American, Antoine Fuqua (*Try Another Day*) and featuring the most enigmatic actor of his generation, John Malkovich as a spirit exorcist bishop of considerable powers, *The Call* is a story about evil, darkness, power and control.

The Bishop is called upon to take care of a powerful demon — played by Naomi Campbell — terrorising some part of town. That's the meat of it. And yet, that's not all it leaves in the audience's mind: the story is problematic in many ways, most of which revolve around Campbell's casting as the devil reincarnate.

Her body is painted black. Her eyes are full of raging red fire and she's kept afloat by these dark, comic-type Count-Dracula sort of wings that renders her an angel of death. The model plays the role with deftness and conviction, so as to leave no doubt in the audience's minds as to who is the evil, and who is the redeemer.

Was Naomi chosen to portray the devil because she's a great actor? Was she cast as an underhand way of confirming her own evil nature as a person? What symbolism does the film intends to convey? That black women are evil, attractive and intriguing? Why are the colours black and the moody ambience used to express evil and not redemption? Why was she exorcised by a man . . . a white man?

Soon after the film, a devastated Dutch woman journalist rushed to my side and asked, 'What do you think, I'm, so disgusted!' Ironically, I was moved to ask in retort, 'Why do you ask me: Is it because I am black, like Campbell, or the devil? What's my name, Idi Don Dada?' Though that last one, I didn't ask.

There were some murmurings amid the hand clapping and angling to ogle Lady Campbell. I pushed towards the creative director, Rodriguez, for a comment.

'Uhm, it's a personal choice, really', he commented, not saying much, but not needing to. It's all part of the public relations gumpf.

They didn't flow ungrateful reporters from all their sad little offices all over the world to ask if they believe the image of black women equates to good or evil - who do we take this people for, Marcel Proust society? Rodriguez continued, 'There's really nothing to it other than what you saw. It's about Pirelli tyres, you see?' In short: Get a damn life!

Act III
Regards to my dad, Nelson Mandela:
I'mma come home, soon

Luckily, Lady Campbell was brought to the question-and-answer session. Barely covered in a mini, chiffon-ish, green floral-number dress, the woman carried off a bygone aura of Hollywood period (1940s) beauty, while the rest of us boiled in thick wool. Her film mate, Malkovich, was out of town, so, she'd handle us. Staple diet.

She deflected questions with a smile and the movement of her eye pupils. Of course, she homed how enriched she was after working with Malkovich. I mean, loll!

Did we expect her to tell on him: about how he does not wash his socks, and what a bossy son-of-a-gun he is? Not that he is.

The question-and-answer session flashed by with a bullet speed, but not before I got my one-to-one in the full glare of Italian and world television after being plucked from the crowd. I sauntered to the stage, and even before sitting down — crumbled on the chair besides her, like waist, when she shot me a 'now-whatdayya want to know' look.

BM: [Licking my lips, not in a leery way, but as way of calming myself.] Ms Campbell, why did you play the devil?

NC: Jus' call me Naomi, ok? Cool. Devil? I am not one. It's just a role.

BM: Films: is it where you are steering your career to ?

NC: S'cuse me?

BM: Is film your next outlet?

NC: S'cu-u-u-ze, meee?

BM: [Cough-cough] I meant, do you want to be a film star?

NC: Oh that? Dunno wha' I be doing nes'- time. Itz all work ya know . . .

BM: You wrote a book that went nowhere some time ago, how long do you want to be our object of desire, I mean you have been around for some time.

NC: So, what yaah'sking?

Right then she tossed her silky dark weave sideways, and, with a trained eye, looked at the interview organisers with that 'next one please' eye. A look that muttered 'somebody better and not so foolish as this man next to me.' Right then I got the hint and pulled a gold out of nowhere: Madiba!

BM: Uh, I'm from South Africa, we are very aware of your sterling work and association with Mandela Children's Fund. A-maaay-zeeng, Naomi, ah tell ya.

Flip, what jackpot! Her usually slanted eyes brightened up and a genuine smile covered her face, ear to ear.

NC: Are you? Great! Me, you — blood. Am coming over there in three weeks.

With those words, she signalled that I am family — whatever that means. Would I miss an opportunity to beam back at the squadron of clearly surprised journalists, crouching like tigers next to Her Majesty, would I?

Ever a gum-shoe sticker that I am, I sought out her personal bodyguard and driver, who gave me her number. But there was this last question I wanted to ask: Will she really agree to meet for a full interview, and invite me to come chill over, is that what she meant, or was that a throw off?

The bodyguard, the driver and two assistant hands winked at me, flashing a 'you've made it big, boy' look, trained, of course at making suckers like me feel like a billion dollars. I still have to get some sort of an answer from her, I thought. Nail her to some agreement.

In ten minutes she was whisked to change, and I beat if after her, my jacket up in the air, like parachute, and purple tie whizzing ahead of me, I felt like I was a flying saucer. Lady Campbell disappeared somewhere behind a team of Italian beefcakes in black suits:

'Uh, uh ah *senor* — wait. Jus' wait dere, will ya?'

She resurfaced after three minutes, a new Naomi Campbell. What passed me, in a long cashmere jacket, denim pedal pusher, knee-length Jimmy Choos or *whatchmacallit*, and wearing the same *Matrix Reloaded* goggles I saw her in her face in that picture with King Mike, was like a ghost I knew too well.

What's this? Sucking up to cheap love for celebrity messing with my head?

As she got into the waiting bullet-proof black shiny Mercedes, she rolled down her window, and the man next to her barked at me, 'Card! Your card, sir!' Followed by a soft, lilting one: 'Will you ever have lunch with the rest of the crew?'

I could have been imagining this. Did she really speak to me? In my ten years of journalism, I have not seen Naomi Campbell speaking to the members of her hounding club - aptly known as the watchdogs. But then again, I don't live in her neighborhoods.

A voice rang in my head: 'South African in two weeks, right?'

BM: Right, 'Sah . . . uhm . . . Mam! Two weeks, in two weeks!'

It's over some months now. I am still waiting. Why would I want to chill with Naomi Campbell? That's an unfair question. I mean why does Madiba love shooting the breeze with Lady Campbell?

Credits

Variations of many of the pieces in *Hot Type* were first published elsewhere. The publishers would like to gratefully acknowledge the following publications:

The Hip

Don King In Soweto: I lurve S-a-we-doo, son! *Sunday Times* 6 June 2004
John Perlman Uncensored *Sunday Times* 8 February 2004
'Hi, I'm The New Bob Mabena: Pleased To Meet'cha' *Blink!* March 2006
Free Mbizo, Freedom, Free Jazz: Elegy For Johnny Dyani
    Sunday Times 5 December 2004
Koto Bolofo: The poet laureate of fashion photography goes to Bizana
    Sunday Times 30 July 2006
Salif Keita: The muezzin from Bamako *City Press* 16 December 2001
Mbongeni Ngema: not Sarafinished yet *Sunday Times* 13 June 2004
Ooowie, Hughie! Masekela's rock 'n roll *Sunday Times* 11 July 2004
Brandford Marsalis: gonna kick yo' ass *Sunday Times* 20 August 2006
Obelix and Asterix: Somregi Ntuli and the Tough Luck Gang
    Sunday Times 7 December 2003
Amu, hip-hop's warlord *Sunday Times* 1 June 2003

Pop's the New Revolution

Danny Glover: Kicking the revolution at the Hyatt *Sunday Times*
   7 November 2004

Goodbye Tata: The young man throws toys out of the court of public
   opinion *City Press* July 1999

Prof. Malegapuru Makgoba gaan jou bokkor! *City Press* 2 December 2001

Young Gifted and Whacked

Makhendlas: Menwana phe*zulu*: In memoriam
   Mail & Guardian 5 November 1998

Mandoza: Uzoyi thola ka Njani Impilo *Sunday Times* 11 April 2003

Tupac Shakur: Am I my brother's keeper?
   Sunday Times 13 September 2003

Adam Levin's write stuff among the non-believers
   Sunday Times 18 September 2005

The Wiggah Triology

Gentleman: Reggae superstar — blacker than tar
   Sunday Times 7 August 2005

Eminem: Genius, *Homo sapiens* or white radical chic?
   Sunday World 2 February 2003

Divas

Rita Marley: In Bob I trust *Sunday Times* 22 August 2004

Miss Gay Soweto: Open up darling, that's how we do it!
   Sunday Times 12 October 2003

Makeba: Lunch With Mama *Sunday Times* 19 September 2004

Makeba: Even if you were a Black Fiend Mama, You were still a Black Queen
   Mama *Sunday Times* 10 April 2005

Dear Soul Sister: I am not feeling you *Sunday Times* 24 December 2006

Credits

Dear Soul Brother: The One Love Movement will heal
   Sunday Times 24 December 2006
FreshlyGroundNut: One love, one voice, one mom
   Sunday Times 6 February 2006

Running with The Wolves: The Rebel Divas
She: In search of my childhood fantasy *Sunday Times* 22 February 2004
The Brenda Fassie Triology
   Life Is Going On Till When ? *Marie Claire* 1 August 2004
   Mirror Mirror On The Wall   *City Life* August 2002
   Ain't No Sunshine When She's Gone *Sunday Times* 23 November 2003
Life is A Funk : Busi Mhlongo says 'I can retire anytime I want! Not'.
   Sunday Times 17 October 2006
Where's Diego Garcia? Barefoot Indian Ocean's diva's blues
   Sunday Times 21 November 2004

Acknowledgements

Without these two souls — Terry Morris; Pan Macmillan's Managing Director, and Jonathan Williams — a rising star at Pan Macmillan, and in publishing circles — this would book would have remained in the cold recess of my mind.

Take a bow.

The book editor, Kirsty von Gogh, as well as the designers and the entire Picador Africa team are highly acknowledged. Working in the book industry is not as sexy as it sounds - so, there.

I'm also eternally indebted to hardworking, hilarious, crazy, deep, brilliant, unbelievable, believable, sweet, nasty, paranoid, sublime, adventurous, egocentric, ego-less artists, personalities, musicians, actors, chance takers, icons, stargazers, thugs; people whose work and every move journalists like me scrutinise and feed to readership that can't get enough of panty-less

Britney's pictures, or emotional meltdowns and phoenix like rise of a Busi Mhlongo: to you, salute!

I thank you for opening and revealing yourselves in the ways you have.

Lastly: one woman who will not rest till I actually go and steal JM Coetzee's Noble Peace Prize, or _____ Prize, bring it to her office and say thank you, man — it's been a helluva ride — Laurice Taitz, my editor at *Sunday Times Lifestyle*.

Go on, pat yourself on the back with both hands, loll!